HOPEFUL GIRLS,
TROUBLED BOYS

HOPEFUL GIRLS, TROUBLED BOYS

Race and Gender Disparity in Urban Education

NANCY LOPEZ

ROUTLEDGE
New York & London

Published in 2003 by
Routledge
29 West 35th Street
New York, NY 10001
www.routledge-ny.com

Published in Great Britain by
Routledge
11 New Fetter Lane
London EC4P 4EE
www.routledge.co.uk

Routledge is an imprint of the Taylor & Francis Group.
Printed in the United States of America on acid-free paper.

10 9 8 7 6 5 4

Library of Congress Cataloging-in-Publication Data

Lopez, Nancy, 1969–
  Hopeful girls, troubled boys : race and gender disparity in urban
education / Nancy Lopez.
    p. cm.
Includes bibliographical references (p.   ) and index.
  ISBN 0-415-93074-X (hardcover)—ISBN 0-415-93075-8 (pbk.)
  1. Education, Urban—New York (State)—New York—Case studies. 2.
Caribbean Americans—Education (Secondary)—New York (State)—New
York—Case studies. 3. Sex differences in education—New York
(State)—New York—Case studies. I. Title.
  LC5101 .L66 2002
  370'.9173'2—dc21
                                                    2002011253

To all those who struggle to end oppression.

Contents

Acknowledgments

Throughout my work I have been blessed with many guardian angels. First and foremost, I would like to express my gratitude to my dissertation committee, Julia Wrigley, William Kornblum, and Michelle Fine. Julia, thank you for sparking my interest in education and for chairing the committee. I am equally indebted to Bill for his insights into community studies and to Michelle for reminding me about the "messiness" of gender and race. In your own special ways, each of you has contributed to my development as a sociologist and teacher.

A special gratitude is due to my second, albeit unofficial committee, Philip Kasinitz, John Mollenkopf, and Mary Waters. Working on the Second Generation Project at the Graduate School and University Center, The City University of New York was a wonderful experience. I am indebted to the faculty and staff at the Gaston Institute for Latino Public Policy and Community Development and the Sociology Department of the University of Massachusetts, Boston. I am also blessed with the support of students, faculty, and staff in the Sociology Department at the University of New Mexico. Thank you for your unconditional support. I would also like to thank the staff at Routledge, especially Ilene Kalish, Kimberly Guinta, and Nicole Ellis for all your guidance.

Special thanks also to some very inspiring people: Ramona Hernandez, Belkis Necos, Ginetta Candelario, Dae Young Kim, Silvio Torres-Saillant, Andrés Torres, Catherine Wong, Raul Ybarra, Juleyka Lantigua, Evelyn Erickson, Tatiana Tresca, Jenny López, Silvia López-Estrada, Laura Ortiz, Heather Dalmage, Robin Isserles, Milagros Ricourt, Nicole Holland, Patricia Tovar, Lisa Farrington, Ivette Estrada, Rhonda Johnson, Maritza Williams, Rosemarie Roberts, and Addette Williams. I would also like to thank my family, who always gave unconditionally of their love: María López, Ramon López, Ramona López, Neyda Gutierrez, Anivelca López, Raymond López, John Sikes, Tiffany Montenegro, Azalea Montenegro, Richard

Knecht, Carlos Gutierrez, Ricardo Gutierrez, Alan Gutierrez, Brian Gutierrez, María Elisa Peña, Lissette Peña, Oneida Rodriguez, Rosa Peña, Jorge Peña and Jorge Peña, Jr., Emma Romero, Gilbert Espinoza II, Elaine Romero, Justin Romero, Talisha Romero, Gabriel Henry Romero, and Ana Espinoza. I extend my deepest love and admiration to my husband Augustine Romero and daughter Sierra Luz Romero. Your love and support nourish me.

Finally, I wish to acknowledge all the people I had the pleasure and pain of interviewing, especially the students and staff at Urban High School. Thank you for allowing me to enter your lives and share your struggles, triumphs, and inspirations.

CHAPTER 1

Unequal Schooling: Race and Gender Disparity in Urban Education

On a glorious bright summer morning in June 1998 a long-awaited graduation ceremony was under way for Urban High School seniors in New York City.[1] The service was held in a majestic gothic cathedral located in an upper middle class Manhattan neighborhood—miles away from the dilapidated housing and urban blight enveloping Urban High School's low-income Dominican immigrant neighborhood.

Perched in the balcony of the cathedral, I had a bird's eye view of the ceremony. Dressed in their finest clothes and with their invitations in hand, several generations of bubbly family members—parents, siblings, grandparents, and godparents—beamed with pride as they entered the church to see their loved ones awarded a high school diploma. For these immigrant families, the sacrifices and hardships they had endured through the vagaries of the migration processes had paid off; their United States–born children would in most cases be the first in their families to have had an opportunity to graduate from high school and pursue higher education—well on the way to fulfilling the American dream of a better life.

To the familiar tune of the "Pomp and Circumstance" graduation march, triumphant young men draped in blue caps and gowns escorted jubilant young women in white caps and gowns down the aisle of the cathedral. Toward the end of the march, Ms. Polanco, a proud mother sitting beside me, turned to me and exclaimed in Spanish, "Mira! Hay más muchachas que muchachos!" [Oh look at that; there are more girls than boys!] Indeed, several rows of young women had to be paired up with each other.

1

The gender breakdown of the graduating class of Urban High School is part of a long established but seldom studied trend in educational attainment. In the United States as well as in other industrialized countries across the globe, such as England, women attain higher levels of education than men.[2] In 1996, there were 8.4 million women enrolled in U.S. colleges, compared with 6.7 million men, even though there were slightly more college-age men than women in the population at the time.[3] Women also had higher college completion rates than men: 26% to 29%, respectively.[4] Not only did women outnumber men in institutions of higher learning, they also earned better grades and outperformed men on reading and writing tests.[5] Women also comprised the vast majority of students in honors classes. It is predicted that as early as the year 2007, the gender gap will reach 2.3 million, with 9.2 million women enrolled in U.S. colleges compared with 6.9 million men.[6]

The gender gap in education is most pronounced among racially stigmatized groups, namely Blacks and Latinos. During the 1990s twice as many African American women as African American men earned college degrees.[7] In the Boston public schools it was estimated that for the high school graduating class of 1998, for every 100 Black and Hispanic males attending a four-year college there were 180 Black and Hispanic females.[8] In the New York City public schools, home to over a million students, where the majority of the student population is also Black and Latino (86%), more women than men graduated from high school. In 2000, 44% of Latinas graduated compared to 35% of Latino men; for Blacks 49% of women graduated versus 39% of men.[9]

The race-gender gap is already discernible among the new second generation—the children of post-1965 immigrants from the Caribbean, Latin America, and Asia.[10] In Florida and California, in a longitudinal survey of second-generation Black, Latino, and Asian youth, it was found that young women outperformed their male counterparts in terms of educational attainment, grade point averages, and educational aspirations.[11] Among second-generation Vietnamese youth in New Orleans, Louisiana, and Mexican-origin youth in San Antonio, Texas, we see similar patterns.[12] A targeted sample of second-generation Dominicans surveyed for the Second Generation in Metropolitan New York Study found that twice as many women (18%) as men (9%) were enrolled in two-year or four-year colleges.[13] The same pattern held for college degree holders: twice as many women (10%) as men (5%) had earned associate's degrees or bachelors degrees. Not surprisingly, 5% of women went on to graduate school, compared with only 1% of men.

Throughout the 1990s, at the City University of New York City (CUNY), where the majority of students are Black and Latino, most of whom are from the Caribbean, women comprised the majority of enrolled Black and Latino undergraduates—up to 70% in graduate programs.[14] These statistics bore out during my adjunct teaching (1993–1997) at CUNY campuses. In any given semester anywhere from two-thirds to three-quarters of the undergraduates enrolled in my introduction to sociology classes as well as courses I taught on Dominican studies were women. Even over the course of the seven years I attended graduate school (1992–1999) (the Ph.D. program in sociology at the graduate school and University Center of the City University of New York), there were six Dominican Ph.D. students, and all but one of us were women.

Despite the fact that historically women have enrolled in schools at higher rates than men, there is a dearth of studies exploring why this is so, particularly among racially stigmatized groups. In the words of the president of Columbia University's Teacher's College in New York City: "We need to be concerned that higher education is losing poor and minority men, that more African American men are going to prison than to college."[15] These trends beg several questions: What accounts for the race and gender disparities in education? How is it that men and women who belong to the same racial and ethnic group, attend the same schools, grow up in the same social and economic circumstances, and live in the same neighborhoods have different outcomes in terms of their educational attainment?

This book grew out of a compelling need to understand the dynamics that contribute to race and gender disparities in urban education. To unravel these dynamics, I focus on how race and gender intersect in the lives of the children of the largest new post-1965 immigrant group in New York City—second-generation Caribbean youth.[16] The children of Dominican, Anglophone West Indian, and Haitian immigrants provide fertile ground for investigating the race-gender gap in education because they share many commonalities. First, Dominicans, Haitians, and Anglophone West Indians immigrants generally enter the United States as permanent residents, in contrast to other Caribbean immigrants, such as Puerto Ricans, who are United States citizens, and Cubans, who are considered political refugees. Second, women predominate in Caribbean migration flows.[17] Consequently, these communities have fairly high rates of households headed by women. Perhaps the most central commonality shared by the vast majority of Haitians, West Indians, and Dominicans is that they are primarily of discernible African phenotype and thus provide an interesting test case of post–Civil Rights race relations in contemporary U.S. society.[18]

My interest in second-generation Caribbean youth also stems from my personal history. My mother emigrated from the Dominican Republic to the United States during the 1960s, and I, along with all my four siblings, was born and raised in the Lower East Side of Manhattan. Although my father eventually joined us during the 1970s, my parents separated in the 1980s. This pattern is not uncommon, as at some point in time women head many Caribbean families. (I attended New York City public schools, where the overwhelming majority of my classmates were from the Caribbean—mostly Puerto Ricans, West Indians, Haitians, as well as African Americans and a sprinkling of Asians.) Over half of the youth interviewed for this study grew up in circumstances similar to mine—in a mother-headed household, a low-income family, and de facto segregated and stigmatized neighborhoods.

Understanding the educational trajectories of the children of immigrants is key to understanding their incorporation into U.S. society because education remains one of the most important measures of an individual's prospects for social mobility and economic well-being. In this chapter I describe the theoretical frameworks that have been used to examine the second generation; I also describe my methods and propose a race-gender experience framework for unraveling the race and gender disparities in education. I end with a description of the chapters that follow.

The hegemonic approach for studying the second generation generally rests on the laurels of the ethnicity paradigm.[19] In the ethnicity framework, uncovering how the cultural characteristics of a given immigrant group and examining whether the values of a given ethnic group have facilitated or stunted their process of becoming "American" via assimilation is the central concern.[20] Segmented assimilation theory emerged in an effort to explain the "divided fates" or the multiple educational and labor market trajectories of the children of post-1965 immigrants.[21] Acknowledging that assimilation can mean upward or downward mobility, segmented assimilation theorists were interested in uncovering which sector of United States society a given immigrant group would assimilate into.[22] Portes and Zhou (1993) have argued that the United States currently has a pattern of segmented assimilation, or multiple ways in which immigrant groups are incorporated into distinct sectors of U.S. society. They suggest three distinct paths. First, a given immigrant group may assimilate into white mainstream middle-class society and experience upward mobility. Second, a group may assimilate into the racially stigmatized lower classes and experience downward mobility. Finally, a group may carve out an alternative route, whereby it preserves its immigrant identity and experience upward mobility. Portes and Zhou (1993) posit that the type of assimilation a given ethnic group undergoes depends largely on its

types of assimilation

mode of incorporation, its color, and its place of residence, as well as its social networks and the cultural capital of its respective ethnic communities.

Segmented assimilation theory has been instrumental in dismantling the assumption that losing ethnic distinctiveness and conforming to mainstream cultural practice was a prerequisite of intergenerational upward mobility. However, among the shortcomings of the segmented assimilation theory is the reduction of racialization processes to the static notion of "color." Instead of exploring how the second generation is assigned racial meaning, segmented assimilation theorists simply acknowledge that the second generation comes in different "colors." Race, which in this framework is operationalized simply as "color," takes a back seat to ethnic differences. For segmented assimilation theorists what is central to the education and social mobility of the second generation is their cultural values and networks, not how they are racialized.

Another pitfall of the segmented assimilation theory is that gender is treated as a static independent variable, rather than a central analytical focus of inquiry. Race and gender not only are categories of identity, but also embody social relations, social organizations, and lived experience. As we will see, the second generation is treated like racialized and gendered bodies, not as "genderless" ethnics or "raceless" genders. Thus, a real weakness of segmented assimilation theory is that its central analytical category—assimilation—neglects the fact that the very social networks, neighborhoods, schools, job opportunities, and family arrangements that are open to the second generation are racialized *and* gendered.

We need a new approach to understanding the race-gender gap in education—one that incorporates the notion of intersecting race and gender processes that can be examined as lived experiences. In this book I examine intersecting racialization and gendering processes as key to understanding educational trajectories. While mapping the ethnic identity formation of the second generation is an interesting endeavor, it is my contention that unraveling their educational trajectories requires a grasp of their racialization in U.S. society first and foremost. Instead of asking, How is the second generation assimilating into the American mainstream? I ask, How is the second generation racialized and gendered? How do they experience race and gender in daily life? How do *racialized* and *gendered experiences* shape life perspectives? How do race-gender experiences in public spaces differ for men and women? How do formal and informal institutional practices within schools "race" and "gender" students? How do family life and gender roles influence how young men and women view the role of education? What is the impact of the race-gender experiences men and women encounter in the workplace on their outlooks? How can oppressive racialization and gendering processes be revealed, interrupted, and rearticulated to create more equitable and liberating educational opportunities, particularly for low-income urban second-generation youth?

This book pioneers a conceptual bridging of diverse bodies of literature in education, sociology, and anthropology, which seldom speak to one another regarding racial formation theory, critical race theory, sociology of education, segmented assimilation theory, critical race feminist theory, Black studies, and Latino studies.[23] In working toward a race-gender theoretical framework, I bring race and gender from the margins to the center of the analysis. I challenge the notion that ethnicity predicts social mobility and instead focus on how the race-gender meanings that are assigned to the members of the second generation influence the type of education that is available to them, as well as the types of experiences they have throughout their youth and young adulthood.

The *race-gender experience framework* employs two central concepts for unraveling experiential differences with race and gender processes, namely *race-gender experiences* and *race-gender outlooks*. *Race-gender experiences* are the social interactions that take place in a given social sphere, such as public spaces, schools, work, and the home, in which men and women undergo racial and gender processes. *Experiential differences* with race(ing) and gender(ing) processes have important implications for how men and women view the role of education in their lives.[24] Over time, the cumulative effects of *race-gender experiences* shape men's and women's *race-gender outlooks*. *Race-gender outlooks* are life perspectives and attitudes about how social mobility is attained.

The unifying thread of this book centers around an analysis of the distinct race-gender experiences second-generation Caribbeans are confronted with throughout their youth and young adulthood. I illustrate how race-gender experiences accumulate and ultimately affect how men and women come to understand the role of education in their lives as well as their prospects for social mobility. Because of their disparate experience with race and gender processes, young men and women from the same ethnic and class backgrounds come to view the role of education in their lives in vastly different ways. Differing outlooks and life perspectives on education arise not because men and women are "essentially" different but rather because of the different *race-gender experiences* they have undergone throughout their lives.

This book does not examine "ethnic differences" among Dominicans, Anglophone West Indians, and Haitians. Rather, I believe a much more fruitful and insightful venture for understanding the growing achievement gap by race and gender is to examine the racialized and gendered meanings that are assigned to these youth in their everyday life. The strength of the race-gender framework is that it focuses on the ways in which race and gender are overlapping *lived experiences*. It examines how the children of immigrants are assigned racial meanings that are gendered and how these definitions come to be seen as seemingly "innate ethnic" differences, when indeed they are socially constructed processes. Another strength of this study is that it attempts to link the larger institutional practices to the lives of the second generation, and in doing so it marries the micro and macro levels of the social construction of race and gender.

It is important to highlight that the *race-gender experience framework* emphasizes that there are no *essential* and innate differences between men and women. Rather, the differing *race-gender outlooks* that men and women articulate arise because of differences in experiences, not biology or cultural differences. *Experiential differences* are the outcome of social interactions and structural relationships, not essential differences between men and women.[25] In an attempt to underscore that race and gender are socially constructed *processes*, throughout the book I refer to "race(ing)" and "gender(ing)." In other words, people are not innately White or Black; rather they are racialized as Whites or Blacks, etc. Race and gender are not static essences; they are contextually based, historically variable social relationships that are continually being created at both the micro and macro levels.

The paucity of quantitative data sets on second-generation Caribbean groups and the need to examine the life course and *lived experiences* of second-generation youths led me to rely on qualitative methods. Quantitative data from survey research can provide important information about individual outcomes on certain measures, including marital status, labor market participation, and educational attainment. Although surveys allow for the creation of representative samples of the population under study and provide snapshots of individuals' life experiences, they often force participants to choose responses from categories determined by the researcher. Moreover, surveys generally lack *experiential depth* and thus do not capture the life history of participants. As a result they do not produce data that enable us to examine the texture, range, and meanings embedded in an individual's life course. For instance, national surveys, such as the census and National Education Longitudinal Survey (NELS-88), do not capture the contextual, real-life, everyday experiences of the individuals interviewed. Finally, and perhaps most importantly, surveys are usually ahistorical and tend to essentialize race and gender, that is, treat them as a priori, rather than examining the processes that create these categories.

Qualitative approaches rely primarily on the skills of the researcher, as an empathic observer, in collecting detailed descriptions about the character, range, and depth of participants' experiences. The qualitative researcher aims to uncover an individual's own narrative about his or her life experience and outlook. Qualitative techniques generally include participant observation, ethnography, in-depth interviews, and focus groups. Whereas a survey may simply record an event, such as high school graduation, an in-depth interview seeks to understand the significance of this event in the life course of the individual, the community, or the phenomenon under study. Although qualitative methods provide rich contextual data, a common limitation is that only a small number of cases can be studied in this intensive fashion.

For my analysis of the race-gender experiences of the second generation I used an eclectic research design that included multiple sites of qualitative data sources. Over a two-year period in 1996 through 1998, I conducted focus groups with college students, life history interviews with young adults, as well as six months of participant observation at Urban High School, a neighborhood high school in New York City.[26]

As a part of the Second Generation Project at the Center for Urban Studies GSUC-CUNY, two focus groups, one with Dominicans and the other with West Indians and Haitians, were conducted with college students attending CUNY. Focus group participants were selected randomly from a list of second-generation students enrolled at CUNY campuses.[27] The focus groups served two purposes. First, they helped fine-tune the survey instrument by providing a forum for pretesting themes, and second, since these focus groups were conducted with CUNY undergraduates, they also allowed us to explore educational issues relating to working class urban college students living in New York City.

Focus groups were conducted in a classroom at CUNY, and they were tape-recorded and transcribed. There were five participants in the Dominican focus group—three women and two men. In the second focus group there were two West Indian men, one West Indian woman, and one Haitian woman, aged 18 to 30. The analysis of focus group transcripts revealed many important themes that were eventually incorporated into the survey instrument. For example, the second-generation Caribbean youth spoke about the neighborhood transitions that had occurred in their communities during the 1970s through the 1990s. "White flight," or the abandonment of the urban areas for the suburbs by White residents, followed by increased residential segregation and pockets of gentrification, "colored" the memories of many of the participants.[28] Other important issues were men's negative experiences with the police and their discourse on ethnic pride as a resource for contesting negative stereotypes about their groups.[29] In contrast, women spoke about the prominent role of family in their lives. Changing gender roles were also a central theme in the narratives of the women. Both men and women also spoke about the importance of educational opportunity programs in terms of gaining admission to college. The focus group participants' accounts of growing up in New York City provided invaluable leads for our next task—designing survey and in-depth interview instruments.

The bulk of the interview quotes that I include here come from my second source of data: follow-up interviews with 40 second-generation Dominican, West Indian, and Haitian youth who grew up in New York City during the 1970s–1990s. The sampling approach was door-to-door solicitation of surveys and later follow-up interviews in block-level census tracts with high and low concentrations of Dominicans, West Indians, and Haitians. Although their selection was not random, participants resided in census tracts with high concentrations of their respective ethnic group, most of which was low-income. In total, 66 second-generation Caribbean young adults, aged 18 to 30, were surveyed: 31 women and 35 men. Respondents included 27 Dominicans, 22 West Indians, and 17 Haitians. The Dominicans comprised 12 men and 15 women interviewed; among West Indians there were 15 men and 7 women; and for Haitians there were 8 men and 9 women. Participants were all from low-income households; none of the participants had two parents with college degrees.

Of the sixty-six participants, only four women had earned four-year college degrees. Although none of the men held college degrees, 63% of them had pursued educational training beyond high school, compared with 77% of the women.[30] Women were concentrated in traditional service-sector pink-collar work, such as clerical jobs (33%) and sales (30%). A cluster of women worked in public-sector jobs (27%), such as health care services. Over half of the men (52%) had worked in the service sector and were concentrated in traditional male-dominated work, such as security and stock personnel (37%), with a smaller concentration in sales (15%). Less than one-fifth of men (18%) had worked in the public sector, compared with almost a third of the women. Four times as many men as women had worked in the informal economy (12% compared with 3%).

Follow-up life history interviews were conducted to explore the racializ(ing) and gender(ing) processes second-generation Caribbean youth undergo during job searches and while working. In total, 40 of the 66 survey participants were reinterviewed for the follow-up in-depth life histories.[31] Interviews were usually conducted in participants' homes and generally took two to four hours. All of the interviews were audiotaped and transcribed.[32] Participants were selected with a view to striking a balance between age and gender. An effort was made to interview people with varied educational attainment and differing employment status. Respondents included ten Dominican men, eleven Dominican women, six West Indian men, six West Indian women, five men Haitian men, and three Haitian women. See Appendices A and B.

It is important to conduct qualitative studies of racialization processes because the terms "Latino" and "Black," which are used in survey research, may obfuscate concrete differences in the lived experiences of people with different phenotypes, genders, sexual orientation, etc.[33] All of the young men and women I interviewed were of varying dark skin complexions. According to the U.S. one-drop rule, all of the participants could have been racially categorized as "Black," whereby any trace of African ancestry defines one as Black. Participants reported that other people sometimes thought they were African Americans. None of the lighter-skinned Dominicans, Haitians, and West Indians reported that strangers mistook them for Whites. However, a few of the lighter-skinned participants said that other people thought that they were Puerto Rican.

Finally, to capture more vivid snapshots of race and gender processes that occur in the school setting, I also thought it would be useful to observe what actually happens in a high school that has a large concentration of second-generation youth from the Caribbean. The strategically located participant observation at Urban High School was important for my study of the race-gender gap because it allowed me to observe how young men and women interacted with teachers and other school personnel, as well as how race(ing) and gender(ing) took place at the macro and micro levels. Over a six-month period, from January to June 1998, I regularly observed four social studies classes for tenth, eleventh, and twelfth graders at Urban High School, which was mostly Dominican: specifically, two economics courses for seniors taught by Mr. Green, an American history course for juniors taught by Ms. Gutierrez, and Mr. Hunter's global history class for sophomores.[34] Each of these classes had between 25 and 30 students, with even numbers of young men and women. Only Mr. Green's economics classes had unequal gender proportions. Less than a third of his first class was female. Conversely, only a third of his second class was male.[35] This skewed gender balance in the classroom proved quite useful for examining how race and gender intersect in the school setting. Mr. Green was a self-described biracial man who was White in terms of phenotype. Ms. Gutierrez was a second-generation Latina who could not "pass" for White in terms of phenotype, and Mr. Hunter was a man who was racialized as White. All of these teachers were in their late twenties and had been teaching for less than five years.[36] In addition, periodically I accepted invitations from teachers who wanted me to visit their classes, such as those housed in the trailer classrooms and bilingual special education classes.

The race, gender, and class location of the researcher and participants *always* shape the framing of an issue, the questions asked, and the dynamics of the interview, regardless of whether one utilizes qualitative or quantitative data or a combination thereof. In establishing rapport with second-generation young adults, I conveyed that I was a U.S.-born Dominican woman in her mid-twenties who was raised in a low-income family in a New York City public housing project and attended New York City public schools. Not surprisingly, the interviewer–interviewee dynamic usually took the form of a friendly conversation between co-ethnics. During the interviews West Indians, Haitians, and Dominicans often said, "You know how it is. You know how they [Whites] see us." This indicated that participants viewed me as an insider to the community. Indeed, a number of second-generation Caribbean participants specifically said that they were eager to participate in the study because they felt very strongly about the misrepresentations of their respective communities. This is not to say that researchers who were not from the Caribbean would have necessarily been viewed as outsiders. Nevertheless, it is imperative that researchers discuss how they navigated the insider–outsider borders, as well as their race, gender, class, age, and sexual preference, and how these differences are incorporated and reflected in their questions, data collection, and analysis.[37] Therefore, in my analysis I also felt it was important to describe some of my own race-gender experiences and clarify my standpoint.

Throughout the book, I use the term "second generation" as a heuristic device to describe U.S.-born youth who had at least one immigrant parent or youth who had most of their schooling in the United States. Among interviewees the average age upon arrival for both men and women who were born abroad was seven, indicating that they had received most of their schooling experiences in the United States. It is important to note that at no point did any of the youth I spoke with identify themselves as second generation. This may be quite different from the experiences of longer established immigrant groups such as the Japanese, who consistently differentiate among the generations. Although the term *West Indian* can be used to refer to people from the whole Caribbean area, in this study it refers exclusively to immigrants from the Anglophone Caribbean, such as Jamaica, Trinidad and Tobago, Guyana, etc.[38] The term *second-generation Caribbean men and second-generation Caribbean women* refers to Dominicans, Haitians, and Anglophone West Indians as a collective group.

Although my research design includes three distinct sources of data—focus groups, life history interviews, and participant observation—the unifying thread that weaves the chapters together is a description of the *race-gender experiences of the second generation*. Highlighting how the life perspectives of the second generation are not simply related to their individual everyday experiences and social interactions at the micro level, but rather are also a by-product of the macro level of large-scale institutions, such as public discourse, criminal justice laws, schools, and workplaces. These qualitatively different lived experiences with race and gender led men and women to formulate surprising outlooks toward the role of education in their lives.

Organization of Chapters

Throughout the book we will be flexing our sociological imagination to witness how the individual lives and circumstances of second-generation Dominicans, West Indians, and Haitians were inextricably affected by the race-gender experiences they encountered and negotiated on a daily basis as they traversed a number of institutions. To allow second-generation Caribbean youths to speak for themselves about their experiences, extensive segments of the in-depth interviews are included in the book. Chapters 2 through 7 depict men and women's *lived experiences* and *outlooks* based on the race and gender processes they have undergone in a variety of social spheres in four key social spaces, namely public spaces, schools, work, and family life. In chapter 2 we enter public spaces to bear witness to some of the race and gender processes second-generation Dominican, Anglophone West Indian, and Haitian youth juggle every day in a variety of situations involving social interaction with strangers in public spaces. Through a series of social interactions with strangers, second-generation men often encountered violent or aggressive treatment, while women were subjugated in more subtle ways. Notwithstanding the language and other cultural differences that exist among Dominicans, West Indians, and Haitians, they were racialized in very similar ways along gender lines.

Chapter 3 brings into focus some of the race-gender experiences men and women coped with in the school context. Both men and women were subjected to "ghetto schooling," yet they had qualitatively different experiences. Men's experiences can be described as a process of institutional expulsion, whereas women's experience can be described as a process of simultaneous institutional engagement and oppression. In chapters 4 and 5 we go inside Urban High School. I dedicate chapter 4 to the experiences of young men. Here, I detail how seemingly neutral school practices at Urban High School were racialized and gendered and mirrored the larger racial stigmatization of men. I focus on the classroom as a space in which oppressive race(ing) and gender(ing) occurs. Chapter 5 tours the world of women at UHS. Both men and women made social critiques of the ghetto schooling they were subjected to, however, this social critique took different forms.

Besides schools, another arena that needs to be examined is the gendering that takes place in family life. In chapter 6 we visit the sphere of the family life, specifically examining gender relations, which have an important influence on educational outlooks. Homegrown lessons learned in family life provided second-generation men and women with key vantage points from which to evaluate their decisions regarding the role of education in their future.

Chapter 7 examines how the changing postindustrial economy sets the backdrop for the views men and women held about opportunity structures, and illuminates how their experiences at the workplace shaped their ideas about social mobility. Chapter 8 outlines the *race-gender experience framework* for unraveling how *race-gender experiences* shape youths' outlooks toward education. It also highlights the main findings of the study and suggests ways in which oppressive *race(ing)* and *gender(ing)* processes may be dismantled for future generations.

As we take a journey through the lives of low-income second-generation Dominican, Anglophone West Indian, and Haitian youth growing up in New York City during the 1980s and 1990s, I invite you to reflect on your own race-gender experiences throughout your childhood, youth, and young adulthood, as well as your current experiences. What were your first instances of awareness of race and gender differences? Perhaps your first experiences occurred in your family, in preschool, or possibly you had an experience much earlier than that while playing in a park or walking down the street. Was it stigma, privilege, or a combination of the two? How have your race-gender experiences affected your life perspectives and outlooks toward schooling? Whatever the place when you became aware of race and gender hierarchies, it is important that you think about how these cumulative race-gender experiences became part of your own worldview and life perspectives. Perhaps the most important task at hand is reflecting on how we can interrupt the oppressive gender and race processes that happen in our schools, our places of work, the media, public spaces, and the family. As a mother and sociologist, I am deeply disturbed by the inequality that exists in our society, particularly in our urban schools across the country. I hope that the answers to these very important questions will guide us in unraveling and dismantling race and gender disparities in education and beyond.

CHAPTER 2

From "Mamasita" to "Hoodlum": Stigma as Lived Experience

Once you're born in this country and you're not white . . . you're a Dominican . . . you become a statistic. White people look at you and say, "Oh, he's going to end up in the streets," or "We have to help him," or "We have to watch out for those kind of people. He will probably come inside a store and steal a candy bar." They always look at you that way.

Joaquín, 20-year-old Dominican man

In the United States' racial landscape, racial meanings permeate every aspect of interpersonal relations.[1] Upon leaving the protected spaces of their homes and the warmth of their families, one of the first places where second-generation Caribbean youth are racialized is public spaces. Joaquín, the 20-year-old Dominican man quoted above, who grew up on the Upper West Side of Manhattan, captured a sentiment shared by second-generation young adults from the Caribbean who grew up in New York City—visceral and ever-present awareness of race-gender stigma. An examination of the distinct racialization and gendering processes men and women were subjected to in public spaces is the first step in understanding their outlooks toward education.

I begin this chapter with an overview of how I conceptualize race and gender, followed by a brief discussion of the historical incorporation of Caribbean immigrants into the United States. Next, I draw upon the life-history interviews and focus groups to describe the range and texture of race and gender processes experienced by second-generation Caribbean men and women as they go about their daily lives. Seemingly mundane and insignificant social interactions with neighborhood residents, police, storeowners, realtors, and bank officials in business establishments and with strangers in the streets and in public parks expose men and women to very distinct race-gender experiences. At a very early age second-generation youth learn that they are not viewed favorably in the larger society. Over time, divergent race-gender experiences accumulate and begin to shape the life perspectives of men and women in fundamentally unexpected ways.

Before unveiling the race-gender experiences of the second generation in public spaces, I first want to clarify what I mean when I speak about race and gender. Most people tend to think about race and gender as innate biological essences, something one is born with and cannot change. Biological definitions of race in the United States can be traced back to the initial conquest of the Americas.[2] The essentialist perspective assumes that the concepts of race and gender reflect meaningful differences that exist independently of societal perceptions. Rooted in social Darwinist assumptions about the evolution of superior "races," biodeterministic theorists presumed that people of different phenotypes comprised distinct hierarchical biological "races." Indeed, research has re-adopted the essentialist perspective to argue that the existence of biologically distinct races has resulted in genetically distinct groups of people who possess immutable amounts of intelligence.[3]

While there is no biological basis for categorizing people according to race, biological definitions of race still seep into people's everyday practices. Many individuals in the United States refer to themselves in terms of the biodeterministic discourses. For instance, individuals and institutions continue to describe themselves or other people as being half-White, a quarter American Indian, or a quarter Japanese. Again, this understanding of race as biology becomes hegemonic "common sense," which reifies the notion of race as a measurable biological essence.

Historically, whether an immigrant group is defined as racially Black or White has had significant consequences for social mobility in terms of housing, schooling, and labor market opportunities.[4] Partly because of the legacy of African slavery and segregation in the United States, people who are deemed to be of African descent have been subjected to the "one drop rule," whereby any discernible trace of African ancestry is enough to classify a person as Black. One contemporary example would be the media's description of tennis professional Tiger Woods as the first African-American to win the coveted Master's trophy, despite his description of himself as both Asian and African American.

The ethnicity framework arose as a challenge to biodeterministic theories. Studies operating under the ethnicity paradigm embarked on documenting how the different cultural practices of ethnic groups, in terms of their language, values, religious beliefs, foods, and other aspects of everyday life, accounted for differences in social mobility.[5] In the ethnicity paradigm, "race," which is operationalized as the "color" of a given immigrant group, is viewed as secondary to their more significant "ethnic" or cultural background.[6] During the twentieth century, biodeterministic essentialist theories were simply replaced by cultural essentialist definitions about race. Moreover, the ethnicity paradigm tends to examine race and gender as if they were separate and discrete categories. Essentially, for ethnicity theorists "race" is synonymous with "color" and gender is synonymous with "sex."

The social constructionist perspective posits that race and gender have no inherent meanings beyond those constructed by the society that employs them.[7] Like race, gender has no biological basis. Accordingly, the defining characteristics for race and gender are completely arbitrary. Gender refers to the historical processes by which socially constructed behavior patterns are defined as appropriate for men and women in a given society. Gender is a process of assigning difference and meaning to the behaviors a given society believes to constitute the "masculine" and the "feminine" social spheres. Gender is not interchangeable with sex, which is also a social construction that refers to the physiological, hormonal, and reproductive differences between males and females. Because gender and racial subordination are relational in nature, they may not apply equally to all members of a given category. The meanings of race and gender are constantly being created and re-created through popular culture, state policies, laws, and social interactions.[8] Race is part of "the historically contingent social systems of meaning that are attached to morphology and ancestry."[9] Race is different from phenotype, which refers to the features of an individual's physical appearance that are socially defined as indicators of race, including skin color, facial features, and hair texture.[10]

Since the colonization of the Americas, the founding of the United States, and throughout the end of the twentieth century, race and gender hierarchies have been fundamental organizing principles in U.S. society.[11] Racial hierarchies permeate social structures at all levels, such that individuals and groups who are defined as "White" comprise the top of the racial pyramid, while those who are defined as having one drop of African blood are relegated to the bottom.[12] Other groups, such as those labeled as belonging to the Asian or American Indian "races," fall somewhere in the middle of the bipolar White–Black continuum. Although some state entities use

"Hispanic" as a racial category for statistical purposes, "Hispanics/Latinos" are not considered a racial group as designated in the 2000 Census. European immigrants have had experiences that were very different from those of immigrant groups who were of African phenotype.[13] While there is no question that European immigrants, such as the Irish and Italians, were not initially considered members of the "White" race and were subjected to negative stereotypes and discrimination upon entering the United States, they were never defined as the direct descendents of African slaves and thus were not subjected to Jim Crow laws or de jure and de facto segregation. Class, not color, mediated the social mobility of second-generation European young adults during the nineteenth and twentieth centuries.[14]

In their groundbreaking work on the social construction of race, Omi and Winant (1994) unveiled the trajectory of racial formation processes in the United States during the 1980s and 1990s. Using Gramsci's (1971) notion of hegemony, which examined how dominant social actors acquire the consent of subordinates, Omi and Winant defined race as "a concept, which signifies and symbolizes social conflicts and interests by referring to different types of human bodies."[15] Omi and Winant argued that racial subordination is accomplished through a series of hegemonic ideologies and practices. A key concept for understanding the social construction of racial hierarchies in the United States is Omi and Winant's (1994) notion of racial projects. Racial domination has been accomplished through a synthesis of ideological racial projects that were operationalized at the macro level of societal institutions and the micro level of everyday social interaction[16]:

> An alternative approach is to think of racial formation processes as occurring through a linkage between structure and representation. Racial projects do the ideological "work" of making links. A racial project is simultaneously an interpretation, representation, or explanation of racial dynamics and an effort to reorganize and redistribute resources along particular racial lines. Racial projects connect what race means in a particular discursive practice and the ways in which both social structures and everyday experiences are racially organized, based upon that meaning.[17]

Racial projects accomplish the work of both signifying and structuring social groups.[18] Race is not simply an unchanging status, but is the combination of an individual's or group's lived experiences in the political, economic, and cultural spheres of a given society. In practice, the racial meanings that are assigned to a given immigrant group or individual have major implications for that group's access to housing, education, and job opportunities, as well as for the general treatment its members receive in the larger society.[19] Race and gender discourses and hierarchies are continually being created and re-created through political, legal, and economic institutions.

Racial formation processes can be viewed at two distinct levels: (1) macro-level processes—social action rooted in the large institutions of the larger society—and (2) micro-level processes—social action performed in the everyday social interactions of individuals within that society. The United States is replete with racial projects, both large and small. Perhaps the most far-reaching racial project was the ideology used to maintain African slavery throughout the Americas. The belief that bodies of African phenotype—dark skin, so-called African facial features, and hair texture—are a biologically distinct species has been quite enduring. Consequently, in the United States, people who are defined as having African heritage are subjected to a unique form of stigma and social exclusion in the wider society.[20] "All persons of any known or discernible African ancestry, regardless of somatic characteristics, are considered 'black' and have been subjected to all of the social and legal disadvantages that this implies."[21]

What if we just stopped talking about race? Omi and Winant (1994) cautioned that simply removing the word "race" from our discourse will not make the fundamental relationships of power, subordination, and contestation disappear. To be sure, during the 1980s and 1990s the new code words for "racial others," included terms such as "inner city," "welfare mother," "urban youth," and indeed "CUNY (City University of New York) student." Although these terms do not make overt references to specific racial groups, they are impregnated with racialized social meanings that are widely understood to signify racially stigmatized groups. These code words have become part of the 1990s backlash against the Civil Rights Movement.[22] For example, since the 1970s CUNY had had an open admissions policy; however, during the late 1990s this policy has been phased out. In was argued that CUNY must improve its reputation and deny admissions to students who fail to pass "objective" entrance examinations. Therefore, racial projects are not simply stereotypes, but are politically damaging representations that have real material consequences in terms of resource allocations in the education, criminal justice system, housing, and health care, as well as in other key institutions. Relationships of domination, subordination, and contestation do not simply whither away when we stop talking about them.

One area that Omi and Winant unearthed that merits further research was an examination of the intersection of race and gender:

> It is crucial to emphasize that race, class and gender are not fixed and discrete categories and that these "regions" are by no means autonomous. They overlap, intersect and fuse with each other in countless ways . . . In many respects race is gendered and gender is racialized. In institutional and everyday life, any clear demarcation of specific forms of oppression and difference is constantly being disrupted.[23]

It is important to emphasize that race and gender are mutually constitutive and inseparable, and they cannot be examined independently of one another.[24] Besides its connection to gender, race is lived through class, religion, nationality, sexual identity, and region.[25]

New York Immigration and Racialization

New York City has been a historic magnet for immigrant flows. One-third (33%) of all housing units in New York City were occupied by immigrants.[26] The Latino population is about one-third (29%) of the city, followed by the Black population (26%) and Asians (10%).[27] Since the 1960s, close to a fifth of the immigrant flow to the United States resided in New York.[28] In the 1970s 63% of New Yorkers were categorized as non–Hispanic Whites; however, in 2000 only 35% can be described as such. Whereas nationwide only 13% of immigrants admitted to the United States during the 1990s came from the Caribbean Basin, in New York City about a third of all immigrants were from the Caribbean Basin. Among the top five source countries were three nations: the Dominican Republic, which accounted for 17% of all immigrants, Jamaica (5%), and Guyana (5%).[29] Two other Caribbean nations, Haiti and Trinidad and Tobago, were also in the top ten. As a result of the huge influx of immigrants from the Caribbean, New York City has become more ethnically diverse and decidedly Caribbean, and the annual West Indian Day Festival and Parade in Brooklyn has become the largest in New York City.[30]

In most encounters race has overpowered ethnicity. Kasinitz's (1992) study of the emergence of a West Indian identity among first-generation immigrants from the former British Empire found that West Indians in the United States were labeled as Black, independently of how they identified themselves ethnically. Waters (2000) also found that while West Indian immigrants enter the United States with much optimism about their prospects for social mobility, their continued experiences with racial discrimination began to taint their visions of achieving the American dream. Dominicans, who tend to have more African heritage than any other Spanish-speaking group, may be subjected to even more racial discrimination based on skin color than lighter-skinned Latinos.[31] In the 1990 census, two-thirds of Dominicans identified their race as Dominican. Nevertheless, according to the U.S. one-drop rule the vast majority of Dominicans could be defined as racially Black.

As a New York City-born and raised daughter of Dominican immigrants who is of discernible African phenotype, I have also been subjected to the one-drop rule. While teaching courses on race in the public universities in New York City, Boston, Massachusetts, and now Albuquerque, New Mexico, on the first day of classes I often begin my courses by passing around small slips of paper and asking students to anonymously guess my race. Anywhere from 60% to 85% of students define my race as Black. When I tell my students that I define my race as Dominican, they seem perplexed. For many of my students, race is synonymous with skin color. According to the one-drop rule, students "see" my race—skin color, facial features, hair texture—as Black, regardless of how I define myself.

Neocolonialism and Racial Subjugation

Before turning to the race-gender experiences of the children of Caribbean immigrants in New York City public spaces, it is imperative that we highlight the nature of the relationship between the United States and the Caribbean. Although Dominican, Haitian, and Anglophone West Indian immigrants speak different languages, namely Spanish, Haitian Creole, and Patua/English, they share a common history of European colonization, the decimation of indigenous populations, and the subsequent importation of Africans as slaves. Since the mid-nineteenth century Caribbean nations have also shared a common economic and political relationship to the United States. During the 1870s, the United States attempted to annex the Dominican Republic. Not surprisingly, U.S. congressional debates were peppered with concerns about the dubious racial background of Dominicans, as the annexation of a "Black" country to post–Civil War U.S. society posed a racial quandary. The Dominican Republic's contested border with neighboring Haiti—the first republic of former African slaves in the Americas—was also seen as problematic and inherently undesirable.

Although the annexation attempt was aborted, U.S. imperial aspirations in the Dominican Republic and the rest of the Caribbean proceeded unfettered. In a quest to expand their overseas markets, the United States invaded Haiti (1915–1934), the Dominican Republic (1916–1924, 1965–1966), and Grenada (1983). These military occupations not only altered the economy, politics, and class structure of these countries; they also radically altered the cultural practices and consumption patterns of the people. By the time U.S. troops withdrew from the Dominican Republic in the 1920s, the island's economy had been transformed from a diverse agricultural economy to a one-crop market rooted in sugar production. At the time of the withdrawal from the Dominican Republic, entrepreneurs from the United States controlled 80% of the sugar-producing land.[32] More recently, through trade agreements such the Caribbean Basin Initiative (1983), free trade zones, and International Monetary Fund policies, as well as the continued surveillance of elections, the United States continues to exercise considerable economic and political hegemony in the Caribbean, making these states de facto neocolonies.[33] Paradoxically, although the Caribbean has become a popular tourist destination for U.S. vacationers, in many respects these small island nations have become the backyard of the United States, as well as a source of plentiful cheap labor and expanding markets for U.S. goods.[34]

Perhaps the most significant by-product of the neocolonial linkages the United States established with the Caribbean has been the displacement of people.[35] The U.S. military presence, coupled with the increased penetration of U.S. capital into the Caribbean region, displaced agricultural workers from their traditional modes of production. Economic dislocations triggered the massive migration of hundreds of thousands of peasants, beginning in the 1960s.[36] The imposition of export processing zones as a developmental strategy has not stemmed the tide of immigrants, as the miserly wages paid to workers did not adequately meet their subsistence needs. Ironically, many of these laborers migrated to the United States in search of economic opportunities.[37]

Given the history of U.S. intervention in the Caribbean, it is not surprising that since the 1960s Caribbean immigrants constituted the largest number of immigrants to New York City.[38] Significantly, women have comprised the bulk of the migration flows.[39] Unlike other Caribbean immigrants, such as Puerto Ricans, who are United States citizens, and Cubans, who are considered political refugees, Dominican, Haitian, and Anglophone West Indian immigrants enter the United States as permanent residents or sometimes without documentation.

Dominican, Haitian, and Anglophone West Indian immigrants, as well as other colonized and racially stigmatized groups, such as African Americans, American Indians, and Puerto Ricans, may be viewed as neocolonial subjects in the U.S. political-economic landscape.

The same original social relations established by conquest of the Southwest were part and parcel of transnational processes that were replicated throughout the Greater Caribbean Basin. These processes established social structures beyond the Southwest into which all Latinos in the United States find themselves inserted. It is on the basis of these relations that a Latino national minority is emerging.[40]

Imperial ideologies of Manifest Destiny, coupled with the capitalistic goals of United States, contributed to the neocolonial relationship the United States has imposed on the Caribbean. For these reasons Ogbu and Simons' (1998) classification of Dominicans and Anglophone West Indians as voluntary immigrants and Haitians as political refugees is problematic because it ignores the neocolonial relationship between the United States and these island nations.

Upon entry to the United States, Caribbean immigrants are confronted with rigid U.S. racial(ized) and gender(ed) social structures.[41] Because they are primarily of African phenotype, Caribbean immigrants and their children fall to the bottom of the U.S. White/Black racial pyramid. Orfelia, a 20-year-old Dominican woman who grew up in Corona, Queens, gives us some insight into where racial meanings are created and deployed:

> If you put on the news, anyone who does anything bad, if he's not Black, he's Hispanic and that makes us look bad. It makes us look shameful. You watch the news and you see that when any white guy does something, you won't see their face. They might just say it and that's all. But if it's a Dominican, a Hispanic, a Black, they put him on for about two minutes, so that you can know him.

Orfelia's social critique points to how the national and local narrative on race and crime has scripted men of African phenotype as potential criminals and drug dealers. The racialization of dark-skinned men as "hoodlums" was the quintessential racial project of the "war on drugs" of the 1980s and 1990s. In 1998 a New York advertising firm circulated a memo warning clients that specialized in marketing to Black and Latino communities that they should want to market to "prospects not suspects."[42]

Andrés, a 24-year-old Dominican man who was raised in Elmhurst, Queens, and enrolled in the police academy, offered his views on why he felt Dominicans were viewed in such a negative light in the New York City political-economic backdrop:

> According to whites we are all criminals and sell drugs. Unfortunately they talk about it in the newspapers. If I were a white person reading newspaper articles about Dominicans getting busted all the time, I would start to think the same thing.

"Much of the media and scholarly work has been devoted to white perceptions of Black men as threatening and the justifiability of that perception" (Feagin & Sikes, 1994:74). In the words of Alfredo, a 19-year-old Dominican who grew up in Elmhurst and Corona, Queens, "I guess the government sees us as trouble makers, trying to stereotype us, that's what I think, especially in the media and all the negative stuff they show about us."[43]

Regardless of intentions, cultural representations, whether journalistic accounts or social scientific endeavors, are inescapably political, even if they claim to be "politically neutral" and "objective."[44] The 1998 *New York Times Magazine* cover story on teenagers across the country provided an important window to how most racially privileged communities across the United States come to know youth who are defined as racial others. Through a collage of photojournalistic accounts, the article depicted a "diverse" group of 13-year-olds across the country.[45] In keeping with the "colorblind" understanding of race, which posits that to mention race is racist, the cover story does not directly mention race once. Yet, hegemonic narratives of "white" middle-class "normal" youths are braided with those of "dysfunctional" racial minorities, namely Latinos and Blacks.

In one photograph a 13-year-old Latino boy from California displayed a "gang" tattoo of a rabbit on his arm. He is smoking something that appears to be a cigarette, but that could easily be interpreted as an illicit drug. Another two-page spread depicts two Latino teenagers clad in baggy pants and white T-shirts kicking and punching another young man during a so-called gang initiation rite. In direct contrast, their White counterparts are depicted as "normal" teenagers who merit emulation. The young White men in these photo essays are portrayed as true "Americans" who possess the proper work ethic, as exemplified by one young man who at the tender age of 13 started his own business. White young men were represented as bright, independent, and politically conscious, generously performing charity work and volunteering at nonprofit organizations. Unlike their Latino counterparts, who were portrayed as criminals who violently prey on one another and turn to illicit drugs for recreation, young White men's sports included getting tans during spring break, as well as horseback riding. In the end, two opposing images of young masculinity become etched in the collective consciousness of the U.S. public: that of the law-abiding and creative young White man and that of the menacing and violent racial other, and no direct mention of race is ever made.

Racialization processes in public spaces are also gendered. The photo essays of the young women featured in this article were represented quite differently from those of their male counterparts. Two images of White teenage girls emerged—the hyperfeminine princess and the frumpy intellectual. The privileged princess worried excessively about her appearance and displayed her femininity by wearing the latest fashions. One two-page spread depicted blonde, blue-eyed, "all-American" young women donning formal halter dresses, curling their hair, and putting on lipstick as they prepared to go out to a party, presumably the prom.[46] The second image is that of the frumpy academic superachiever. Tomboyish, sporting T-shirts and jeans, these no-nonsense young women had another obsession—their college entrance examination scores.

The images of Black and Latina young women were decidedly less threatening than those of their male counterparts. Among the few women who were included in the so-called gang initiations, Latinas appeared only as props to the "real" Latinos—their hypermasculine and menacing male counterparts. In keeping with the narrative of African Americans as athletically gifted, the sole picture of a "superachieving" young African American woman is that of a muscular wrestler in a gym locker room.[47] Interestingly, the only African American man in the article was represented as a young man who "controlled" his anger through participation in sports.

The aforementioned ideological representations of race, gender, and sexuality are central to the social construction of racial and gender hierarchies in contemporary U.S. society. Racialized and gendered bodies are defined in relation to one another and become more than simple stereotypes or prejudices. They become part and parcel of the urban policy debates that have dominated the national discourse over the last few decades, rendering hegemonic racial narratives and explanations for poverty, violence, educational failure, and drugs in U.S. society. Racial representations become "controlling images" that are used to justify contemporary policies regarding urban youth, criminal justice, and education.

Washington Heights, a predominantly Dominican neighborhood in Manhattan, has been depicted as one of the centers of the drug industry in New York City.[48] Not surprisingly, men living in this neighborhood spoke about living in constant fear of any type of interaction with the police that might result in police brutality.[49] José, a 25-year-old Dominican man who grew up in Washington Heights, Manhattan, had dropped out of high school but eventually received his General Equivalency Diploma (GED). According to José, police officers routinely drove around his block looking for criminal suspects, sometimes taking snapshot pictures of young men who were sitting on park benches or standing in front of their apartment buildings.

The prevalence of racial profiling and the imminent threat of police brutality was an ever-present reality that men of any discernible African phenotype navigated on a daily basis. When queried about the safety of his neighborhood in a housing project in Brownsville, Brooklyn, Mark, a 24-year-old West Indian man whose mother was born in Jamaica and whose father was born in St. Vincent, replied: "The police are the only people I fear when I'm walking down the street." On his way home from class one night, Mark faced a scenario that echoed the experiences of men:

> That night I was the only Black person who came out of the train station. As I exited the police approached me and started questioning me about a shootout that had just occurred. I explained I was in college and they finally let me go.

Mark admitted that he gets extremely angry when he is stopped by the police for questioning simply because he fit the profile of a "suspect."

On a separate occasion police officers even came to Mark's apartment and interrogated him:

> Another time the police came knocking at my door in the projects and they said that I robbed somebody. My dad looked at them like they were crazy. I was in the house all day. My dad said, "Get out and stop talking foolishness and leave," and finally they left.

Mark feared being the victim of "mistaken identity" because he might be jailed and have to put up bail money if he could not give a satisfactory explanation of his whereabouts.[50] To protect himself from the "hoodlum stereotype," Mark carried his college identification card and was always careful to speak politely to the police.

The hegemonic racial project of dark-skinned young men as suspects was not limited to racial profiling by law enforcement officials or people who are racialized as Whites in general. Mark lamented that he felt extremely uncomfortable when women, many of whom were themselves members of racially stigmatized groups, instantaneously clutched their purses and walked away from him. One of the ways in which Mark coped with the hoodlum narrative was by wearing a walkman and listening to music so that he might distract himself from the many "hate stares" that he was subjected to on a daily basis.[51]

Among West Indian and Haitian high school students in New York City, young men were more likely to say they experienced racial discrimination and police harassment than women.[52] Fine and Weis (1998) found that all of the African American men in their study of two large northeastern cities reported incidents in which police had stopped and questioned them. These young men were frisked for no apparent reason other than the fact that they were young men who were dark-skinned. MacLeod (1995) found that Black and Latino young men living in public housing projects were also periodically questioned by police officers in the Northeast.

In 1997, Abner Louima, a Haitian immigrant, was savagely beaten and sodomized while in police custody. In 1999, police officers fired 41 shots at Amaduo Diallo, an African immigrant, after mistaking him for a rapist. Civil rights activists have coined the term "racial profiling" to describe the new form of state sanctioned racial oppression in the twenty-first century. Racial profiling, the use of race as a legitimate category for stop-and-search practices, is common practice in many police departments across the country. Supporters of racial profiling maintain that since the majority of crimes are committed by racially stigmatized minorities, racial profiling is a legitimate crime-reducing tactic in law enforcement that is commonly used in federal and state investigations.[53] Indeed, a manual used for police training across the country stated: "Jamaicans/Rastafarians have been known to operate and transport narcotics in the following types of vehicles." and suspicious cars "may display the Ethiopian flag . . . red, yellow and green, Jamaican paraphernalia."[54] Those who oppose the practice maintain that racial profiling is a form of institutional discrimination that unjustly targets Black and Latino youth, particularly males.

Racial profiling is also a global problem. Caribbean families living in England have suffered the alienation of their sons and constant threats of police brutality.[55] Sam, a 26-year-old Haitian man who was a small business owner, reflected on the negative experiences he had when he traveled to Japan. Upon arriving at the airport Sam was detained and searched under suspicion of carrying drugs. Regrettably, after the September 11, 2001, terrorist attacks on the World Trade Center and the Pentagon, numerous attempts to justify racial profiling at airports as a legitimate form of policing both in the United States and abroad have surfaced.

Not only were men subjected to constant surveillance in their own neighborhoods; some business owners actually demanded that they leave their establishments altogether. Denzel, an 18-year-old West Indian man who was still enrolled in high school, recalled that his dark skin color and the fact that he was a young male were enough evidence for storeowners to immediately assume that he was a criminal. Denzel remembered an awful experience he had when he entered a convenience store in his Crown Heights, Brooklyn neighborhood. An Asian storeowner bolted in front of Denzel yelling: "No, no, no! Get out! Get out! We don't want you in here!" Denzel shot back: "I have money! I don't want to steal your cheap bubble gum!" and stormed out of the store. Numerous "hate stares" and interactions with strangers taught men that they were not truly accepted and that they were viewed with contempt in U.S. society.[56]

Paven, an 18-year-old West Indian man who grew up in Bushwick, Brooklyn, and who was attending a community college, described an unpleasant experience he had one weekend at a Brooklyn department store when he was out shopping with his cousin:

> The security guard kept following us and my cousin was like, "Why are you following me for, man?!!! I am not going to steal your shit! I could buy whatever I want!" And then the guard just flipped out. The guard grabbed him or something. I think you're not allowed to do that but it happens.

The prevailing view of dark-skinned men as hoodlums was so hegemonic that members of racially stigmatized groups also shared it. Men recalled that many of the security guards who harassed them were also dark-skinned. Taxi drivers, many of whom were also members of racially stigmatized groups, also presumed that young men of African phenotype were potential criminals. Time and time again men recounted episodes in which they had to walk home in the pouring rain because no cabs would stop for them, especially if they were in groups of two or more. Men recalled that some taxi drivers forced them to pay in advance and then left them several blocks away from their destinations because they feared that they would mug them.[57] Men coped with the discrimination they faced in stores by displaying their cash in their hands as they walked in, to "prove" that they were not potential criminals and that they had a right to be there.

Jahaira, a 30-year-old Dominican woman, who grew up in Bushwick, Brooklyn, devised a clever strategy for hailing a cab late at night. Late one evening Jahaira and her partner, a Panamanian man of African phenotype, tried hailing a cab after dinner and a movie in Times Square, Manhattan, however, cabs continually passed them by and proceeded to pick up White clients. Jahaira then asked Carlos to stand away from her, and before the cab driver could protest she had waved Carlos into the cab. In *Race Matters* (1990) Cornel West described how his class status did not protect him from racial discrimination when trying to hail a cab. I have also had many difficulties in obtaining cabs in New York City. On one such occasion, I was leaving a downtown hospital in Manhattan with a sprained ankle in the pouring rain. While balancing myself on crutches, I tried for over thirty minutes to hail a cab, but they consistently passed me by and proceeded to pick up White passengers. Finally, one cab stopped and made me get off after I told him that I was headed to my apartment in Washington

Heights/Inwood Manhattan because he did not go to so-called dangerous neighborhoods. On another occasion, I tried hailing a cab near the World Trade Center in lower Manhattan while accompanied by my teenage nephew. For over half an hour we tried hailing a cab and consistently cabs drove by us and proceeded to stop for people of European phenotype.

The reality of racial stigma was not limited to face-to-face interactions; it was literally conveyed through the very air the second generation breathed. Every day, as they walked through their neighborhoods and attended dilapidated and overcrowded schools, second-generation Caribbean youth were reminded of their racially stigmatized status. As I walked through the neighborhoods of the second generation, I noted that garbage was piled up in the streets, potholes were commonplace; in general sanitary codes were not met. Many of the train stations in the neighborhood I visited were dilapidated and had leaks when it rained, and some even lacked lighting on the platform. Denzel, an 18-year-old West Indian man who was born in Trinidad and Tobago, but raised in Brooklyn explained:

> In my neighborhood, Crown Heights, it takes twenty minutes for a train to come, but when I went to Bay Ridge, the white neighborhood, a train comes every five minutes. And the streets are cleaner! Also Jews have the mayor [Giuliani] under their control. The government gives them better transportation and everything. It is more for them. Better schools, housing.

In comparing their neighborhoods with those of racially privileged communities, second-generation Caribbean youth realized that they could not count on the same type of social services, including transportation, sanitation, and schools, as those who resided in communities that were racialized as White neighborhoods. One common thread in the narratives of youth was that the only contact they had with Whites in their neighborhood was mostly with Jewish immigrants. Thus Jews became the de facto White group of reference. Throughout the 1990s Crown Heights had been the site of much racial tension.

National studies of the contours of racial segregation across the United States continually find that African Americans and other groups of African phenotype, such as Dominicans, experience extremely high degrees of residential segregation and that only groups subjected to the one-drop rule were the only ones that continue to do so.[58] In New York City, throughout the 1990s, 34% of Dominicans, 22% of Caribbeans and Africans, and 27% of African Americans were living in apartments that suffered from rat infestation, lacked water or heat, and had no kitchen or bathroom.[59] In contrast,

European immigrants from similar class backgrounds were able to obtain better housing.

Sam, a 26-year-old Haitian business owner, who grew up in Flushing, Queens, hoped to purchase his first real estate investment property; however, his plans were stunted:

> I was making enough money to buy the co-op in cash and they wouldn't let me in. This was in Flushing, Queens, near Union Turnpike. It was an all-white area, mostly Jewish. I had the proof of the loan but the people in the co-op were not cooperating. They basically didn't tell me that but they didn't give me certain paperwork the people giving me the loan needed—the prospectus—so they could see the property's value. And the people that were going to give me the loan said, "Look, save yourself some problems, forget about this co-op. You want another co-op someplace else, fine. As long as they abide by our rules, we'll give you the loan. But these people don't want you in this place."

This experience led Sam to formulate doubts about his prospects for social mobility. Sam, who did not plan to pursue a college education, gave a scathing critique of racial discrimination in the United States: "Police officers, bankers and the people who give mortgage loans—those are your gangsters."

Wilson (1987) has posited that the Black middle class can escape discrimination and the plight of the urban ghetto via their class status; however, the experiences of second-generation Caribbean youth calls into question the assumption that race has declined in significance. Racial discrimination continues to play an important role in the housing options of immigrant and native-born communities of African phenotype, regardless of their class background.[60] The deliberate concentration of Blacks in "certain" suburban areas illustrates how residential discrimination continues to be a powerful problem for racially stigmatized groups, regardless of their class backgrounds.[61] Sam eventually moved to a middle-class suburban neighborhood; however, it was predominantly Black. Sam reflected bitterly on the reality that even in his new neighborhood he was suspect:

> I was driving and I didn't come to a complete stop at a stop sign. The police officer had me get out of the car and he wanted me to get on my knees. I told him, "I'm not going to run, you have all my paperwork. If I were to get on my knees in front of another man, I don't think I could actually ever look my father in my face, knowing that you could have a gun to my head and you could practically kill

me. I couldn't be a man anymore if I do that." And finally he was like, "Okay, then just have a seat."

According to Sam it did not matter what kind of car he drove, the combination of his dark skin, dreadlocks, and gender was used by police officers as enough evidence to categorize him as a "suspect." The emasculation ritual described by Sam has historical origins. During slavery and postemancipation, many African American men were castrated.

Like Sam, who had many difficulties in securing a home in a middle-class neighborhood, Jahaira, the Dominican woman who worked as a research assistant at an investment bank, and her partner, a Panamanian man who was of African phenotype, encountered many roadblocks during their apartment search:

> We tried to go through a real estate agency and for some reason they would showed us the ugliest apartments. It wouldn't be like up here, it would be closer to Ridgewood in the area where I "belonged." It was weird! The type of apartment that I would pay for . . . I told them I'm not going to pay any more than $800 rent. I can't afford to pay more than that. Even $750 is rough, but they could have done better than that.

Jahaira eventually found an apartment in Flushing on her own. She happened to be walking in the neighborhood, scouting for "apartment for rent" signs, and an elderly White woman invited her to come and look at an apartment. Unlike Sam, who had endured numerous negative interactions with real estate brokers and the police and therefore had developed a worried outlook about his prospects for social mobility, Jahaira hoped to pursue a graduate degree in business administration.

In addition to experiencing troubles in securing decent housing, middle-class people of African phenotype continue to confront discrimination when they enter traditionally White middle-class public facilities, such as restaurants, hotels, department stores, and recreational facilities. A national study of the experiences of middle-class African Americans provides a provocative framework for analyzing the effects of the discrimination that African American are subjected to in everyday social interactions. Feagin and Sikes (1994) posit that the glances that African Americans are subjected to on a daily basis from strangers are not merely inconvenient; they have a significant psychological impact on the worldviews of African Americans as individuals, as well as on the community at large.[62] These incidents reverberate and accumulate to form part of the life perspectives of African Americans.

The use of a White-sounding voice was a coping strategy that many people who are racialized as Blacks use to navigate racism in their everyday lives.[63] During the course of opening his restaurant, Sam also had to contend with a range of other publicly humiliating experiences. To circumvent some of the discrimination from wholesalers that he was confronted with, Sam sometimes asked a White male friend of his to place his phone orders because he had a so-called White-sounding accent:

> It's really interesting to have my [White] friend Tom around because a lot of experiences that I've had, he would never really be able to relate to until he's been with me and he sees what I go through with police harassment and discrimination. When we go out I tell him, "First of all, Tom, you're with me now, you're no longer white. You're black now. And you're a traitor, so you're even worse."

Sam remembered that Tom confessed that he did not believe that Sam endured racial discrimination until he witnessed it.

The racialization of women in public arenas took on forms qualitatively different from those encountered by their male counterparts. Nicole, an 18-year-old West Indian woman of Jamaican ancestry who grew up in St. Albans, Queens, was always at home taking care of her baby sister while her mother worked as a home attendant. When I asked Nicole about how she thought Blacks were viewed in the United States, she spoke passionately about a social interaction she often confronted while walking in the street with her baby sister:

> What I hate is how people view African Americans up here. It is really hard for me when I'm on the street with my little sister because everybody is looking at me. I don't want them to think I'm some girl who just went out and sleeps around. So, I tell my little sister in a loud voice, "We're going to see Mommy now!" I make it obvious that she is not my daughter. And even my little sister plays along because she starts screaming: "I want my Mommy! I'm going to tell Mommy!"

These experiences provided Nicole and her baby sister with their first lesson on where they fit into the U.S. racial pyramid. Mere glances from strangers in public spaces were impregnated with multiple racial and gender meanings that cast dark-skinned women, such as Nicole, primarily as sexual objects.[64]

The "welfare queen" myth emerged as one of the many race-gender narratives that permeated the lives of women.[65] According to this hegemonic story, young women who are members of racially stigmatized groups are prone to succumb to early sexual activity and become teenage mothers who have numerous children out of wedlock at the expense of "hardworking [read: White] taxpayers."[66] What is key here is that race-gender experiences in public spaces were not merely unpleasant episodes, but more importantly affected the ways in which young women viewed the role of education in their lives. A case in point: after having repeated race-gender experiences in which assumptions were made about her sexuality, Nicole was determined to go to college and become a medical doctor so that she would not become another teenage mother statistic. Nicole had an A grade point average in high school and was a member of the honors society.

In the latest edition of the welfare queen story, Dominicans were regularly featured in the mass media as abusers of the welfare system.[67] Yvonne, a 22-year-old Dominican woman who grew up in Williamsburg, Brooklyn, but was now living in Inwood, Manhattan, had a counternarrative on the welfare queen story:

> A lot of them [Jewish immigrants] were involved in the Diamond district. You would think that they had no jobs or anything, but they were diamond traders, very rich, rich people that were on welfare too. You walk into these houses, because these people they're religious because of the Sabbath, Friday when the Sun goes down, they are not allowed to touch anything electrical, so many times, we were the only Spanish people on the block, so many times their air conditioning would go haywire and they needed someone to unplug it, and they could not touch anything electrical, so we would walk into these houses and many times we would walk in and see a chandelier that clearly was like $25,000. They were on public assistance. And they don't believe in birth control, or abortions or anything like that. So here they are with 10 kids and they are getting checks, and I'm talking about huge checks.

Yvonne resented the fact that immigrants who were racialized as White are viewed as deserving poor, while immigrant groups who are considered racial "others" are cast as immoral and undeserving in the mass media.[68] Indeed, immigrants from the former Soviet Union have the highest rates of public assistance usage of any immigrant group; however, they are not stigmatized in the media.[69]

Cultural essentialist narratives were part and parcel of the public policy discourses on poverty and race. In *Killing the Black Body: Race, Reproduction, and the Meaning of Liberty*, Roberts (1997) critiques the racial bias evidenced in the dominant discourse on reproductive liberty. Roberts argues that the liberal American ideals of individual autonomy and freedom from government are routinely primarily concerned with the interests of middle-class women who are racialized as Whites. This individualistic discourse is narrowly focused on the right to an abortion, while the procreative choices of low-income and working-class women, particularly those from racially stigmatized groups such as African Americans, were circumscribed through state policies that coerce them into undergoing sterilization. Ignited by the resurgence of the eugenics movement, sterilization technologies continue to be imposed in racially stigmatized communities.[70]

Second-generation youth protested the negative ways in which their immigrants were represented in the media. Cassandra, a 27-year-old Dominican woman who grew up in Washington Heights, gave a biting critique:

> I think immigrants make a great contribution for the City. We are just being judged by a few of us that come here and do bad things. There are a lot of hard-working people here that are paying their taxes and they don't see that. Believe it or not, every person in New York is an immigrant. Every person. If you find a complete pure New Yorker in New York, please let me know. Every person is an immigrant, so why does the media call only certain groups immigrants?

Counterhegemonic discourse is part and parcel of women's critique of racism in U.S. society and their commitment to education.

Cristina, a 21-year-old Dominican woman who participated in the focus groups at the public university of New York, commented on how the negative racialization of Dominicans formed the very backdrop against which she carved her own ideas about her dreams and aspirations:

> Ever since I came to the United States I kept hearing all these bad things about Dominicans—drugs and welfare. And it's so unfair! Because a few do bad things, that's all you hear. You never hear about Dominicans winning scholarships and excelling in business. That's part of the reason I finished high school and I am now going to college. I want to change that image. I want to be a writer so that people can know that I am a Dominican writer.

For Cristina, pursuing an education was a way of "proving the racists wrong"—a way of contesting negative stereotypes circulating about Dominicans as lazy people, drug dealers, and welfare queens.[71]

Politically damaging representations of urban minority youth in the media contributed directly to the negative stereotypes men and women have to contend with in public spaces, and these "commonsense" truths permeated every aspect of their lives, from friendships, to housing, workplace relations, and education.[72] Janet, a 26-year-old Dominican woman who grew up in Washington Heights, Manhattan, recalled how students at the predominantly White out-of-state college she attended perceived her neighborhood:

> When I went away to college, there was a stereotype drawn of what Hispanics were like and I remember enlightening the group because they were ignorant. They had this image of Harlem being the drug capital of the world and Washington Heights being right there behind it. They'd say, "I'd never go to New York." Or they'd say, "You come from New York? How do you survive?" They thought it was like a guerrilla camp or something where people were constantly shooting at you.

For Janet what was most appalling was that many of her college peers had never even been to these communities, but they had "learned" about these neighborhoods through the media. Janet eventually transferred back to a university in New York City because she was tired of the constant racial harassment she was subjected to in the upstate school.

While men reported having negative interactions with the police, none of the women reported being stopped and searched by the police. Although women had little personal experience with police officers, they spoke about numerous incidents involving their brothers, husbands, and male friends. When asked why they thought this was so, Cassandra, a 27-year-old Dominican woman who was raised in Washington Heights and lived in Inwood, Manhattan, offered her insights:

> I think it has to do with my sex because often, especially here, I see a lot of police officers around my neighborhood checking out women. They like to check out women, especially when they are driving around in their cars or when they are on foot patrol.

Cassandra added that at times while she was walking in her neighborhood with her younger cousin, White male police officers directed sexual comments to them. Sexual harassment in the form of comments and gazes from male police officers appeared to be among the reasons why women said that they also did not trust the police.[73] Again, this experience reminded Cassandra that in public spaces she was seen first and foremost as a sex object. In response to her stigmatization, Cassandra spoke about pursuing an education as a vehicle for counteracting these racist images.

Cassandra also gave a biting social critique of the racialization of public safety resources in her Washington Heights, Manhattan neighborhood:

> This used to be a Jewish neighborhood before. There's a Jewish syn-agogue right here and for the holidays they had cops on each corner. So I asked Mom, "What happened? How come the cops are out-side?" "Oh no, it's the Jewish holiday now. They have the cops out there because they don't feel safe around us." Hello!!!??? We've been here just like you guys. What are we going to do to you?

The stigmatization of poor minority communities is a process of assigning "symbolic taint" and "territorial stigmatization."[74] Territorial stigmatiza-tion of Black and Latino neighborhoods contributes to the intensive police surveillance racially stigmatized immigrant communities are subjected to.

Women coped by making jokes or dismissing the discrimination they were subjected to as ignorance. Marie, a bubbly 19-year-old Haitian college student who grew up in East Flatbush, Brooklyn, chuckled as she explained how she dealt with being treated like a potential thief in public spaces:

> When you go to department stores to buy clothes, they constantly have people watching you! No matter what store you go to. For ex-ample, all of a sudden a store employee has to fix something that is in your aisle. I love that one! Sometimes we will make jokes like, "Did you put it in your pocket?" Jokes like that. It's not funny but it is so true.

Women also reported that in some cases, salespeople simply ignored them because they thought they were not really going to buy anything. At times sales personnel reminded them that the products they were looking at were "expensive." Yvelise, a 24-year-old Dominican woman who grew up in Washington Heights, Manhattan, described her experience:

> When you go downtown, to nice neighborhoods and you are going to buy something, they look at you like you don't have fancy clothes and maybe you're wearing some jeans and a leather jacket or what-ever and they are wearing nice clothes. I don't think they really think anything about it. They think that all Dominicans are low lives. They think we are dealing drugs on the corner; the little girls are coming up pregnant.

While women recalled incidents in which they were subjected to oversur-veillance in department stores, these episodes seldom involved physical confrontations, as they did with men. Instead, women were reminded of their stigmatized racial status in more "subtle" ways. While men painfully recalled vivid accounts of blatant face-to-face discrimination in stores, women spoke about dealing with more "discreet" forms of discrimination in upscale department stores.

Conclusion

The way in which a given ethnic group is racialized has quite important consequences for its members' life chances and social mobility above and beyond its assigned cultural traits.[75] In this chapter I examined how second-generation Caribbean youths were assigned racial meanings in public spaces and how if at all these processes differed for men and women. Although Dominican, West Indian, and Haitian immigrants are different ethnic groups originating from Caribbean countries with different languages and cultural backgrounds, they were subjected to similar racialization processes in the U.S. context of racial stigma. In essence, the social mobility of the second generation is a "colored" process. Since the majority of Caribbean immigrants are of discernible African phenotype, they were defined automatically as Black. The racialization of a given immigrant group as "Black" has quite an enduring and unique stigmatized status, which did not simply evaporate across the generations.[76]

In their narratives, men and women alike pointed to the media as perhaps the most important institution that created and circulated their racially stigmatized status in the national narrative. The portrayal of Black and Latino communities as hotbeds of criminal activity loomed large in the media.[77] Time and time again, second-generation Dominican, West Indian, and Haitian men spoke about being treated with suspicion, resentment, and in some cases fear by police and strangers who automatically assumed they were hoodlums. In their everyday interactions with strangers, service providers, and civil servants, second-generation Caribbean men learned that they were unpalatable in U.S. society. Men painstakingly described numerous incidents in which store owners cast them as thieves, women automatically assumed that they were rapists, and taxi drivers refused them service. The hegemonic images of dark-skinned men as potential criminals was so powerful that men reported many instances in which they were treated as "suspects," not only by members of the dominant group, but also by their own communities. Men expressed particular concern about their interactions with some police officers who racially profiled them as potential criminals as they walked the New York City streets, solely because of their skin color.

The psychological costs to the individuals and groups subjected to this type of experience included repressed rage, humiliation, frustration, resignation, and depression.[78] Men's encounters with negative stereotypes served as painful reminders that they were racially stigmatized and not truly accepted by the wider society. Social rejection and face-to-face discrimination were realities that not only were humiliating and stressful, but also had a lingering effect that shaped the life perspectives of the second generation in surprising ways. In due course, these experiences contributed to men's worried outlooks about their prospects for social mobility through education.

Women also spoke about encountering racial stigma in public spaces; however, it was markedly different from that encountered by men. The racialization experiences of Dominican, West Indian, and Haitian men were more similar to one another than to that of their female counterparts. Women's racialization stemmed from stigmatized notions of them as exotic, sexual objects. Through social interactions in public spaces, women learned that strangers viewed them as sexually promiscuous "mamasitas" and welfare queens.[79] Women carved their identities and life perspectives against the backdrop of hegemonic narratives that cast them as sexual objects and in response spoke about the importance of an education in dismantling these racist images.[80] The racial meanings assigned to the second generation by strangers in public spaces stemmed largely from images depicted in the mass media that portrayed Blacks and Latinos as dysfunctional, menacing, and exotic—the cultural antithesis of Whites, who are represented as "normal" Americans.

What is significant here is how men and women responded to their distinct race-gender stigma. Episodes of stigmatizing and racializ(ing) social interactions in public spaces left indelible imprints on their life perspectives and views about the role of education in their lives. While men often encountered violent or aggressive treatment from Whites, women's race-gender experiences were somewhat less confrontational than those the men were subjected to. Women spoke about the importance of attaining an education in terms of contesting widely held stigmatizing beliefs about their immorality and sexuality as urban minority women.[81] Men, on the other hand, responded to their racial stigma by expressing some doubts about education as a route for upward mobility for them. As we wade through the following chapters we will learn that some of the race-gender lessons imparted to men and women while in school also begin to sculpt their views about education in fundamentally distinct ways.

CHAPTER 3

"Urban High Schools": The Reality of Unequal Schooling

There is something about the educational system here in the United States, especially in those formative years, from kindergarten, first, second and third grades. There is something that is missing here that I got there in the Caribbean. I remember when I came here I got skipped a grade because I was more advanced than the other children my own age. And now, I have an eight-year-old brother who is in school here, and the things that he does now, I was doing when I was six. So the systems are geared totally differently and I think I would like my children to be raised in that kind of educational system in the Caribbean, at least at first.

Hazel, 22-year-old West Indian woman

Hazel's concerns about the quality of the education available to racially stigmatized groups in the United States are provocative. Like most immigrant parents, Hazel's parents came to the United States in order to provide better educational opportunities for their children. How can we explain the apparent irony that small island nations offered a more rigorous education than one of the world's biggest superpowers? This paradox can be understood in terms of how Caribbean youths are racialized in the U.S. context.

The social and political landscape faced by the new second generation is qualitatively different from that faced by older second-generation groups. When the children of European immigrants entered the public school system during the post–World War II economic boom, public investment in education was considered a national imperative. During the 1980s and the 1990s, racially stigmatized immigrant communities have faced a political-economic culture that has consistently disinvested itself of public education.[1] It is against the backdrop of a political backlash against the gains of the Civil Rights Movement, women's rights, bilingual education, and affirmative action programs that the second generation entered U.S. schools.[2]

In 1993 Robert Jackson, a parent from Washington Heights, Manhattan, and District 6 School Board member, along with the Campaign for Fiscal Equity, brought a lawsuit against New York state for its chronic underfunding of New York City public schools. As a plaintiff, Mr. Jackson argued that 74% of New York state's Black, Latino, and Asian children lived in New York City, yet there was a $2000 discrepancy per child between the funding received by schools in New York City and the statewide average. As a defendant in the case, Governor Pataki contended that the state only had to provide students with a ninth-grade education. The defense for New York state argued that since poverty and troubled families were the key causes of student failure, better-funded schools would not make a difference. However, State Supreme Court Justice Leland DeGrasse begged to differ:

> Demography is not destiny. . . . The amount of melanin in a student's skin, the home country of her antecedents, the amount of money in the family bank account, are not the inexorable determinants of academic success. . . . The court finds that the City's children are capable of seizing the opportunity for a sound basic education if they are given sufficient resources.[3]

In January 2001 Justice Leland DeGrasse of Manhattan decreed that New York state had violated the federal Civil Rights Act of 1964 by depriving New York City public school students, the vast majority of whom are Black, Latino, and Asian, of "a sound, basic education" guaranteed by the New York state constitution.[4] Judge DeGrasse argued that the underfunding of New York City public schools confined racially stigmatized youth to low-wage jobs in today's high-tech job market. Despite the historic ruling, Governor Pataki appealed the verdict.

During the mid-1990s, at the local level, New York City Mayor Giuliani campaigned aggressively for the right of police officers to gain access to public high schools' yearbooks as a way of apprehending criminals. Despite local opposition from parents and community leaders, armed police officers finally gained control of the security operations at all New York City public schools in the fall of 1998. Given that the overwhelming majority of New York City public school students are Black and Latino, regardless of intentions, this demand can be interpreted as an oppressive *racial project*.[5] By intimating that delinquents attended New York City public high schools, government officials discursively linked low-income, urban, dark-skinned youth to illicit activities.

Both Governor Pataki and Mayor Giuliani's public policies point to how state and local officials create, circulate, and enact racial and gender meanings. Most importantly, the creation of these meanings in public discourse has concrete implications for the ways in which racially stigmatized students were treated in the school setting. In this chapter I examine how the racialization and gendering arising from public policies and institutional practices affect the experiences of young men and women attending public schools. I focus on their high school experiences because it is there that the race-gender gap is solidified.

As we sort through the narratives of second-generation Dominican, West Indian, and Haitian men and women, we learn of their critique of the substandard education they were subjected to and their differing race-gender experiences in the school setting. Over time, differing cumulative race-gender "lessons" again left significant but contrasting imprints on men and women's outlooks toward education. Regardless of intent formal and informal institutional practices within schools "race" and "gender" students.

Since the founding of the United States, access to public education has been a racialized and gendered privilege. Until the 1850s only a few states offered elementary schools for girls, as women were generally excluded from high school until the 1820s. However, once public education was made available to women, they always enrolled at higher rates than their male counterparts.[6] In spite of the landmark desegregation case of *Brown v. Board of Education* (1954), de jure segregation has been replaced by de facto segregation. My own experience growing up in a public housing project on the Lower East Side of Manhattan during the 1970s and 1980s is emblematic of the de facto segregation that has become commonplace across the United States. Although my predominantly Latino and Black housing projects bordered a neighborhood that was racialized as White, I never once sat in classrooms with students who were racialized as Whites until I went to college.

The dumbed-down curriculum made available for the majority of low-income urban youth has contributed to their growing disenchantment with the schooling process. José, a 25-year-old Dominican man, had dropped out of high school in the eleventh grade. While sitting in his crowded Washington Heights, Manhattan, apartment living room, I asked José about his aspirations and he remembered that he loved working with numbers but became bored by the dumbed down curriculum:

> In high school the teachers used to get me sick! I would go to class and they would teach me the same stuff that I already knew, that I had learned a year before that. It was boring! I always wanted to be an architect and draw buildings. I have always liked drawing. I don't know why. I should have kept on with my dream, but I don't even think I would go back to school. I mean, I want to go college but I don't know what to take.

Since they were exposed to low-curriculum tracks, second-generation Dominicans, West Indians, and Haitians were often underchallenged in their classes and responded by engaging in willful laziness.[7] Jose responded by becoming disengaged and withdrawing from school. José credited his younger sister and mother with motivating him to eventually earn a (GED). Although José recognized the importance of schooling, his previous experiences left a lack of trust in the school system's ability to prepare him for higher education and therefore he did not plan to continue his education. When I asked José about how he had ended up at that particular high school, he grimaced:

> They told me to fill this form but they just sent me there. I didn't want to go that school. . . . At my high school, in the fifth floor, it was all Dominicans and Hispanics. The blacks hung around in the first or eighth floor. There were no whites at my school. White people have more money, so a Hispanic guy might be smart and everything, but he won't get into a good school. He has to go to the whack school. So that's what messes them up.

José's experience of attending a de facto hypersegregated low-curriculum-track school resonated with the experiences of the second generation. José's description of his high school as "whack" revealed that he is painfully aware of the unequal schooling he has been exposed to through the years. In due course, José learned the lesson that as a racially stigmatized youth he was not expected to succeed in U.S. society.

Rodrigo, a 23-year-old Dominican man who had dropped out of high school in the tenth grade, but also eventually earned a GED, had grown up in my childhood neighborhood of the Lower East Side in Manhattan. Rodrigo lamented that he had applied to the elite specialized public exam high schools, but he had not been admitted:

I first wanted to go to the specialized high school because I was doing really well out of the regular people in junior high school. But the problem is that they never put me in a special program. They did not help me enough so that I could have passed the exam to go to the specialized high school. Then they said my second choice was my local high school. I started out real good [in elementary school], but then I didn't end up good. At the end of my high school years, I ended up mediocre because I was thinking that I couldn't really do it. I was average.

A pattern that emerged among the few men who had been initially been placed in "smart classes" while in elementary school was that by the time they had reached high school, they had been demoted to the "regular" classes, which usually meant low-curriculum tracks.

A handful of specialized elite New York City public high schools are accessible only through competitive entrance examinations. Although some of the second-generation Caribbean youth in this study had heard about these schools and had even applied, they, like Rodrigo and myself, were not accepted. The term "public school" actually refers to two different types of educational institution. The elite public high school just two blocks from my vocational high school had a student population where only 10% of the student population were classified as low-income and less than less than 8% were Black and Latino students. At my high school over 80% of the students were low-income and 80% of the students were Black and Latino. While at my high school my peers and I were learning how to make beds and take orders as a part of their nursing assistant track, my White peers were being trained to be scientists.

The 1980s and 1990s the backlash against equal opportunity programs at institutions of higher learning has trickled down to the elementary school level. In this debate, access to elite public high schools has been constructed as a racialized property right for deserving students.[8] Affirmative action programs that aimed to rectify historical and contemporary forms of educational discrimination have been framed as "racial preferences" for the beneficiaries of these programs. In this discourse, high test-scoring White students "lose" spots in highly competitive schools to low-scoring "unqualified" racial minorities, most of whom are Blacks and Latinos.[9] Embedded in this discourse are biodeterministic assumptions about intelligence and the intimation that any "minority" student, such as Blacks and Latinos, who gain admission to an elite school are inherently inferior to any of the White students who were not accepted.[10]

One of the reasons that curriculum tracking and unequal resource allocations are virtually uncontested in U.S. public schools is that most people subscribe to the "commonsense" ideology that we live in a meritocracy. Individual students' cognitive abilities are believed to be inherently unequal; therefore, one of the primary functions of schools is to foster academic competition among students in an effort to select and reward those best equipped to benefit from a quality education. In accordance with these principles, students are tested throughout their academic career, beginning in preschool. On the basis of these test results students are placed in "honors," "regular," or "remedial" tracks. In spite of the fact that tracking has been shown to benefit primarily those middle- and high-income students who are placed in the higher tracks and penalize low-income students who are placed in the lower tracks, the use of tracking is pervasive. As described by Fine (1991) in *Framing Dropouts*, in low-income immigrant neighborhoods "public" schools are ultrabureaucratic institutions that educate some youths, but more often alienate them and push them out. For wealthy communities, "public" schools were those that "privilege the already privileged and exclude others."[11]

In response to the dumbed-down classes they were subjected to, men described earning average grades because they were simply bored with the classes being offered. Men talked about not studying as hard as they should and cutting class, boasting that they were often "chilling" and "hanging out with the fellas." When asked about why he received Cs throughout high school, Alejandro, a 23-year-old Dominican man who had grown up in Elmhurst, Queens, grinned: "School was easy; C is all I needed to pass and I never tried to do better. I guess I was just lazy." According to Deren, an 18-year-old West Indian man whose parents were from Guyana: "I was smart in elementary school. I was always doing work, work, work, but in high school, you goof off." "Goofing off" can be understood as a response to the low-curriculum tracking that men were exposed to.

Sam, a 26-year-old Haitian man who attended a Catholic high school, but had earned Cs throughout high school, explained his disillusionment with his education:

> I gave enough to pass. I wasn't interested in what they had to show. I was interested in music and my idea of music wasn't what they wanted to show me. I'm glad that they taught it to me—the Mozart and the classical music—because now I'm actually interested in it, or curious about it and I can appreciate it. But they didn't really teach us about jazz or about pop or the modern music that we listen to today, which was what I was going into at that point and time.

Men's ambivalent attitudes about the role of education in their lives were also tied to larger social critiques about how the curriculum gave the impression that White men were superior to other groups.[12] In typical low-income public schools, racially stigmatized groups are subjected to academic violence.[13]

Since their cultural backgrounds and interests were deemed insignificant and omitted from the "official" curriculum, men responded by disengaging from their studies.

Sam expressed his doubts about succeeding in higher education:

> My mother told me, "Look, you need to go to college because you need to have something to fall back on." I want to be in the music business and right now it's more on-field training that you need besides the diploma. Well if I go to school to be a doctor and I don't become a doctor, what do I have to fall back on after I spent all that money? That's why I didn't go to the university.

Lurking in Sam's consciousness was the idea that he would fail in his educational endeavors.

Denzel, an 18-year-old West Indian man who was born in Trinidad and Tobago, but whose parents were born in Grenada, was old enough to have graduated from high school, but he was still enrolled in high school. When I asked Denzel about his C average he responded:

> I just try to work on my basketball game and get good enough grades to make sure I am in a good position to get a free ride to college because my mom, she can't really afford to send me. She wants to send me but I don't want to put that much pressure on her. If I go to college and I mess up, she will owe people money and stuff, so I try to get a free ride. That way if I mess up and lose the scholarship, I don't lose anything. But if my mom had to pay, I would have to take her money and trust in me. I would feel so bad if I messed up and cost her all that money. That's why I work on my game to get a free ride to college.

Throughout our interview at his kitchen table located in the small hallway leading to the door, Denzel appeared distracted. Denzel continually checked his watch so that he would not miss a baseball game with his older brother at the makeshift court located just outside of his Brooklyn neighborhood apartment building in Crown Heights. I asked Denzel if he thought it was better to work on his basketball skills than his schoolwork:

No, I study too, but not as often as I should. I think it is better if you can get a free ride because if you mess up you really lose nothing. You can go back. You get money. But if you take money and you mess up, you can't get any more money because the bank gave money in the past and you lost it, so they won't want to trust you anymore. I think its better to get a scholarship.

Why does Denzel fear he will "mess up"? Here it is important to distinguish worries over succeeding in academic endeavors from an oppositional stance toward schooling. Denzel aspired to become a lawyer and recognized the importance of higher education, but he was unsure whether it is a realistic goal. Denzel's primary concern centered on the notion that he would "waste" his mother's money because he may flunk out of college. At a subconscious level, Denzel may be worried that the education available to him at his local public high school has not adequately prepared him to go to college, and therefore pursuing a basketball scholarship might be his only hope for admission to college. Far from being oppositional, Denzel's views on education can be understood as ambivalent or vacillating—part of the worried outlooks shared by many men.

Perry was an 18-year-old Haitian man who lived with his mother and four siblings in a crowded one-bedroom apartment in Prospect Heights, Brooklyn. Perry's mother worked full-time as a cashier to support her family of five and therefore was not home during the daytime. I noticed that Perry's apartment was quite crowded, so we conducted the interview at a local fast-food establishment. I was heartbroken when several times during the interview, Juny, Perry's youngest sister, came by to get a bite from Perry's sandwich. When I asked Perry why he was not eating he explained that he was saving it for later.

Perry aspired to become a medical doctor. I asked Perry, who was still enrolled in the tenth grade in high school, if he had ever heard anyone say that if he did well in school he was "acting White." Perry was perplexed:

I'd think he's an idiot. . . . Why he's an idiot? OK, if that person is doing good in school, he got good grades, and then he's at the top of his class and he finishes school, why do you have to say that he's acting White? Because if he wasn't smart he would never be where he was, so why would you go saying things like that? Just because he got good grades in school doesn't mean that he's acting White.

Instead of locating the problems of urban schooling in individual students or their families, Perry articulated a counterhegemonic explanation for the academic problems of racially stigmatized youth: "The government sometimes isn't doing the job that they are supposed to be doing." For Perry larger social structural inequality, not individual student behavior and identity, was the most important influence on the life chances of youth.

Some of the literature on the education of racially stigmatized youth has pointed to the presence of an oppositional identity among stigmatized minorities.[14] The phenomena of declining grades and low academic attainment among stigmatized minorities have traditionally been explained in terms of Ogbu's (1995a, b) cultural frame of reference theory, and Steele's (1992) disinvestment theory.[15] In these frameworks, low academic achievement and other oppositional behaviors among involuntary minority groups are seen as responses and adaptations among minority groups that were incorporated into the receiving society through a process of slavery or conquest. Accordingly, these youths are not doing well in school because they have adopted an adversarial stance that equates schooling with losing their identity as minorities and "acting White."[16] Other studies have suggested that men may not want to pursue academic success because they may be accused of being feminine.[17] Fordham (1996) found that some of the high-achieving African American male students in Washington, DC, high schools faced more pressure to reject school achievement than women because they feared that their peers would accuse them of being homosexual. Waters (2000) also found a similar dynamic among second-generation West Indians and Haitians in New York City. Similarly, Arnot (1999) and Willis (1981) argued that the new boyish antischool culture is one of the consequences of economic decline and one of the reasons for boys' failure in schools.[18]

The men in my study did not define academic success as a feminine trait. Some studies have begun to challenge the assumption that African Americans do not do well academically because they fear being accused of losing their identity. In a study of African American adolescent female high school students, Schultz (1996:534) found that the notion of "acting White" was nonexistent.[19] Instead, the young women believed that it was foolish for them not to try to do well in school.[20] Similarly, Tyson's (1998) study of African American children in a southeastern city also found that academically successful Black elementary school students were not ostracized by their peers for achieving academic excellence. Rather, students strove to be "smart." This response to schooling was quite similar to that of the second-generation Caribbean men in this study, who in spite of the worries they had over their chances for upward mobility, still believed in the value of an education.

Men who had earned As and Bs throughout high school explained their success in terms of serendipity.[21] Shawn, a 25-year-old Haitian man who had grown up in Prospect Heights, Brooklyn, and who was enrolled at the public university, said that he received good grades in high school because "I had a 'knack' for it. When I listen, I retain the information. I didn't really used to study." Similarly, when asked about how he was able to earn a B average one marking period, Reynaldo, the Dominican young man who was struggling in a community college, replied: "I must have gone crazy."

Besides willful laziness, another response men had to the dumbed-down programs they were offered was involvement in a variety of non-academic activities. Playing sports, hanging out, and talking to girls became the most engaging aspects of high school. Joaquín, a 20-year-old Dominican man who had dropped out of high school and was attending a GED program at a local community college, explained that he had received mostly Cs in high school because "I was there for the basketball." Young men from racially stigmatized groups may place more emphasis on being good at sports and games because curriculum tracking and poor preparation in their local high schools have left them with many doubts about their academic potential.

Men lamented the lack of academic support they had received from some teachers in their schools. I asked Carlos, a 19-year-old Dominican man who participated in the focus group and who was enrolled at a four-year college, about his relationships with his teachers:

> My high school counselor told me I was not made to go to college. That's when I was slipping and my grades were low. I was like, "Why are you telling me this? I want to go. Let me find out on my own." So my counselor was not really supportive. My parents wanted me to go to school, but I really didn't have a teacher that was saying, "Go to school." So you have to give yourself support and not depend on other people.

Through their interactions with school personnel, men often received both subtle and overt messages that intimated that they were viewed as problematic youths who were not expected to do well in school. Men from racially stigmatized groups have been most likely to believe that teachers did not encourage them to pursue their goals.[22] Teachers tend to discriminate against young men who misbehave, so that late maturing boys are more likely to be tracked into low-level curriculum programs.[23] Black men are given less praise for their work in school and are more likely to be diagnosed as retarded or emotionally disturbed than are their White counterparts.[24]

Isidro, a 21-year-old Dominican man, had attended some elementary school in the Dominican Republic and had grown up in Flushing, Queens. He was completing his baccalaureate studies in economics at a four-year public university. He expressed nostalgia about schools he had attended back home:

> I wish I had finished school over there [the Dominican Republic]. You used to get into fights and stuff with other kids, but it wasn't that bad. You used to like the teachers a lot—have a good relationship with the teachers. . . . We knew where they lived. I used to pass by their house and do whatever. It was more . . . como se dice eso? [how do you say] Sometimes they became your parents. They were more involved in your education and not just your education, but how you grow up.

interesting

Isidro remarked that the only teachers with whom he had a good relationship in the United States were his gym teachers: "I used to play volleyball in a team and we had a good relationship with my coach, she was good. Sometimes I see her and her kids. It was a good relationship. . . . I think the sports did that." Like Isidro, few men could recall having good relationships with teachers other than their gym teachers.

Although the average age of the foreign-born youth in this study was seven at the time of arrival, a handful of them had completed a few years of schooling in the Caribbean. Young men, mostly Dominicans and West Indians, spoke about being sent to schools in their home country for short spells of one to three years for disciplining.[25] Andrés, a 24-year-old Dominican man who had grown up in Corona, Queens, but lived in Elmhurst, Queens, was attending the police academy. Andrés explained that his parents worried about the safety of their children in New York City, so when the time came for him to enroll in high school they moved back to the Dominican Republic:

> My parents were afraid you would become a criminal here so they just shipped my whole family. First an uncle of mine sent his kids out there and they thought it was a good idea and they sent us and another uncle sent his. We wound up, the whole family, all the young kids being in DR together. . . . I think it worked. Everybody they sent out there, when they came back, none of them are in jail; none of them are in trouble.

It is ironic that they sometimes sent their children back to their homelands so that they may be protected from the problems that were commonplace in the United States.

In comparing the curriculum he was offered in the United States with
that which he had had in the Dominican Republic, Andrés articulated a biting social critique of the low-curriculum tracking and pedagogy:

> It's very different because over here [the United States] you have
> tests (A, B, C). You aren't going to see that over there [the Domini-
> can Republic]. Over there, it is, "What is this?" BLANK. No multi-
> ple choice. And over there, you have to read chapters 1 and 2 and the
> next day you got to go in front of the class and say what chapter 1
> and chapter 2 was about. Everybody is supposed to be prepared. She
> won't tell you who's going to talk, so everybody has to read it and
> then the next day she will start going around—sometimes they just
> use the list. She will say, "Student number one, come up please.
> What did you learn?" You got to give a speech saying what you
> learned. . . . It works! You're scared when you first got there that
> you're not going to know anything, so you read it two or three times.

It is ironic that racially stigmatized second-generation youth, whose parents
came to the United States seeking better educational opportunities, felt that
the education they would have received in their home countries was superior to that available in the urban low-income schools they were confined to
in New York City.

A common thread in the narratives of young men was ethnic bantering
that led to fights while in school. Rodrigo, a 23-year-old Dominican man
who had grown up on the Lower East Side of Manhattan, recalled dealing
with ethnic teasing while growing up:

> They used to call me, like, "Hey, platano." I used to be like, "Who
> you . . . ???!!!" You know it was like I used to take it as an insult be-
> cause it wasn't said as a good thing. It was said like derogatory thing.
> I mean, like if my friend would say, "Hey, platano," I wouldn't
> mind. But, these guys are like trying to put me down for some rea-
> son for being Dominican. I would get into fights sometimes. In high
> school and junior high, I would say I was little less mature. I would
> be like, "Aghhh, what you . . . what's wrong with you?" And I'd just
> get into fights, sometimes verbal fights and physical fights; all that
> sort of thing.

Men described these confrontations as stemming from male rites of passage,
which they referred to as "testing." Testing or proving one's masculinity is
experienced by young men across racial, ethnic, and class lines, however, for

more masculinity

second-generation Caribbean young men, this process was intertwined with their stigmatized racialization process.

Alejandro, a 23-year-old Dominican man who was attending the police academy, remembered a similar experience while growing up in East New York, Brooklyn:

> When I was growing up being Dominican mattered a lot. My junior high school was mostly Black people and Hispanic people. Being Dominican caused you to be in fights. It made you become a victim of maybe an African American person or a Puerto Rican, so it was dangerous. I had a couple of friends, Black friends, Puerto Rican friends, but I mostly hung out with my cousins. It was basically who you knew.

Alejandro remembered that some of the same young men who engaged in fights with him would turn around and attempt to date his sisters: "It's different for girls. They are not tested in the same way because women are pretty and feminine."

While Dominicans reported being mocked for their clothing and culinary preferences, Haitians harbored many painful memories of virulent ethnic badgering that often resulted in unprovoked physical attacks. Perry, a Haitian man who at 18 years of age was still enrolled in the tenth grade, remembered the racial epithets hurled at him, particularly throughout his junior high school years:

> They would say: "Haitians stink, they don't shower, they don't know how to take care of themselves, they don't know how to do this or that." Sometimes that hurts. A long time ago that was the only thing I used to hear in my ears. That's actually when I would be getting into fights. Getting suspended for like two weeks at a time. If you ignore them, they're just going to keep it up.

The virulent racial stigmatization faced by Haitians is captured in the music being produced by the second generation. Wyclef Jean, a second-generation Haitian New York-based hip-hop musician, refers to the humiliation faced by Haitians in his album *Carnaval*: "When I went to school, Americans used to curse me. They used call me black boy, they called me little Smoky. The way they talk, I see they're uncivilized. They way they talk, I know they don't know God."[26]

Perry had frequent problems at school that stemmed from the way in which he responded to ethnic bantering:

> In 1992 when I was in elementary school, kids in my school were call-
> ing people Haitian and this and that. They were calling us boys some
> bad words. They didn't like Haitians, so all of us who were Haitian,
> started following them for that. We got suspended like two weeks or
> four weeks. . . . Every time the American kids did something to us we
> went and told her. She would just say get out of here you little Hai-
> tian this and that. Since we were still being picked on by them, and
> she didn't do anything to them, we did something to them.

Upset that his teacher had not done anything about the teasing, Perry and his
friends decided to take matters into their own hands. Not surprisingly, these
types of incidents led men to have bad relationships with their teachers.

Deren, an 18-year-old West Indian man who was born in Guyana and
came to the United States at the age of five, had grown up in Corona,
Queens. Although Deren had earned a GED and was attending a local community college, he admitted that did not enjoy high school because of his interactions with some teachers:

> The worst part about high school was that some teachers and security
> guards had bad attitudes and things like that. The way they would
> treat you! They'd treat you like a kid. They wouldn't treat you like an
> adult. Some teachers spoke you so low [condescending] like you're
> stupid, like you're low and they are all so intelligent. They always
> thought of you as a kid and you're always going to be a kid.

In part because of the stigmatized racialization of "Black" and "Latino"
young men as "problems" in the mass media, all of the young men recalled
at least one very negative interaction with a teacher. I was struck by how
men's narratives were laced with stories about constant problems with
teachers. When asked about his relationships with his teachers, Reynaldo,
an 18-year-old Dominican man who had grown up in Washington Heights,
echoed the sentiments of the men: "All of them were problems. Some of
them made my life impossible! They used to say that I was a pain in the
butt." Rodrigo, a 23-year-old Dominican man who had grown up on the
Lower East Side of Manhattan, grimaced as he recalled his elementary
school days: "Uhhh! My sixth grade teacher, for some reason he disliked me
so much and he was like, you know, he was nasty with me for some reason. I
don't know why." Likewise, José, the 25-year-old Dominican man born and
raised in Washington Heights, Manhattan, recalled: "In the fourth grade,
the teacher hated me, so I used to talk back to her every day." Men's negative interactions with teachers culminated in larger disciplinary actions in-

volving other school administrators. This was the case with Denzel, an 18-year-old West Indian man who recalled having "spats" with teachers who regularly sent him to the dean's office.

Even young men who earned above-average grades recalled having difficulties with teachers. Mark, a West Indian man whose mother was from Jamaica and father was from St. Vincent and St. Grenadine, had maintained a B average throughout high school. Mark recalled being expelled from class by his social studies teacher: "She just had a bad attitude. She gave us hell so we gave her hell." Shawn, a 25-year-old Haitian man who grew up in Prospect Heights, Brooklyn, and had maintained an A average in high school, was attending a four-year public university. However, when I asked Shawn about his relationships with teachers, he just bowed his head, "I'd rather not talk about it," refusing to revisit the painful memories.

These problems were not just confined to the public schools. Men who had attended private schools were not exempt from the generalized view that they were "problems." Sam, a 26-year-old Haitian man who had attended a Catholic junior high school in a predominantly White neighborhood in Flushing, Queens, grunted when he remembered how he learned about racism at an early age: "Mr. DeMaggio, the Catholic school principal, treated us like animals. He didn't treat us like kids. He told our class stuff like, 'You all should try to go to a school where there is more of your kind.'" For Sam, these interactions were painful reminders of the fact that his dark skin "tainted" him as a problematic student, even before he had even set foot in his school. Sam explained that he did not plan to pursue postsecondary education because he felt that the only way he would gain respect in this country was through opening up his own business and making money.

Schooling "Young Ladies"

Recollections about negative experiences were largely absent from women's narratives about their schooling trajectories. I met Rosy, a 19-year-old West Indian woman who was born in Trinidad and Tobago and had grown up in parts of Flatbush and Bedford Stuyvesant, Brooklyn, during lunchtime at a deli near her place of employment at one of the large department stores in midtown Manhattan. Rosy had been an average student throughout high school; however, she was attending the City University of New York and had a B average. Rosy aspired to a Ph.D. in psychology after graduation. Rosy remembered a time when she was not doing well in high school. When I asked her about how her grades had improved, Rosy reminisced about how her grades improved dramatically after she followed her teacher's advice:

My math teacher was my favorite teacher because she pushed me a lot. She knew I could do more than I was doing. I was playing around a lot during my second year in high school and my math teacher really kept behind me. I used to dress real boy! With a hat on backwards and everything! She would say, "You know, Rosy, you can be a lot more if you just apply yourself and dress like a young lady." So I did. By her telling me all this, she kind of changed my whole attitude. And I just changed. I graduated with a B+ average in high school.

Although she was still a teenager, Rosy had mastered the art of conforming to her gender role. A far cry from the jeans and baseball hats Rosy had sported during her early adolescence, for our interview Rosy was impeccably dressed in a cream-colored silk shirt and brown pants; not a hair was out of place; her make-up looked like she had just visited the cosmetics counter at a large department store. Thus, among the many lessons Rosy learned in high school was how "young ladies" should dress to succeed in the business world. When asked about problems with teachers, Rosy was perplexed: "Me personally? I was a really good student and very quiet," indicating that she equated her own silence with being an exemplary student.[27] Given that grades sometimes measure how much students follow school rules, at some overcrowded authoritarian schools "good students" are simply quiet and "ladylike." Increasingly, as low-income urban public schools became more authoritarian, they begin to prize so-called feminine traits, such as conformity, silence, and passivity.[28]

Unlike men, who were generally hard-pressed to describe positive relationships with teachers, women spoke of having a good rapport with their teachers. Marie, a 19-year-old Haitian woman who had grown up in Crown Heights, Brooklyn, but lived in the Flatlands area of Brooklyn, spoke fondly about one of her high school teachers:

There are certain teachers that you go to and they just put the work on the board and whether you do it or not they really don't care because, like they always say, it's not their education. They are still getting paid. That's what certain teachers said. But, there was this one particular teacher, he took very much interest in what we did. He also prepared us for college. He would give us college books to read. It was an English class. He would make us do certain college-level work. He would make us write essays and research papers like college students would do.

Studies have found that teachers tend to favor young women over young men because teachers think that young women are smarter and they like being around them more and have higher expectations for them.[29] Moreover, women are generally seen as less menacing than their male counterparts even if they misbehave. This may be due in part to the fact that the majority of teachers in the United States, excluding colleges and universities, are women. As a result, young women receive more positive messages about their capabilities and future prospects. Although Marie had a C average, at CUNY she was quite optimistic about achieving her career goal of becoming a registered nurse.

Women who had participated in bilingual programs remembered having very special relationships with their teachers. Cassandra, a 27-year-old Dominican woman who had grown up in Washington Heights, spoke nostalgically about her bilingual classes:

> When it was a bilingual class I was more close to my teachers. You know every teacher by name and the teacher was more concerned about you. . . . The teacher could tell you this is Dominican; this is Puerto Rican; this is Jamaican. They knew everybody. In a regular class you were just all the same. Everybody was just the same.

Likewise, Lidia, a 20-year-old Dominican woman who had grown up in Inwood, Manhattan, but was sent back to the Dominican Republic for part of her childhood after her mother passed away, remarked that she had had wonderful experiences with her teachers:

> I never had a teacher that caused me real problems. There were a couple of teachers that they always used to be nice with me. There was an English teacher that got me a summer job. I think he was Colombian or Cuban; I don't remember. There was this other one that he was Dominican and he used to teach history too. He was the favorite of all students. We used to love to take his class. . . . forget it; he used to love us to death.

As Lidia explained, besides good grades, women's friendly relationships with teachers sometimes materialized into bridges to job opportunities. Teachers seemed to more readily recommend women than men for jobs and internship programs.

Notwithstanding women's good overall relationships with teachers, they, like men, were also subjected to low-curriculum tracks. Katia, a 19-year-old Dominican woman who had grown up in Flatbush and Canarsie, Brooklyn, but had attended a high school in my childhood neighborhood of the Lower East Side in Manhattan, alluded to the racial dimensions of curriculum tracking:

At my high school you would not see a single Chinese person in ESL (English as a Second Language), but Dominicans were in ESL eleven! Easy courses like low-level math. Even though many of the Chinese were immigrants, they are taking chemistry. They're making it to private elite colleges. Dominicans go to community colleges, not universities. I was kind of disappointed at my high school graduation because I didn't see that many Dominicans receiving awards or making speeches. It was all Asians. You would be so surprised because our school is mostly Hispanic, Dominican.

Katia aspired to become a pediatric registered nurse; however, she was struggling with a C average at a community college. Katia had never taken biology or chemistry classes at her high school.

School practices (re)produce racial and gender inequalities by using race, class, and gender as markers to track students within schools, even within de facto segregated schools. Whereas Asian students may be stereotyped as college-bound "model minorities" who excel in mathematics and science, their Black and Latino peers are often stereotyped as academically inferior and steered into vocational tracks.[30]

At my high school, although I was placed in a vocational track that prepared me to become a licensed practical nurse, Ms. Wilson, an African American woman who was one of my favorite teachers and a retired registered nurse, recommended me for one of the few Regents-level classes offered in the school. Whereas my "regular" classes were exclusively Black and Latino, the Regents-level classes were mostly Asian, with a sprinkling of Blacks and Latinos, mostly second-generation youth from the Caribbean. Since my high school did not offer advanced placement courses, Mr. Healey, my ninth-grade science teacher, made provisions for several Asian students to attend these courses at the elite specialized high school located a few blocks from our high school; however, this invitation was never extended to any of the Black or Latino students, despite the fact that many of us had A averages.

Studies have shown that informal social practices within classrooms socialize White and Black girls to occupy dominant and subordinate positions in the larger society. A study of Black and White elementary school girls concluded that the gender and racial order in the classroom nurtured Black and White girls to develop different aptitudes. Whereas classroom experiences encouraged African American girls to perform emotional labor and develop their social skills, White girls were encouraged to develop their intellectual capacities and pursue high-paying, high-prestige occupations.[31] In this environment, Black girls were socialized to pursue service-oriented jobs, while White girls learn to assume that they will dominate racial "others" women in the workplace.[32] All of these practices occurred largely without any malicious intent on the part of counselors, teachers, or school administrators. These practices are part and parcel of the institutional discrimination that happens at many low-income urban schools across the nation in spite of the "good intentions" of school administrators.[33]

Another dimension of tracking was related to sex segregation. Women spoke at length about being placed in pink-collar vocational tracks.[34] Among the "majors" that women were funneled into during their high school careers was secretarial studies. Thelma, a 21-year-old West Indian woman who had moved to Crown Heights, Brooklyn, from Barbados at the age of six, expressed a social critique about her experiences in vocational classes:

> In secretarial studies, they teach you shorthand and how to take notes. It was kind of easy to take notes because I took a lot of notes in shorthand. My teacher taught grammar and the use of punctuation. It was very integrated in secretarial studies and you had to know it. You lose points for putting a comma in the wrong place. It was amazing to me. Although I didn't know what a research paper was, I knew where to place my commas! So, it was hard for me in college. In high school we didn't have any research paper or anything like that. They didn't challenge us at all.

Although Thelma had been an honors student throughout high school, in her secretarial program she had been poorly prepared to deal with college-level work. Consequently, shortly after beginning her undergraduate studies at a four-year college at a public university, Thelma was unable to maintain satisfactory academic progress, and she was asked to leave. Nevertheless, Thelma maintained an optimistic outlook and hoped to complete graduate studies in theology and pursue her vocation of becoming a clergywoman.[35]

How was it that Thelma and other low-income racially stigmatized women were placed in "honors" classes, learned "where to place their commas," and received "good" grades, but were never taught how to write a research paper? "Honors" classes are not equal across public schools, and many working-class and minority students who are placed in them and receive good grades do not necessarily get the same level of education available at the predominantly White, middle- and upper-class public schools in New York City.

Diana, an 18-year-old Dominican woman who was still enrolled in high school, giggled as she described the gender composition of the Cooperative Education Program (CO-OP): "In my first period business class there are a lot more girls! There were like thirty-five girls and about three guys. In my second period stenography class there were no guys. Not one guy!" CO-OP was another example of a vocational track available at many low-income public schools that prepared poor, racially stigmatized, and immigrant women for pink-collar work. Students in CO-OP alternated between classes and work on a biweekly basis. In addition to being graded on their classroom assignments, CO-OP students also received grades for their work performance, including opening mail, answering phones, data entry, and filing papers.

Another popular vocational program that women participated in was again another traditionally female-dominated field, nursing. A number of the women who were funneled into these programs aspired to become registered nurses; however, the nursing classes that women were offered were in preparation for work in the lowest echelons of the health-related industries. Vocational tracking, although well intentioned on the part of school administrators, undermined the dreams of the second generation. Katia, for instance, wanted to complete an associate's degree in nursing and eventually pursue a bachelor of science degree and become a pediatric registered nurse; however, she had only a C average at the community college. Since the vast majority of stigmatized minority students receive low-level academic preparation, they have a difficult time reaching their professional goals, regardless of how high their aspirations might be.[36]

Marie, a 19-year-old Haitian woman who had grown up in Crown Heights, Brooklyn, elaborated on her career goals:

> I always wanted to study nursing. Ever since I was little, in our family, they wanted us to go into nursing or become doctors and lawyers. So I wanted to be a nurse because I learned that in high school. I had so much fun in the nursing classes because they taught you a lot. They taught you vital signs and CPR. I never knew that was very important until I looked it up. And you had to learn it to be a nurse, so I took it. They showed you how to do CPR on a baby and the Heimlich maneuver. I got a certificate for nursing. I took the test and I passed it so I was a certified nursing assistant.

In Marie's case, making the leap from nurse's assistant to registered nurse would be a challenging feat, largely because of the shoddy preparation she had received at her high school. Despite the fact that Marie's community college average was only a C, she remained hopeful, firmly committed to her dream of becoming a registered nurse.

Women's ghettoization in pink-collar vocational tracks led them to formulate a nascent critique of the education they had received. Sedare, a 19-year-old Haitian student who had earned an A average throughout high school but was attending a paralegal vocational school, had some harsh words about the "preparation" she had received in her high school:

> They said my high school had a preprofessional program law program. They said it was a law school. A law school! Ha! There wasn't anything about law! They only offered one class about law and it was the shortest class. They didn't do anything about law! Nothing at all!

Sedare voiced women's disappointment over the inferior education they had received in high school. Although when compared with their male counterparts, women were more institutionally engaged and more likely to be placed in vocational tracks, they were still subjected to an inferior curriculum, which led to their woeful underpreparation for college-level work.[37]

Women who had been schooled in the islands not only felt that they had been exposed to a more solid curriculum in their respective home countries; they also mocked the low-level curricula that they were subjected to in the United States. Jahaira, a 30-year-old Dominican woman who had grown up in Bushwick, Brooklyn, but had completed two years of high school in the Dominican Republic, laughed when explaining the difference between the two school systems:

> In the Dominican Republic it's harder and more demanding! It's not like, read pages five through seven or an open book test, like they do here in the U.S. Over there, you had to get up in the class, close your book and recite, summarize what you learned—in your own words— not what you memorized from the book. And they had tests, pop quizzes every other day. It was really hard! It's not as easy as it is here.

Nicole, an 18-year-old Jamaican woman who had attended elementary school in Jamaica, also shared Jahaira's view of the schooling she had received in the United States:

> The exams up here [in the U.S.] are so easy it is unbelievable! And I wonder how people fail! For real! Down in Jamaica, there's this thing called CSC (I forgot what it stood for). You have to take all your subject classes. You have to choose a profession, say you want to be a nurse or you're doing the sciences or whatever. When you go to high school, you pick out what you really want to focus on. You have geography, you have history and whatever and you're going to take at least seven or eight subjects in school. And you have to take all of them and you have to pass all of them in order to pass the grade.

Second-generation women's critique of the education system raised some interesting questions, given that their parents had migrated to the United States to provide their children with a better future. While it is true that in the United States education is universal in that it is available to everyone, historically stigmatized groups, particularly those of African phenotype, have consistently been funneled into substandard segregated schools that offer little or no preparation for college-level work.[38] In their home countries, Caribbean youth were neither racially stigmatized nor segregated into low-level-curriculum tracks.[39]

Women also maintained an ongoing social critique of funding cuts to education. Maryrse, a 21-year-old Haitian woman who had grown up in Crown Heights, Brooklyn, echoed the sentiments of youth:

> I believe that one of the issues that the Mayor [Giuliani] refuses to pay attention to is education. I mean they are raising tuition on college students and then telling them to stay off the streets. They don't have the money to go to school, so what do you expect them to do? I believe that the government tends to overlook that. Also, there are a lot of abandoned houses around the neighborhood. Simple things like just keeping the neighborhood clean, they tend to worry about other things more than the important issues.

Maryse's comments illustrate the social critique and resistance emanating from low-income, racially stigmatized communities.[40] Men and women alike voiced their worries over the growth of prisons, while disinvestments from education have continued unabated. Continually blamed for the ills of society and relegated to substandard living conditions and social services in their neighborhoods, second-generation Caribbean youth wondered why cuts were being made to the public university system. Three decades of open admissions at the public university was phased out at the four-year colleges over a four-year period (1998–2001).[41] Given that for over a century (1865–1965) the City College of the City of New York had been free of charge, second-generation youth felt that these cuts were targeting them because they came precisely at time when large numbers of low-income members of racially stigmatized groups and immigrants were enrolling in college.[42] In spite of all of the budget cuts in higher education, women maintained a firm belief in the value of an education.

Like men, when asked whether they had ever heard of any academically successful co-ethnics being accused of "acting White," women were perplexed. Maryse explained that she had never heard of this phenomenon:

> Not in the school I went to, kids were not saying that. I see it on TV.
> It's ridiculous to say that to get an education means to sell yourself
> short, how are you selling yourself short if you get an education? I
> don't get that.

Women mentioned that they heard of these terms on television programs or
vicariously through their African American teacher's stories about growing
up during the "second emancipation," the post–Civil Rights era.[43]

Women recalled that their academically successful co-ethnics were
viewed with pride in their schools. Katia explained that her academically
successful high school peers were looked up to:

> They actually applauded you. If you were getting a certain average
> or whatever, people would say "Wow! I'm proud of you." They
> were like, "Wow! You're making a difference because most of us, we
> don't make those kind of grades. You're going to make it!" I knew a
> couple of people like that. You just had to applaud them.

Since the second-generation Caribbean youth in this study did not see academic success as incompatible with retaining their ethnic identity, the explanation that racially stigmatized youth do not do well in school because
they fear that their peers will accuse them of "acting White" was not rele-
vant.

When women were confronted with ethnic teasing, they often dismissed
it. I asked Yvelise, a 24-year-old Dominican woman who had grown up in
Washington Heights, Manhattan, and had dropped out of high school, but
eventually earned a certificate in secretarial studies from a vocational school,
if there had been any times when she experienced problems for being Dominican: "Yeah, maybe somebody didn't like the way I looked or somebody
was jealous." Likewise, Rosy, a 19-year-old West Indian woman who was
earning a B.A. in psychology and hoped to pursue graduate studies in psychology, remembered ethnic teasing as jealousy:

> When I was in elementary school they used to call me names because
> I was West Indian. Some students would say: "You are all coconuts
> or something like that." I would say: "Hey, I'm proud to be one." I
> think it is just an envy thing where they are just jealous that they are
> not from the Caribbean.

In part because some West Indian women spoke with a slight British accent,
they recalled being stereotyped as snobbish by their peers.

Lidia, a 20-year-old Dominican woman who had grown up in Corona, Queens, was attending a GED program at a private community college. Lidia remembered that she often heard negative comments about Dominicans; however, she resisted the urge to engage in fights:

> You know what, sometimes I would get annoyed when people talk bad things about Dominicans. But, I never said anything. I stayed quiet. One day I was coming home from school on the bus and there were these two Puerto Rican girls. I was sitting down and they were standing right next to me and saying, "I hate getting on the bus when all these little Dominican guys are here." So, I just said to myself, "Are we the only ones that have a mouth?" It was annoying. I wish I could tell them something but, then I said, no, forget it.

Cassandra, a 27-year-old Dominican woman who had grown up in Washington Heights, Manhattan, remembered how she dealt with racial epithets about Dominicans:

> When I was a child, whenever people would say negative things about Dominicans, I always said, "I guess you haven't seen much of the world." I just pictured that person as being very limited in terms of their knowledge and ideas about the whole world. That's how I see it.

While Dominicans and West Indians were subjected to a milder form of ethnic bantering than were Haitians, Haitian women recalled that they often felt isolated and were subjected to cruel ethnic teasing. Maryse explained how she coped with the anti-Haitian sentiments at school while she was growing up:

> The things that used to go on, especially in the junior high school I went to! They used to beat up Haitians. I was lucky because I was never in ESL [English as a Second Language] class. I was in an American class. Although I came here at the age of five, my first language was English. I learned how to speak English. So that separated me from the rest of the Haitians, but I used to see what happened to them, especially around Halloween. They used to beat them up! Therefore, when I was growing up I used to be afraid to say I was Haitian. I used to say I was from the Caribbean, but not Haiti. But now that I'm an adult, it's not a problem for me.

Maryse shielded herself from violence by camouflaging her ethnicity from her peers. As Creole speakers, with no other reference groups in the United

States, Haitian students were sometimes subjected to violent ethnic teasing and physical attacks at school and in their neighborhood. While men's responses to ethnic bantering were tied to notions of masculinity, women's approach to conflict resolution was intimately related to women's notions of gender-appropriate behavior whereby "ladies" resolved disagreements in nonconfrontational ways. However, it appeared that men and women coped with this badgering in distinct ways. While men viewed ethnic teasing as an assault on their masculinity, women did not feel that their femininity was under attack and therefore developed a thick skin for ethnic bantering.

Despite the fact that she had dropped out of high school, Yvelise, a 24-year-old Dominican woman who eventually earned a GED, clung to her belief that education is important for social mobility:

> I really want to go back to school. . . . I tell my daughter, the one that is going to school now, go to school. That's all you do. That's your problem and that shouldn't be a problem to you. That's all you do, go to school. . . . I think if you had an education you would be able to do anything you wanted. . . . If you want to do something, you can do it.

Women articulated more hopeful outlooks than men about the role of education in their lives. This was due in large part to the different experiences men and women encountered throughout their schooling trajectories.

The race-gender gap is not unique to the United States and is apparent in other industrialized countries. In England women have also outpaced their male counterparts in their academic endeavors.[44] Here, the gender gap in education is explained in terms of social movements for equality, including feminism, coupled with economic transformations that have radically altered historic patterns that denied educational opportunities to women. Accordingly, both macro-level and micro-level changes, including the forces of social change and the actions of the state as well as teachers have irrecoverably transformed girls' and boys' identities, aspirations, and educational choices.[45]

Conclusions

In spite of the progress made after the Civil Rights Movement, racial and class segregation in the United States has increased during the 1990s.[46] In a national study of residential segregation, Massey and Denton (1994) found that African Americans continue to be segregated residentially. Racial segregation has concentrated disadvantage in the poorest neighborhoods, with the result that overcrowded and dilapidated school buildings have become commonplace in the vast majority of racially stigmatized neighborhoods in New York City.[47] New York City Mayor Giuliani's support of police access to public school yearbooks and New York state Governor Pataki's appeal to the State Supreme Court ruling for equitable funding for New York City public schools are examples of the macro-level oppressive racial projects in urban schooling that are part and parcel of the racialization of Caribbean youth.[48] Robert Jackson's lawsuit is an antiracist racial project. Macro-level racial formations at the level of state and city school policies as well as micro-level racial and gender formations in the form of social interactions are important because it is against these backdrops that the second generation formulated their views on the role of education in their lives. I want to emphasize that both young men and women in second-generation Caribbean communities were receiving an inferior education because of the ways in which their respective groups have been racialized in the United States. Notwithstanding the fact that women were more likely to attain higher levels of education than their male counterparts, it is important to emphasize that they were both subjected to "ghetto" schooling.

In the opening quote, Hazel's vexing question about the quality of the education offered in the Caribbean compared with the United States posed a quandary. How was it that economically exploited countries provided a better education than that available in most of the school attended by the second generation in the United States? Largely because the education offered to racially stigmatized youths in the "formative" years was substandard, by the time students left high school they had been exposed to very little preparation for college-level work. Indeed, most schools attended by racially stigmatized youth did not even offer college preparatory tracks or advanced placement courses.[49] Judging from the low-curriculum tracks that they had been exposed to, it was not surprising that men expressed doubts about pursuing education as a route for social mobility.

Experiences with ethnic bantering were also a source of fights for men, which eventually contributed to their strained relationships with teachers. In addition, with the sole exception of sports activities, men were not as involved as women in school programs or internships. Nonetheless, men also criticized the low-curriculum tracks they were placed in and often responded to boredom in school by not studying. "Willful laziness" was men's basic response to the negative treatment they received within the school system. "Willful laziness" should be distinguished from a forthright adversarial stance toward education. Rather, an ambivalent attitude, which was common among second-generation Caribbean men in this study, can be viewed as a consequence of mistreatment in school, rather than as the cause of their low educational attainment.[50]

In contrast, women remembered episodes in which they were exhorted to behave like "young ladies." In this context, women learned that being a good student was related to social behavior, rather than to academic achievement.[51] Moreover, unlike the young men, who spoke about having extensive problems with teachers, women spoke of positive relationships with their teachers. Overall, teachers were more sympathetic toward young women who broke school rules because as "young ladies" they were not seen as menacing as their male counterparts. While women dealt with ethnic teasing by ignoring it or by hiding their ethnicity, men sometimes coped by engaging in physical confrontations. Nevertheless, women expressed a growing dissatisfaction with the inferior schooling and vocational tracks they had been exposed to, but at the same time they also held an unwavering belief in the value of education for them as women. Whereas women's high school experiences can be described as a process of institutional engagement and oppression, men's experiences can be described as institutional expulsion.

Significantly, the distinct race-gender experiences that youth navigated within the high school setting were cumulative and in turn molded their outlooks on education. Men and women experienced the racialization process differently and therefore reacted differently. The following chapter delves into what I observed during my six months of fieldwork at Urban High School, with a focus on the ways in which young men and women were treated in the school context and how these experiences further shaped their outlooks toward education.

CHAPTER 4

"Problem" Boys

¡Yo siempre tengo que llegar tarde! (I always have to arrive late!)
Juan, senior at Urban High School

One cold and blustery February morning I bumped into Ms. Marín on my way out of the subway on my way to Urban High School (UHS). Ms. Marín was a veteran second-generation Dominican teacher who had worked at UHS for over fifteen years as a bilingual counselor. As she rushed off to her first period class, Ms. Marín hollered, "The Dominican Students' Organization is celebrating Dominican Independence Day, February 27. They have invited a renowned Dominican-born writer to speak during periods four and five. I hope you can make it."

Thrilled that I would have an opportunity to participate in this event, I arrived early, but it was already standing room only. Since the auditorium on the main floor was quite decrepit, the activity took place in an alternative space—another dilapidated fourth floor classroom. Over a hundred students were squeezed into space designed to accommodate perhaps seventy. As usual there was a strong security presence. Positioned at the entrance to the room, uniformed security guards checked students' identification and collected signed permission slips authorizing them to attend the event. Fortunately, my privileged status as a "volunteer" allowed me to circumvent the long line.

Before introducing the writer, Belkis, the president of the Dominican Students Organization, expressed gratitude to its advisor, Mr. Gómez, a first-generation Dominican teacher who helped them organize the event. During the presentation, I could have heard a pin drop. Students and teachers alike demonstrated the utmost respect and reverence for the writer, who appeared to be in his sixties. When the question-and-answer period began, students engaged in a lively exchange. Nelson, a young man in the audience, asked in Spanish, "Does the future of Dominicans reside in the United States?" The writer affirmed, "You will always be Dominican, even if you become United States citizens. You will always have the last name, the color, and you will always be Dominican." Feliciano, another Dominican young man sitting in the crowd, stood up and asked in Spanish, "What do you think about the negative stereotypes that have been created about Dominicans both here in the United States and back on the island?" The writer remarked, "The infamous drug workers are the product of a youth without a future— youth who do not have an education." The reality of the racial stigmatization of the Dominican community is ever present in the minds of the second generation that grew up in New York City during the 1980s and 1990s.[1]

High school is a crucial site for exploring the origins of the gender gap because it is in this institution that it becomes most pronounced. Seemingly neutral school practices, such as security operations and classroom dynamics, are deeply racialized and gendered. Therefore in this chapter I focus on how ordinary day-to-day school practices and classroom dynamics are racialized and gendered and in turn shape second-generation youth views about the role of education in their lives. In an effort to unravel how race and gender stigmatization filter down to the school level, in this chapter as well as the next, I tour the hallways and classrooms of UHS.

I begin with a brief description of the neighborhood and institutional context in which UHS is embedded. Next, I bring into focus some of the invisible race(ing) and gender(ing) processes that occurred at UHS. I focus on two levels: first, the formal and informal institutional practices, in the form of rules, regulations, and policies, and, second, the micro level of social relations and interactions among students, teachers, and other school personnel. I uncovered that ordinary, seemingly neutral day-to-day school practices are racialized and gendered. Although men and women are members of the same ethnic group, attend the same high schools, and come from the same socioeconomic background, they have fundamentally different cumulative experiences of the intersection of race and gender processes in the school setting. These processes are significant because they eventually frame their outlooks toward education and social mobility.

Racialization and Educational Opportunities

UHS is emblematic of "ghetto schooling"—the grossly inferior education available to stigmatized racial groups, such as low-income Latinos and

Blacks.[2] Both inside and outside, the building appeared to be falling apart and bursting at the seams. Scaffolding enveloped the entire four-story, turn-of-the-century building. Sections of the roof regularly collapsed, and pigeons could be found flying around in the auditorium and hallways, sometimes making their nests in the stairwells.

Originally intended to accommodate approximately 2500 students, UHS had a student population of over 3000. To accommodate the overflow of students, all incoming ninth graders were housed in twenty-eight makeshift neon orange trailer classrooms that had been squeezed into the neglected baseball field located behind the main school building. I dreaded using the bathrooms, as even the coveted teachers' bathrooms in the main building were quite unsanitary; they had missing doors, did not flush, and lacked toilet paper and working faucets. Ironically, despite the fact that the trailer classrooms had only one toilet for about forty students, these facilities appeared to be more hygienic than those in the main building.[3] Indeed, during the course of my fieldwork I could not locate a single working water faucet, so I always had to bring a water bottle with me. When queried about the possibility of moving to a habitable school building, Mr. Perez, the middle-aged Latino principal, lamented, "There is no public will to build new schools."[4]

During the first half of the century, the residents in the neighborhood surrounding UHS were mostly Jewish immigrants. Among the former graduates of UHS are several celebrities and well-known politicians. However, beginning in the 1950s, after African Americans and Puerto Ricans started moving into the neighborhood, UHS experienced significant decline in infrastructure, as investments in education faded. During the 1980s and the 1990s, when the Dominican community exploded, making them the uncontested single largest national origin group in the neighborhood, UHS experienced even more decline and lack of resources. Despite the fact that UHS is located in one of the city's most populated neighborhoods that has experienced intensive migration from the Dominican Republic, it is the only neighborhood high school in a six- to eight-mile radius. While the election of Dominican representatives to local and state government has led to the creation of a handful of elementary and junior high schools to address the problems of overcrowding, the dire need for a new high school remains.

In his state of the city address in January 2001, Mayor Giuliani made reference to the needs of New York City public school students; he juxtaposed predominantly White public schools in Queens as needing computers, with predominantly Latino high schools as needing baseball fields to motivate their students. No mention was ever made of the inequities that existed between these schools, namely habitable school buildings, books, supplies, basic necessities, and certified teachers. Not once during his address did the mayor address the "savage inequalities" that have become normalized throughout the New York City public school system.[5] New York City Mayor Giuliani's discourse on the need for different resources and motivators for "diverse" students is but one of many examples of how Black and Latino students have been written off in the minds of some policy makers.

Although the majority of teachers at UHS were White, the student population was officially designated as Latino (90%), mostly Dominican, with a number of Puerto Ricans and Cubans, as well as a sprinkling of Mexicans. The remaining student population is categorized as Black, mostly African American and second-generation youth from Haiti, the Anglophone West Indies, and parts of Africa. The enrollment of Asian and White students was negligible (1%). Not once did I see a White or Asian student in the entire school.

The majority of students at UHS were from low-income families. Seventy-five percent of students were eligible for the free school lunch program, indicating that they were living in poverty. One in four students was categorized as an immigrant who had entered the school system in the last three years, and 49% of students were designated as English Language Learners (ELL). Over half of ninth and tenth graders were overage for their grade, and 7% of students were classified as needing special education and were taught in self-contained classes. Only a quarter of students graduated within the traditional four years it usually takes to earn a diploma, and about a quarter dropped out, leaving the vast majority of the cohort remaining enrolled beyond the traditional four years of high school.

In part because more women graduated than men, it was men who were more likely to remain enrolled beyond the fourth year, making UHS enrollment slightly more male (55%) than female. In the hallways, I often overheard young men remarking that they had been at UHS for five to six years but had not been able to graduate.[6] In an effort to cope with the school overcrowding, in addition to the trailer classroom, UHS, like many other schools throughout the city, had adopted "p.m. school"—extra after school classes designed to deal with the large number of students who were behind in their classes but were too young or did not want to attend GED classes.[7]

Inside UHS

At our first meeting, Mr. Perez expressed enthusiasm about my research project because during his eight-year tenure as principal, he had been observing the race-gender gap for quite some time and was curious to learn what I would find. Mr. Perez quickly introduced me to Ms. Rivera, a middle-aged Latina teacher who was an assistant principal and chair of the social studies department. A vivacious veteran teacher of 20 years who could not remain still for a second, Ms. Rivera promptly took me under her wing, giving me a whirlwind tour of the school. Before joining the staff at UHS, Ms. Rivera had taught for over two decades at another predominantly Latino and Black High School that was plagued by the same infrastructure and resource deficits commonplace at UHS. Although Ms. Rivera had only joined the staff at UHS two weeks earlier, it seemed as if though she knew everyone in the school.

As Ms. Rivera and I made our way to the main social studies department office on the top floor, we stopped off to meet Mr. Matos, the college advisor, and she reminded him to call seniors who had not stopped by to see him. In a flurry of activity that included stopping by the attendance office and the guidance counselor's office, before the end of my first day at UHS, Ms. Rivera had me fixing billboards, distributing flyers to teachers, and taping up the results of the New York State Regents Examinations. As I taped up the examination results for the Global History Regents, I noted that only seven students had passed: five young women and two young men. When I looked over the exam roster for the American History Regents the results were even more dismal—only five students had passed: four young women and one young man. Although the New York State Regents requirements would not affect this year's graduating class, next year, in 1999, all students would be required to pass the English Regents. The remaining subject areas, math, science, history, foreign language, would be phased in gradually.

As we chatted in Spanish, Ms. Rivera commended me for doing research on our community and added that she was pleased that I was a Dominican graduate student who was educated in New York City public schools, because I could serve as a "role model" to UHS students. Ms. Rivera also warned me to ignore all the damaging media depictions of UHS as a dangerous school. Indeed, media representations of the neighborhood were quite negative and included images of drug wars, gang fights, and other criminal behavior at UHS. However, far from the depictions of UHS as a violent school, I noted that students were quite cordial toward each other. Between classes, students exchanged gossip in the hallway in a mixture of English and Spanish. Young men walking in the hallways usually greeted each other in Spanish by gliding, not shaking hands, while young women embraced and kissed each other on the cheek. I noticed that the young men walked in groups, while the young women tended to walk in pairs or by themselves.

strange

While we made our way through the crowded hallways to the department office, I queried Ms. Rivera about why there were classrooms filled with students, but there was not a teacher in sight. Ms. Rivera lamented that at the beginning of every semester there was always a shortage of teachers. Close to a third of the social studies teachers that spring were new recruits. Some of the veteran teachers in the social studies department remarked that the figure for the fall was closer to two-thirds of the department. Ms. Rivera was also part of the teacher revolving door, as she had just joined the staff. The need for teachers was so great that before the end of the semester, Ms. Rivera tried to entice me to consider teaching at UHS, even though I had had no prior experience with high school students and I was not a New York City certified teacher.

Every time I entered the social studies office, I was struck by how dedicated the teachers were despite the fact that they were neither treated nor compensated as professionals. Time and time again, I marveled over how teachers were able to perform their duties when they were lacking even the most basic supplies, such as books, chalk, or even a desk at which to sit and prepare for their next lesson. Although Ms. Rivera was an assistant principal and the head of the social studies department, due to lack of office space, her office had been transformed into a makeshift headquarters for the two dozen teachers she supervised. During their "free" periods, teachers were huddled elbow to elbow, cramped in a space designed to comfortably accommodate perhaps two to four people. In the words of Mr. Benjamin, one of the veteran social studies teachers, "This is really meant to be the assistant principal's office, but we have taken it over." Without access to a computer, teachers filled in attendance sheets, planned lessons, organized school trips, graded tests, advised students, and, in the few minutes that remained, tried to eat their lunches. On a number of occasions, I saw teachers sitting in the back row of each other's classrooms just so that they could have a space to sit and prepare for their next class. Working under such dreadful conditions, even the most student-centered teachers received the message that their job was not important. Likewise, even the most school-oriented students invariably learned that the education of low-income groups that are racialized as Black and Latino, particularly immigrant students, was not important, as in the U.S. context they were not expected to amount to much.

On Overcrowding, Policing, Race(ing), and Gender(ing)

Beyond the decrepit unsanitary conditions of the UHS school building and the lack of even the most rudimentary school supplies and basic resources, one of the most striking aspects of UHS was the ubiquitous security pres-

ence. Ten-foot iron gates surrounded the school grounds, including the dilapidated main building and the shiny orange trailer classrooms. All students
had to enter the main building through a smaller side door because the main
entrance was boarded up. Upon entering, students were required to present
their picture identification cards and pass through state-of-the-art airport-
style full-body metal detectors monitored by video cameras staffed by an assortment of security personnel, including uniformed security guarded and
plainclothes parasecurity school aides. On any given morning, at about 8 AM,
there was always a crowd of students overflowing from the student entrance.
Frequently, video cameras recorded false alarms—metal detectors set off by
keys and belt buckles, all of which contributed to delays. Not surprisingly,
student tardiness for first-period class was a routine occurrence. The only
reason I ever made it to first-period class on time was that my privileged status of "volunteer" meant that I never had to wait in line with students to
enter the school. I had access to a special entrance, accessible only to teachers, staff, and volunteers. Although uniformed security guards were stationed
at the separate visitor's entrance, there were no metal detectors or random
searches of backpacks, and I never saw more than a trickle of people entering
at once. In effect, I was exempt from the intense surveillance and scrutiny
that all UHS students were subjected to on a daily basis.

On a visit to the security office located on the first floor of the main
building, I queried Mr. Castellanos, a Latino man in his fifties who was the
head of security operations: "Why were police officers introduced to UHS
in the early nineties, years before Mayor Giuliani made it a citywide policy?" Mr. Castellanos explained, "UHS is not among the most violent
schools in the system, but it is among the most overcrowded in the city." In
total the security team consisted of over 50 personnel: one armed New York
City police officer (a police officer was on duty 24 hours a day), 15 uniformed security guards, 15 deans who had walkie-talkies, and 20 school
aides who served as de facto parasecurity staff. The occupational hierarchy
of the security personnel also formed a racial pyramid, with a White police
officer at the top, followed by Latino/Puerto-Rican uniformed security
guards, and at the bottom rung of the security forces were Dominican plainclothes parasecurity school aides who patrolled the hallways. In their early
twenties and dressed in T-shirts, jeans, and baseball caps, parasecurity
school aides were barely distinguishable from most of the older Dominican
male students whom they patrolled, barring the ubiquitous walkie-talkies
fastened to their belts.

Crowd control was one of the major functions of the security personnel.
During the five minutes that students were given to walk between their 40-
minute classes, uniformed security guards equipped with bullhorns were

positioned at the corners of the hallways hollering: "Move it!" Long after students were seated quietly in their classrooms, teachers often had to compete with the noise emanating from the walkie-talkies of security guards patrolling the corridors and stairwells.

One afternoon while spending time in the security office at UHS, I asked Mr. Peña, a Dominican security guard in his thirties, about his interactions with female students. Mr. Peña assured me that young women were only involved in frivolous spats over jealousies, unlike male students, who were involved in more "serious" fights over property. Remembering my own experiences in a New York City public high school during the 1980s, I pressed Mr. Peña to describe how he dealt with female students who had been involved in "real" fights. Before Mr. Peña had an opportunity to respond, Mr. Colón, another Latino male security guard, interjected, "We are not allowed to make physical contact with female students; only female guards are allowed to do that." In the event that a female student had been involved in an altercation, the only thing that the male security guards could do was follow them and radio for one of the female security guards. Since there were only two uniformed female security guards in the entire school compared with over two dozen uniformed and plainclothes male security personnel, the informal institutional practice was to police the men, but not the women. Meanwhile, male security guards were allowed to chase, manhandle, and apprehend male students. Although the official discourse maintained that security guards were supposed to protect and supervise all students, in practice the only students under constant surveillance were young men. In due course the problematic student was profiled as male.

I witnessed much physical and symbolic violence directed toward young men at UHS. As I traversed the packed hallways with Ms. Rivera, several times she greeted young men who were hanging out in the hallways, mostly in groups of two or three, and asked them in Spanish to remove their hats. The young men were usually polite, smiled, and obliged. However, one time Ms. Rivera and I bumped into Samuel, who was supposed to be on his way to her class but who instead was walking in the opposite direction. When Ms. Rivera queried him in Spanish about where he was going, Samuel explained that he was on his way to meet with his guidance counselor so that she could change his program. As Samuel continued walking, Ms. Rivera asked Samuel to remove his hat, but he just continued walking. Ms. Rivera then asked an African American male security guard who was patrolling the hallway to chase him down. As the security guard sped off to chase Samuel, Ms. Rivera grimaced and we continued on our journey to the social studies department office.

At UHS, school rules stipulate that no students may wear a hat in the school building. This rule was strictly enforced for young men but never for young women. Public officials view Black and Latino masculinity, including male working-class cultural forms, such as baggy clothing and baseball caps, as adversarial. This in turn contributed to men's higher frequency of misunderstandings with teachers, security, and other school staff. In effect, overcrowding and the subsequent emphasis on social control by security personnel are turning urban public high schools, which are supposed to be institutions of learning, into spaces in which urban low-income second-generation Dominican youth, particularly young men, are humiliated and criminalized through searches and other demeaning encounters, as well as the eminent threat of physical violence. Since public schools have resorted to authoritarian methods as a means of controlling students in overcrowded schools, young men, more than young women, have been regarded and treated as problem students by school authorities.

Security measures in the trailer classrooms were even more extreme. Ninth graders, all of whom were housed in the trailers, were required to wear school uniforms—blue shirt and beige pants—or face penalties, including having their identification card confiscated and losing their lunchroom privileges. Only students with swipeable identification cards were permitted access to the overcrowded lunchroom located in the main building. Not even teachers had keys to the teacher's lunchroom. A security guard positioned at the entrance of the teachers' lunchroom let teachers in, as the doors were locked from the outside. Most teachers, particularly Whites, ate in the cafeteria of a neighboring health facility; however, a few ventured into the decaying teachers' lunchroom. From the vantage point of the teachers' lunchroom, which was relatively empty, the students' lunchroom was overflowing with students. Whenever I entered I could not find a single vacant spot. Despite the sheer overcrowding, students were not allowed to leave the premises. The only exceptions were students who were in the trailer classrooms; a security guard escorted them to the main building for their lunches. Since the ninth graders were required to wear uniforms they were quite easily identified and were often the target of ridicule by older students in the main building, who were exempt from the uniform requirement. Not surprisingly, school administrators, students, and teachers colloquially referred to the trailer park as "Riker's Island," a jail located in New York City.

Security measures were even more intense for special education students, who were segregated on a separate floor and represented 10% of the students. Mr. Wallace was a White veteran teacher in the social studies department who expressed deep criticism of the "savage inequalities" at UHS. According to Mr. Wallace, the special education students were slated to go to the trailer classrooms; however, because of greater security concerns with them, they were housed on the second floor of the main building, directly above the principal's office, within a short distance of security headquarters.

I learned of one fight involving young men who were in the special education program. Mr. Sosa, the plainclothes security guard who intervened in the fight, was wearing a tae kwan do T-shirt and looked barely older than some of the students at UHS. Tired and irate, Mr. Sosa told me that he was a bouncer at a club on the Upper East Side, an upper-class White neighborhood in Manhattan. Understandably, school aides who made only $9 per hour had to moonlight to make ends meet. Mr. Sosa mentioned that five male students were arrested, and they were still looking for more. "I will be pressing charges," Mr. Sosa assured me. Mr. Sosa's brother also worked as a security aide and explained what had happened:

> A fight was going on where a young man was being held down and beaten by a group of other young men on the special education floor. Felipe summoned for help and jumped right in to stop the fight and was hit in the process. At that point the other security guards arrived at the scene to hold Felipe down before he went after the young men.

Mr. Sosa admitted that he tried hitting the students back, but that other security officers held him back. Later another uniformed security guard stopped by the office to say that the reason backup security guards had not been there sooner was that Mr. Sosa had given the wrong code over the walkie-talkie.

Mr. Castellanos, the head of security operations, was very careful about his choice of words when referring to security operations. Instead of using the word punishment, he said that he prefers the term "disciplinary consequence." He explained that the ages of the students affected where they would be disciplined: "Fifteen- and sixteen-year-olds are treated quite differently from seventeen- to eighteen-year-olds." It is worth noting that UHS had a significant portion of overage first-year students, indicating that many of the tenth graders were already seventeen years old. Mr. Castellanos declared: "Crimes will face the maximum consequence."

While we spoke, a young man entered the security office and Mr. Castellanos quickly reminded him, "Sir, your hat." Frustrated by the young man's hesitation, Mr. Castellanos repeated in a sterner voice, "Sir, your hat," and the young man obliged. When I queried Mr. Castellanos about the significance of the hat rule, he remarked that the enforcement of this policy was part of demanding respect from students. However, although all students were prohibited from wearing hats, only young men were penalized for doing so.

On other occasions, while sitting in the security office, I witnessed young men who had been engaged in scuffles being whisked away in handcuffs by the White police officer who was permanently assigned to the school. I asked Mr. Castellanos if the majority of students who were involved in fights were also involved in drugs, and he explained that there were rarely any incidents over drugs: "Most of the fights were primarily due to squabbles over property." According to Mr. Castellanos, it had been over five years since there had been a gun incident at the school. Given the link between overcrowding at low-income schools and increased security measures, it is not surprising that young men who are racialized as Black and Latino continue to be disproportionately arrested and convicted and were quickly forming part of the burgeoning prison industrial complex.[8] One of the worrisome by-products of the school overcrowding I witnessed at UHS was the forging of a pipeline between public urban schooling and the burgeoning prison industrial complex. The criminalization of low-income youth from racially stigmatized communities has become a "normal" occurrence that is considered to be a "common sense" law enforcement measure.[9]

Unearthing Race-Gender Lessons in the Classroom

Classrooms are not impervious to the social narratives and formal and informal institutional practices that "cast" youth who are racially stigmatized groups, particularly young men, as "problems."[10] In *Framing Dropouts*, Fine (1991) poignantly details how Black and Latino students are "framed" as the cause of poor schools, while the structural inequities of society remain unquestioned. Fine argues that much of this "framing" is unintentional and occurs despite the "good intentions" of overworked and underpaid teachers and other school personnel, who in turn are also "depicted" as lazy and unqualified.

One afternoon, I had lunch in the school cafeteria with Mr. Jimenez, a bilingual Latino teacher in his thirties, and he invited me to visit his bilingual special education global history class for ninth graders. Equipped with a walkie-talkie that connected directly to the security office should any student require immediate disciplining, Mr. Jimenez was indistinguishable from the ubiquitous plainclothes security guards. The class consisted of fourteen students, ten young men and four young women. The half-pint-size classroom was quite claustrophobic; it was originally part of a classroom that had been split into two with a makeshift dry wall. The chairs were pushed up against each other, forming two rows, and I was lucky to have found a space to sit in the back row. When I entered the classroom, one young man boasted, "Yo pongo a las mujeres loca!" (Women go crazy over me!) The four young women sitting near the window giggled silently. The young men sitting beside me berated each other in Spanish for misbehaving in front of "la visita" (the visitor). Seemingly preoccupied with acting out their definitions of masculinity, these young men announced their maleness through their disruptive behavior and sexual posturing.

Before Mr. Jimenez made his entrance, Ms. Flores, the teacher's aide, a Latina woman in her fifties, patrolled the tiny classroom, urging students to settle down and be quiet. While Ms. Flores looked over students' home-work, Mr. Jimenez opened the class by drilling students with true or false questions about ancient Asian civilizations. Next, he asked for volunteers to read passages from their textbooks in both Spanish and English. I was amazed to see that this class actually had textbooks for in-class use. After each reading students applauded each other, or, in cases where it was evident that a student had difficulty with reading, they mocked each other. Throughout the class, I was quite distracted by Ms. Flores, who spent much of her time working on a one-to-one basis with a young man seated in the front row. I noticed that although some of the readings were in Spanish some students still had quite a bit of trouble reading. I wondered if they had received any formal schooling in the Dominican Republic. Was special education simply a dumping ground for bilingual young men who did not have much formal schooling in their home countries, as well as students who did not "behave"?

Mr. Green's economics class for seniors provides a window to the micro-level race(ing) and gender(ing) that occur in classrooms.[11] On a clammy, rainy February morning on my way to UHS I bumped into Mr. Green at the bus stop. Mr. Green was an economics teacher in his twenties who described himself as biracial but who could "pass" as White in terms of phenotype. Mr. Green was carrying a huge army duffel bag filled with student journals and fresh photocopies that he had just picked up for distribution in that day's class. I almost asked him why he didn't leave them at school and quickly remembered that neither Mr. Green nor any of the social studies teachers had the luxury of a desk or office where they could sit down and prepare for classes, much less grade journals, exams, or any other student work.

That morning students asked Mr. Green about when they would receive their books and he bemoaned apologetically: "We should be receiving books soon and it should be easier. I know it's very hard to learn without a book. Just bear with me. I placed the request but it is centralized." Mimeographed handouts, whenever the machine was not broken, as well as some journal writing every day at the beginning of class, were the short-term solutions. Throughout the semester I noticed that none of the classes I observed had received textbooks. In an effort to compensate for the lack of books, Mr. Green often purchased the *New York Times* and joked: "I spare no expense for this class . . . and it's tax deductible too." To compensate for the lack of basic teaching materials, Mr. Green, along with many other dedicated and self-sacrificing teachers, had no choice but to pay for basic school supplies and reading materials for his students out of his own pocket.

One morning, seconds after the bell rang, Mr. Green, who always wore a shirt and tie to his economics class, slammed the door shut and announced: "You will have exactly seven minutes to complete this quiz. Please take off your hats." Students usually kept their coats on as they shuttled from class to class because they were not permitted to have lockers. Since the doors were locked shut from the outside, all latecomers had to knock to be let in and they were required to sign the late book. I was often late for class myself, as the five minutes that students were given to change classes was not enough time to get to their destinations in a timely fashion.

While students were completing the quiz, Mr. Green inched his way down the crowded aisle, grasping his Delaney grade book as a shield, while checking for homework. Mr. Green maneuvered his way around a tight space by walking over desks to get to the next row. As Mr. Green approached Lionel's desk Lionel joked in Spanish, "Hasta la tarea hize yo. Me estoy poniendo bueno. Unbelievable!" (I even did homework last night. I'm actually getting good. Unbelievable!), while the rest of the class laughed. Disappointed at the number of students who did not hand in their homework, Mr. Green warned, "Students, this is unacceptable! Only a handful of you have submitted homework. You have to make sure that you do your homework. It's 30% of your grade; therefore 70 is the highest grade you will get even if you get 100% in your quizzes and on the exam. Many of you will lose points for not handing in homework!"

Feliciano, a young man in the class, called out, "How come you didn't used to give us homework last year?" Mr. Green retorted, "You guys quiet down! Do you want to be here? I suggest that you follow the rules," pointing to the blackboard. A large piece of cardboard stapled over the blackboard listed "Mr. Green's rules for success":

1. Be present every day.

2. Be in your seat when the bell rings.

3. Homework is due at the beginning of class.

4. Do not wear hats, walkmans, or beepers.

5. Be quiet and attentive when some one is speaking.

6. Do not bring food or drinks to the classroom.

7. Raise your hand and wait to be recognized before speaking.

8. Be prepared for school.

9. Treat faculty and other students with respect.

Another rule that was not formally included on the board but was strictly enforced, not only in Mr. Green's class but also throughout UHS, was *English only*. On a previous occasion, Mr. Green had asked students about their favorite musicians and Viscaino called out *La Banda Loca,* a Dominican merengue band that was popular throughout the 1990s. Seemingly annoyed by the Spanish response, Mr. Green continued, "Okay. No music artist," and moved on to the next student who answered in English.

At a day-long teachers' workshop held in the crumbling auditorium on the phasing in of Regents examinations as a graduation requirement, many of the 200 teachers present, most of whom were European Americans, openly expressed their belief that students should speak *only* English while they were in school. At UHS one-third of students were Spanish speakers who were English Language Learners (ELL). However, the hegemonic understanding of bilingual students was that Spanish was a barrier that students had to overcome to become academically successful.

On a number of occasions, some teachers, mostly Whites, stopped students in the hallway and scolded them for speaking in Spanish. In one such instance, I was walking down the hallway and noticed Ms. Perkins, a White middle-aged teacher in her fifties, berating a young man: "Pedro, you should never speak Spanish in my class. You know English. Speak English!"[12] Understandably dejected about the de facto prohibition of his native language in the school setting, Pedro just stared down at the floor while being reprimanded. I was disheartened to see that in over twenty years the hegemonic belief that speaking Spanish is a liability was still in circulation at UHS. Like Pedro, I also received a number of disapproving glances from some other European American teachers and staff because I spoke Spanish with students, personnel, and Spanish-speaking teachers. I remembered my own experience when I attended a New York City public elementary school on the Lower East Side of Manhattan during the early 1970s. Although at the time bilingual education programs were not formally in place at my elementary school, some well-intentioned European American teachers automatically assumed that because Spanish was my first language, I would be condemned to speak Spanglish; I would never learn to speak or write English or Spanish fluently. The stigmatization of Spanish speakers as deficient continued to operate as unquestioned "common sense" at many public schools that served Latino students.[13]

In an ethnography of U.S. Mexican-origin youth in a Houston, Texas, public high school, Valenzuela (1999) found that Mexican youth and their families firmly believed in the value of an education. Families spoke about coming to the United States to provide their youth with the opportunities that were not available to them in their home country. However, schools were organized to undermine the cultural resources of Mexican youth as well as other racially stigmatized youth in that the cultural backgrounds of students were defined as deficient and problematic and therefore something they should move beyond. It was not education per se that Mexican origin youth objected to; rather they were reacting to a schooling system that consistently devalued their families and communities and chipped away at their social and cultural resources. In the end, Mexican students experienced schooling as a subtractive process, whereby their cultural and language backgrounds are defined as "problems" that needed to be stripped from them for them to succeed.[14]

In a similar vein, Mr. Green was a very dedicated teacher who, like many of his UHS colleagues, operated under the hegemonic assumption that assimilation was a prerequisite for academic excellence and social mobility for immigrant students.[15] As a Spanish-speaking group that is predominantly of African phenotype, second-generation Dominican students are often seen through the lens of the deficit model: racial others who are also "limited English proficient" and allegedly live in culturally deprived families. This type of racial stigmatization can be seen as a form of academic violence because it denigrates the culture and language backgrounds of students, and it is premised on the racist notion that retaining the Spanish language is detrimental to the acquisition of English. Against this hostile background, English language learners, particularly Spanish speakers, feel humiliated, devalued, and symbolically violated throughout their schooling process.[16]

Exactly six minutes after the quiz had begun, Mr. Green glanced at his watch and warned, "Okay students, you have one minute." Seconds later he added, "Okay students, time is up. Put your pens down. Put your names and pass the quizzes forward. If I see you writing I will take points off." The fact that Mr. Green had to cover a given amount of material within a 40-minute time block for each of the five classes he taught meant that coverage often took precedence over critical dialogue and substantive learning. Mr. Green was working within the institutional confines of a school system that was grossly inadequate and resistant to change; his classroom often felt like a very controlled environment that had a definite, inviolable time schedule.

Despite his "good intentions," Mr. Green inadvertently "framed" young men from Black and Latino communities as potential drug and crime statistics during classroom discussions.[17] Another morning Mr. Green began class by asking students to talk about the major problems that existed in contemporary society. I noticed that young men and women articulated differing views of the problems in society. Young men called out, "Crime, drugs, pollution." Young women in the class replied, "Poverty, homelessness, unemployment." Mr. Green continued, "Is crime directly or indirectly caused by poverty?" Leo, a male student, replied, "Drugs are a way to escape from reality; therefore we have a drug problem. But poverty doesn't necessarily cause crime. People come from New Jersey, buy their drugs, and what kind of life do they lead?!" Likewise, José chided, "I read about a study in the newspaper that states that 40% of 'weed heads' are in the 'inner city,' but 60% are from the suburbs!"

Affirming their approval for the social critique that had just been aired during class discussion, the rest of the young men in the class cheered and as usual made side remarks in Spanish. Noticeably upset, Mr. Green replied: "Students, I don't need the heckles! You need to raise your hands!" Mr. Green continued in a textbook fashion, "In an indirect way poverty can lead to drugs."

Flustered by the "symbolic taint" that was cast on his community, Leo muttered under his breath, "Just because you're poor doesn't mean that you use drugs." Leo's comments about people from New Jersey, as well as José's comments about the suburbs, were direct references to White suburban youth who came to low-income Black and Latino neighborhoods in New York City to purchase drugs, but they were neither featured in newspaper articles as drug addicts nor systematically racially profiled or targeted by the police for their criminal behavior. Given that the majority of the students at UHS are from low-income Dominican families and that the local and national media have stigmatized the young men in these communities as drug lords, they were understandably upset by Mr. Green's comments.

In an effort to continue the debate, José continued by asserting, "Many of the people who engage in crime do not have drugs." Again, the rest of the class applauded and made supportive remarks in Spanish. Oblivious to his students' social critique, Mr. Green continued to press them to agree with the class-based approach to the study of inequality: "What is the broad social goal of the minimum wage? Come up with alternative methods."

After a deafening silence, which can be interpreted as form of resistance to the racialization processes that had taken place in class thus far, Mr. Green offered another textbook solution: "Tax breaks to employers who create jobs." After another pause, Viscaino offered, "Train people for higher skilled jobs." While his classmates clapped, from his seat, Viscaino took a bow and looked at his friends. But, José chided, "What good is job training if the jobs are not there?" Mr. Green reproached, "There is a demand for skilled workers who make $100 per hour." Incredulously, Lionel questioned, "What kind of job pays $100 an hour?" Mr. Green replied, "Actuaries, they make over $100,000 a year." Lionel rejoined, "You have to understand that there are people out there who have an education but who still sell drugs because the jobs are already taken by people out there who have experience." Missing an opportunity to engage in a substantive dialogue on racism, police brutality, and job ceilings, Mr. Green regurgitated the textbook answers and proceeded with the lesson for the day in his quest to beat the clock.

Time and time again, Mr. Green's laudable attempts to encourage classroom discussion were undermined by his authoritarian pedagogy.[18] "Banking education," in which students are constituted as empty receptacles to be filled with the knowledge of an omniscient teacher, was not conducive to transformative dialogue.[19] It is interesting to note that Mr. Green did succeed in getting young men to participate in a classroom dialogue, but the ways in which second-generation Dominican young men participated—speaking Spanish and cheering each other when articulating counterhegemonic interpretations of the origins of racial and class inequality—were not palatable in the conventional classroom. Students' biting references to job ceilings, racism, and police brutality were muffled by an institutional pedagogy fixated on "covering" a given amount of material and producing "official" responses. More importantly, the young men in Mr. Green's class were once again racialized as disruptive and experienced as problem students.[20]

The gender balance of the class had a visible effect on Mr. Green's social interactions with students. Mr. Green was always on guard for his third-period class, which comprised mostly male seniors. However, Mr. Green's demeanor changed almost instantly during his fourth-period class, where the majority of the students were women. Mr. Green described these two classes as being like night and day.

One morning as students entered Mr. Green's third-period class, students were complaining that Mr. Green had given out chocolate to his fourth-period class and had taken them to the auditorium. Mr. Green retorted, "Sorry to disappoint you. Take your hats off please, gentlemen." I was often struck by how much older the young men appeared in comparison with the young women. Indeed, many of the young men looked only a few years younger than Mr. Green. This may be due in part to the fact that young men were more likely to be held back and remain enrolled beyond the fourth year than were women.

Students jotted down their responses to today's journal questions: "Should pornography exist? If the KKK exists, why shouldn't pornography exist?" In the meantime, Mr. Green walked around checking for homework. A bilingual announcement was barely audible over the ancient loudspeakers: "Tomorrow there will be an entire day of workshops for teachers; therefore, students will not have classes." Student rejoiced. When Mr. Green got to Gilberto, a young man sitting next to me in the back row, he noticed that he was reading a popular rap magazine, and, without saying a word, he quickly snatched it away from him. Throughout the rest of the class, Gilberto just sat silently in class staring off into space. After checking homework, Mr. Green began with today's aim, "How can we explain the results in shift in supply and demand?" A number of students moaned and groaned. I noted that although this was the eighth week of the semester students still did not have textbooks. Barely legible mimeographed worksheets were all they could rely on.

Mr. Green reminded students that the new Math and Science Regents examinations required students to write out a full explanation detailing how they arrived at their answers. "Yeah. But I don't have to take it," challenged Lionel. Toward the end of the class, Mr. Green distributed another quiz for them to work on, and Viscaino asked, "Didn't you give one just last class?" Mr. Green reproached, "I don't want to hear another word." I noticed that Gilberto, the young man whose magazine had been confiscated, did not participate throughout the class; he did not even write his name on the quiz. Relieved to hear the sound of the bell marking the end of the class, Gilberto quickly put his hat back on and raced out the door to his next class.

For his next class, period 4, which is mostly female, Mr. Green was relaxed, less confrontational, and indeed quite congenial toward his students. As Ramfis, a young Dominican man in the class entered, Mr. Green smiled silently, gesturing that he should take off his hat. Mr. Green thanked him when he removed it. As students wrote in their journals, Mr. Green returned yesterday's exams. Juan, one of the class clowns, who was always begging for attention, walked in and announced, "Yo siempre tengo que llegar tarde!" (I always have to arrive late!) and proceeded to his seat in the middle of the classroom. As Mr. Green distributed the quizzes, the young women generally appeared more concerned about their grades than did their male counterparts. Germania whispered to Rosa, "Did you pass? I got a 90." Mr. Green began class by saying, "Let's turn to our favorite graph. The supply and demand curve, so that we can do really well on the quiz today." I noticed that Mr. Green had not given this warning to his previous class, which was mostly male.

Mr. Green added, "I hear the same voices all the time. I want to make sure that everyone understands this for the test on Thursday." Juan protested, "But we have another quiz today." Mr. Green added, "I am very concerned about your learning. Students, let me give you something new. The Regents Exams require you to give written explanations of graphic problems." Ani, also a class clown who sat in the back of the classroom sucking a lollipop and who was always speaking out in class, announced, "I'm going to do my work now during finals." When Mr. Green called on Ani she replied, "I don't know. I wasn't even paying attention." Mr. Green replied gently, "Students, you need this class to graduate. I suggest that you pay attention." Even Juan participated, answering questions about the minimum wage. "But Mr. Green, didn't you say that inflation will result if the minimum wage increases?" Mr. Green responded, "Your answers are too vague."

At the end of class Mr. Green placed the quiz face down on each student's desk. Again, Mr. Green had to literally walk over desks to navigate the pint-sized classroom. Juan got up and announced, "I need a pen." Marisol, a young woman sitting beside him, offered him one. Assured that all students would begin at the same time, Mr. Green commanded, "Go ahead and get started." About half of the class had questions about unfamiliar terms on the quiz. A number of students asked what a tax rebate was. While students worked quietly, Mr. Green distributed copies of the vocabulary words in preparation for Thursday's exam. Upon completing his quiz, Juan could not resist the urge to stand up and announce his accomplishment. "Here, Mr. Green; I'm finished." He delivered his exam to Mr. Green's desk at the front of the classroom. As Juan inched his way down the narrow aisle back toward his seat, Mr. Green took a cursory look at the quiz and reproached, "Juan, you can go into more detail. Have a seat and go into more detail." Juan took the quiz back and resumed his seat, but he did not write another word—an indication that Juan was willing to give only enough effort to pass.

When the bell rang Juan approached me and asked curiously, "Are you checking up on Mr. Green?" Juan had not been in class, when I introduced myself to the class, so I briefed him on my research project, but Juan was more interested in asking me about what part of the Dominican Republic my family was from, and I told him "El Cibao." I queried Juan about his career aspirations, and smiling he replied, "A big-time lawyer." When I prodded Juan about any ideas he had about the colleges he would like to apply to, he said that he did not know. I encouraged Juan to drop by the college office for advice on the application process and financial assistance.

On the day of the exam Mr. Green began his fourth-period class by asking students to raise their hands if they wanted to go to college. Every single young woman and most of the young men in the class hoisted her hands up in the air. I noted that a few of the young men did not. Again, Mr. Green passed out the test, warning students to leave them face down until further notice. Once everyone had a copy, he commanded, "Okay, students. Go ahead and get started." While students were taking the exam, Mr. Green maneuvered his way around the room to collect the journals. Only one young woman and one young man did not bring their journals, compared with seven male students in the previous class. The entire time students were busy answering their quizzes. I was again distracted by the noise emanating from the walkie-talkies sported by security guards patrolling the hallways.

Just as Mr. Green began to take attendance in the Delaney book, Juan, the class clown who always walked in with his baseball cap and nylon sportswear, was late, so he knocked on the door to be let in.[21] While Juan was signing the late book, he asked, "Where's the test?" Instead of handing Juan the test, Mr. Green demanded that he remove his hat. Juan refused and asked why Mr. Green had not asked the women in the class to remove their hats. As I looked around the room, I noted that, indeed, four women were wearing hats despite the fact that school rules stipulate that no students may wear hats on the school premises. Angrily Mr. Green replied, "Ladies can wear it because it's fashion!" Unscathed by Mr. Green's insistence, Juan, who always wore the latest designer sportswear, pointed to his attire, "I'm fashion, too, Mr. Green." At that point, Mr. Green was noticeably irate and threatened to send Juan to the principal's office, but Juan would not budge, "You can send me anywhere, but if the girls don't have to take it off then I should not have to take it off." After an uncomfortable silence, Mr. Green glanced at me as I pretended to look down at my notebook, then glared back at Juan. Finally Mr. Green said reluctantly, "Okay. Okay. Ladies please take the hats off." Only then did Juan finally oblige and take his seat. Toward the end of the class, the "ladies," but not Juan, had their hats back on, without a word from Mr. Green. Shortly thereafter, toward the end of the semester, I noticed that Juan stopped coming to class. Later that month I found Juan in the college office. When asked about what happened, Juan said that he left because he had "problems" with Mr. Green.

The next month in the fourth-period class, Ani, a class clown who, just like Juan, often came in late wearing a baseball cap, as usual greeted her classmates loudly and joked about Mr. Green's resemblance to comedian Pee Wee Herman. In part because of Mr. Green's likeness to the television personality, of course the entire class bursted out laughing—including Mr. Green. In disbelief, a young man sitting beside me turned to another young man and whispered, "Imagine if we had said that he would have kicked us out of the class!"

Mr. Green was generally more understanding and informal in his interactions with young women, sometimes joking and smiling with them, however, he was quite cordial when interacting with his male students on an individual basis. One day after third-period class, Antonio approached Mr. Green, asking about the origins of a landscape painting he had been using as a makeshift window shade. Since the window was broken, Mr. Green propped it open for air circulation with a Webster's dictionary and removed the painting every day at the end of the day so that the night school students would not damage it. Mr. Green explained that he had acquired it on a recent trip to Asia. As they admired the beautiful work of art, Mr. Green prodded Antonio to comment on any differences he saw between Asian and European paintings. Antonio replied, "The people are not so big." Mr. Green added that while traditional Asian paintings revered nature and presented men as subservient to nature, European paintings tended to present humans as larger than life.

When compared with their female counterparts, men from groups that have been racialized as Black and Latino have been more likely to believe that teachers do not encourage them to pursue their goals.[22] Washington and Newman (1991) found that Black men were given less praise for their work in school, and they were more likely to be diagnosed as retarded or emotionally disturbed. Research suggests that teachers tend to discriminate against young men who misbehave, particularly those from groups that are racialized as Black and Latino. Late maturing young men are more likely to be tracked into low-level curriculum programs.[23] Given the rac(ed) and gender(ed) ways in which school rules and policies are implemented at many urban schools, it is not surprising that men who are racialized as Blacks and Latinos comprise a disproportionate number of students who are pushed out, discharged, expelled, or tracked into low-level curriculum tracks, including special education.

Conclusions

This chapter began with the question of how institutional practices in the high schools attended by racially stigmatized youth "race" and "gender" men and women. While the intersecting stigmatizing racialization and gendering processes second-generation Dominicans undergo in educational institutions can be seen at the micro level, such as in the interactions among students and teachers in the classroom setting, they are emblematic of larger racialization processes that occur at the institutional level, as manifested in the dilapidated infrastructure problems at low-income and immigrant schools, the dearth of resources such as books and computers, as well as the lack of a challenging curriculum, as seen at Urban High School. The savage inequalities in terms of resources and basic school supplies that UHS students and staff had to contend with on a daily basis served to remind them that their education and work were not considered important.

Hegemonic race and gender narratives about racially stigmatized communities filtered down to the classroom and ultimately affected the ways in which men and women from the same ethnic group experienced racialization processes. Through the implementation of security measures, young men in particular were profiled and singled out as problematic students throughout the school. Notwithstanding the fact that men were generally more rambunctious than their female counterparts, teachers were generally less understanding of young men and were more likely to discipline them more harshly for the same infractions committed by their female counterparts. In the next chapter we take a more in-depth look at the experiences of women.

CHAPTER 5

Rewarding Femininity

I want to be a strong and independent woman.

Lissette, junior at Urban High School

At the Dominican heritage celebration Melania, the president of the Dominican club, presented the guest of honor with a plaque, praising him for being a source of pride not only for Dominicans, but also to the larger Latino community. As the entire board joined the writer for a picture, I noted that all but three of the nine board members were women.

While in the previous chapter I focused on men, in this chapter I look at women's experiences at UHS. I sought to uncover how day-to-day school practices and classroom dynamics were racialized and gendered and in turn shaped women's views about the role of education in their lives. In doing so, I combined my focus on the macro-level organizational structure and the micro-level concrete lived experiences of young women. My focus questions included: How were women's lived experiences linked to institutional practices? What role did classroom pedagogy play in creating and circulating feminist critiques of patriarchy? How did women respond to low-curriculum tracks they were subjected to within the high school setting?

I begin my analysis of women's race-gender experiences at UHS by visiting a cross section of social studies classes. Besides Ms. Gutierrez's American history classes for juniors, we visit Mr. Hunter's global history course for sophomores and Ms. Mastri's global studies class for ninth-grade students revisit Mr. Green's economics class for seniors. I found that women's relationships with their teachers, as well as with the rest of school staff and personnel, were quite cordial. Women were not disciplined as harshly as men, even when they engaged in the same behavior that young men were punished for. Most importantly, women, more so than men, actively voiced their social critique of substandard schooling by demanding an education.

On Feminist Ideologies and Pedagogy

On a windy March morning, Ms. Gutierrez began class by challenging her students, mostly juniors, in her American history class to analyze a cartoon she had distributed on the American Revolution: "What do you see represented here?" Rafelo called out: "Men who founded the nation." The cartoon depicted several European colonists aboard a ship spotting North America territory after their long journey across the Atlantic Ocean. At the bow of the ship was the mascot—a sculpture of a scantily clad and buxom woman. Ms. Gutierrez pressed: "Who is missing from the cartoon?" Lissette and a number of cacophonous young women called out in unison: "Women!" Smiling, Ms. Gutierrez asserted, "Although throughout history women have represented freedom, they have been treated unequally." Vindicated by Ms. Gutierrez's feminist discourse, exultant young women nodded in agreement.

Another morning as she waited for students to stroll in, Ms. Gutierrez declared, "I'm tired of the assembly line." Ms. Gutierrez was a fireball that would never stand still. In an attempt to enhance student interaction, Ms. Gutierrez then asked students to move their desks and chairs around and form a semicircle. As I helped rearrange the desks, I could not help but notice that many of them were broken, chipped, and filthy—stuffed with gum-wrappers, dusty paper, and grime—seemingly they had not been cleaned in months.

Students began writing that day's aim in their journals:

What is *your* aim? What do you hope for spiritually, physically, physically, and materially? How far is your dream—the "American" dream—a house with a white picket fence, 2.5 children, a car, and a dog? What can prevent your dreams from coming true? Can the government help or stop you and your dreams from coming true?

After a few minutes of free writing, Ms. Gutierrez asked for volunteers to share their thoughts with the rest of the class. As always, Lissette, Analiza, and several young women shot their hands up in the air; however, Ms. Gutierrez called on Eduardo, who seemed distracted: "Tell us your dream." Eduardo boasted: "I want to be a millionaire, to be famous, to make history, like Michael Jackson; although I'm not going to be gay or anything." Of course the entire class burst into laughter. Although seemingly playful, Eduardo's comments pointed to the underpinnings of hegemonic masculinity across the globe: wealth, power, fame, and heterosexuality.

Women gave differing visions of their goals. Beaming with a mixture of pride and restraint, Lissette raised her hand and volunteered her desires: "I want to go to a good college and become a lawyer so I can become a strong and independent woman." Interestingly, Lissette's assertion was not simply that she wanted to attend college, but a "good" college, so that she could go on to law school, indicating that she had been planning for her future. Analiza continued: "My dream is to become an independent woman. I will build schools for the homeless. I also want to have a family and children—at least one child."

Roberto, who always wore a baseball cap to class, smirked: "It's interesting that you mention one child. I want five children. My father had fourteen children." Betsy affirmed, "People don't have children because they are busy with their jobs. Women don't want to stay at home and take care of children." Ms. Gutierrez interjected, "The best birth control is education," while women nodded in agreement. Ms. Gutierrez pressed, "Do you think your dreams would have been different if you had been born in the Dominican Republic?" Lissette asserted, "All the women in my family have been independent." Women spoke about coming from a legacy of strong and independent women, many of whom had children, ran their households, and provided for their families for generations in their home countries and now in the United States.

Ms. Gutierrez continued, "Do you think that the government is involved in your dreams? How do you plan to go to college?" Roberto seemed skeptical: "Miss, you don't need a college diploma. You can work for a lot of offices and you don't need a college diploma." Carmela had a more buoyant outlook: "Financial aid. Loans." Although they were juniors, women seemed more knowledgeable about reaching their goals and about the college application process.

Ms. Gutierrez nudged students to draw parallels between multiple forms of oppression: "Do we have slavery today?" Alex called out, "No. But we have racism." Ms. Gutierrez moved on to discuss the amendments to the Constitution and asked students, "Do we have equal protection under the law?" All students unanimously roared: "No!" Ms. Gutierrez rejoined, "What can we do about it?" Just before the bell rang, Ms. Gutierrez cited the Civil Rights Movement and the women's rights movement and ended the class by affirming, "Freedom is a struggle, not a privilege. The pen is mightier than the sword. Your education—no one can take that away from you."

In a departure from conventional lectures, Ms. Gutierrez always stressed critical thinking. The following week Ms. Gutierrez brought the Industrial Revolution to life by having students simulate a nineteenth century sweatshop in lower Manhattan. The aim for the day read "How did industrialization change the economy of post–Civil War America?" Students formed assembly lines by lining their desks into rows. Their task consisted of putting a paper dress on a paper doll. Before starting, Ms. Gutierrez added an incentive: "Remember workers in the rows who do not make the piecework quota will not be compensated for your time. Which ever row finishes first will get a plus and those who finish last will get a minus." After time was up Ms. Gutierrez asked, "How do you feel doing this?" A discussion ensued where students articulated biting critiques of capitalism and the exploitation of laborers. Through her classroom lessons and pedagogical practices, Ms. Gutierrez actively created spaces for the social critique of racism, capitalism, and patriarchy.

Through her classroom pedagogy, Ms. Gutierrez conveyed that she valued the cultural knowledge that students brought to the classroom, as she made their life experiences an integral part of the "official" curriculum. Ms. Gutierrez always drew on culturally sensitive examples to illustrate the relevance of history to the present-day lives of her students. Recognizing that most of her students came from the Dominican Republic, Ms. Gutierrez used the *bodega* (grocery store) as an example to explain how the Dow Jones works. Ms. Gutierrez shared some of her own family's experiences as immigrants: "When my mother first came to this country from Latin America, she worked in a toy factory. Later she went to school and became an accountant." Ms. Gutierrez added that her family, parents, and siblings were pooling their resources to put together a down payment toward a multi-unit family home that would serve as an asset for the entire family for generations to come.

Before the end of class, Ms. Gutierrez discussed the semester-long project. "The research paper must be 15–17 pages long. Before going on the trip to the American Indian Museum you must have completed five pages. Remember that the research paper is a year-long project." Rafelo protested, "Why do we have to do five pages?" Ms. Gutierrez retorted, "Because you are honors." Although Ms. Rivera, the head of the social studies department, denied the existence of an honors track, Ms. Gutierrez treated all of her students as college bound. Honing critical thinking and student-centeredness were the cornerstones of her pedagogical practice.

Ms. Gutierrez apologized: "I know that I have a large emphasis on the Native American experience, which is not really on the Regents, but there is no way to rush up to the 1990s, so I made a time line. Your homework is to do the scantron from the Regents booklet. I went through hell to get the Regents booklets, so you should not lose them." While Ms. Gutierrez reminded students to bring parents as chaperones for the trip, I looked around the room and noticed the absence of any textbooks, a situation that lasted throughout the entire semester. Mimeographed cartoon sheets and newspapers served as the only written work students could count on.

On the morning of the school trip to the Native American Museum students arrived early. As one of the chaperones for the trip, I chatted with students and several mothers who came to assist with the trip. Students were understandably elated because they would have an opportunity to leave the decrepit UHS school premises. Just as we prepared to leave, a monitor from the principal's office came to tell Ms. Gutierrez that the trip had been canceled. Determined to make this long-awaited trip happen for forty of her students, Ms. Gutierrez left me in charge of the classroom while she made her way down to the principal's office to find out what was happening. Shortly thereafter, Ms. Gutierrez reappeared, grinning. We would be leaving after all and headed toward the subway for our ride to the southernmost tip of Manhattan, just blocks from where the World Trade Center Twin Towers once stood.

Mr. Quintana, a Latino man in his twenties who wore his hair in a long ponytail, eagerly awaited our visit; he began with a brief lecture on the injustices that were currently being committed against Native Americans in the United States, as well as other indigenous communities across the globe. Students made linkages between the European colonization of Native Americans in the United States and the Caribbean. Then we saw a short video on the indigenous populations in Mr. Quintana's native South America. During the question-and-answer period, Mr. Quintana alerted students that the remains of American Indians were currently on display at numerous museums across the country and students expressed their outrage.

After spending all morning wandering through the museum, Ms. Gutierrez treated the class to pizza and soda, out of her own pocket. While we picnicked at a nearby park overlooking the New York City harbor, it was evident that students behaved like members of an extended family—each cooperating pouring soda into little plastic cups and making sure that everyone had enough to eat. Students were actively engaged in their learning and displayed an enormous amount of respect for Ms. Gutierrez, in part because she embodied the politics of caring.[1]

Through her teaching and actions Ms. Gutierrez had not only communicated basic content learning; she also conveyed an ethic of love and respect for her students, and they reciprocated. At the end of the semester, students organized a party for Ms. Gutierrez, where they presented her with tickets to *Freak*, a one-man off-Broadway play by John Leguizamo, a second-generation Colombian man raised in New York City. Through semi-autobiographical references, Leguizamo poignantly detailed his own racial stigmatization as an aspiring Latino actor struggling to find a leading role that did not cast him in the stereotypical role of drug dealer or criminal.

On another sunny and breezy spring morning, as Ms. Gutierrez waited for a critical mass of students to arrive, she asked the early birds to help straighten up the room. Before beginning class, Ms. Gutierrez posed a dilemma she faced as the coordinator for the junior prom: "There are 700 juniors, but UHS only has funding for 300 students. What should we do? Should it be open to only those students who are passing their classes or should it be open to everyone?" Curiously, the young men in the classroom were the most vociferous about insisting that it should be open to everyone. The women maintained that it should be based on grades.

The "Do Now" on the board read: "Define: Exploitation; Revenue; stock; trust; Carnegie; Tycoon; Capital; Monopoly; Technology; Eighteen-fifty; factory; laissez-faire; Urbanization; exploitation; slum; capitalist." As a few more students trickled in, several young women entered class with the familiar black smudge of ash on their foreheads, in remembrance of the Catholic holiday of Ash Wednesday, which marked the beginning of the 40 days of Lent.[2] Although several young men were wearing baseball caps, Ms. Gutierrez generally did not enforce the hat rule; she was usually too busy keeping her students engaged in classroom work. Not surprisingly, young men appeared to be at ease in this class, as their displays of masculinity were not threatened. On the rare occasion that Ms. Gutierrez did request that young men remove their hats, such as the day that representatives from the state Department of Education came to visit, she did so by gently smiling and gesturing by touching her hand to her head. Young men always obliged.

Ms. Gutierrez continued: "Jorge, are you ready for your oral presentation?" and Jorge shook his head. Next she moved on to Miguel, and he, too, said that he was not ready. Ms. Gutierrez then called on Rosalie, who responded gleefully, "We all did it together." Jardin, Rafelo, and Rosalie took center stage at the front of the classroom and performed a play about intergenerational conflict in a Latino immigrant family. The main character, Rosie, was a young second-generation Latina woman growing up in New York City during the 1970s, portrayed by Rosalie. Rosie wanted to leave her home and to go to Hollywood and pursue her dream of becoming an actress. Of course her parents, portrayed by Rafelo and Jardín, resisted the idea, citing the dangers of a young woman leaving her family and living on her own, miles away from her family. Against her parents' wishes, Rosie left her home and later became a famous actress—Rosie Perez.[3] At the end of the play, Ms. Gutierrez commended Rosalie, Rafelo, and Jardin for their performance and lauded them, saying that she would post their work on the bulletin board. The play embodied the independent will of second-generation women.

Later that evening I attended a workshop and dance performance, again spearheaded by the leaders of the Dominican club, most of whom were young women. The evening workshop, titled "Cultural Reflections: The Revival of Dominican Identity," featured invited panelists from the Dominican consulate. The audience, a mixture of parents, students, and teachers, welcomed guests with a round of applause. First they showed a video about the origins of merengue, the national dance of the Dominican Republic, and followed up with a discussion. Representing the consulate, Ms. Bellini, a Dominican woman in her thirties, made her remarks in Spanish about the origins of Dominican culture:

> La identidad es la manifestación de cultura. Necesitamos conocer a nuestra cultura para que nuestros niños tengan una identidad. Yo todavía no soy madre, pero temo que mis futuros hijos solo hablaran el inglés porque no se le está ensenando el español. . . . Qué paso en 1492? Este fue el momento donde se encontraron los indios con los españoles. Por eso nuestras raíces tienen tres fuentes: Taino, español y el africano. Los españoles se mezclaron con los indios y luego los hombres españoles con las mujeres africanas. Somos todos mulatos—no de raza, pero de color. La cultura african nuestra es nuestra tercera raíz. El negro se ve como feo; lamentablemente se habla de pelo malo, pero esto tiene que cambiar. Los padres deben de reconocer su cultura y debemos de ser orgullosos de ser dominicanos. Somos mulatos.

> (Identity is the manifestation of culture. We need to know our culture so that our children will have an identity. I am still not a mother, but I fear that my children will only speak English because we are not teaching them Spanish. . . . What happened in 1492? This was the moment when the indigenous people of the island first came into contact with the Spanish. That's why our roots have three

foundations: Tainos, Spanish and African. The Spanish mixed with the Indians and later the Spanish men with the African women. We are all mulattos—not in terms of race, but in terms of color. African culture is our third root. Unfortunately, Blackness is seen as ugly; we hear people talk about "bad" hair; but we have to change that. Parents should recognize their culture and we should be proud of being Dominican. We are mulattos.)

Next, we had a merengue dance performance. As homage to the Dominican flag, young women wore red shirts, blue mini skirts, and the platform shoes that became ubiquitous in New York City during the 1990s. The Dominican flag was draped across the stage. All but two of the ten dancers were women. Young women choreographed the performance for the group, appropriately named "Las merengueras" (The merengue girls). Although women simulated playing plastic toy instruments typically used in a merengue band—the tambora drum, saxophones, trumpets, and *guiros*—the music was provided through a soundtrack. For the last performance two young Dominican men in traditional cream-colored *guayabera* shirts, the customary dress shirt throughout the Caribbean, moved to the fast-paced beat of a merengue rap from La Banda Loca. I noticed that when two young men entered the auditorium, security guards promptly escorted them out.

The College Office

On several visits to the college office, I noticed that there were always more young women than men present, filling out applications and planning interviews. Mr. Matos, a Latino man in his fifties who was the college advisor, confirmed that there were always more women in his office than men. "Only the students we think are graduating are ranked—four hundred students—but there's another 400 students who are just floating," lamented Mr. Matos. On his list of the top ranking fifty seniors, barely a quarter of the students were young men.

As we chatted in Spanish, Maciel dropped by to inform Mr. Matos that one of the four-year colleges in the state university system had invited her upstate for an interview, but they had still not received her official transcript. Mr. Matos smiled, assuring Maciel that he would send the transcript; however, I noticed that he was not taking any notes. I looked around the room and saw that there were no computers, copiers, or other staff in this small room. A simple a makeshift desk piled with a few college catalogs where the only furnishings. After Maciel left Mr. Matos bemoaned the fact that one of his biggest problems was completing basic day-to-day operations: "We have not computerized the application process and we do not have access to a photo-copier. I don't even know where I can make photocopies." Chronic resource deficits such as these had serious implications for the educational opportuni-ties available to UHS students, as well as other racially stigmatized students at schools across the nation. Not only were UHS students severely short staffed in the college office; simple tasks such as sending a transcript to a college ad-missions office represented insurmountable feats.

While Mr. Matos was out to lunch, I chatted with Ms. Sanchez, a Latina teacher in her twenties, who was on duty at the college office during lunchtime. Ms. Sanchez lamented that even her younger sister, who coinci-dentally was attending my former high school, was having a hard time ap-plying to college because of the cost of preparing for the SAT, as well as college application fees. As I listened to Ms. Sanchez's struggles with her younger sister, I recalled my own experiences in applying to college. I had attended an overcrowded New York City public high school with a student enrollment of 4000, who were categorized as 60% Black, 30% Latino, and 10% Asian.[4] Over 80% of the students qualified for school lunches, indicat-ing that the majority of us were from low-income backgrounds. Only a quarter of students graduated within a four-year period, and of these less than 1% received academic Regents diplomas.[5] Our college advisor, Ms. Johnson, an African American woman in her fifties, was available only dur-ing two periods; her office, the size of a closet and piled with papers and col-lege catalogs, could barely accommodate two people. Not surprisingly, meeting with Ms. Johnson was a challenge.

Despite all of the factors that would lead most people to label me as "at risk," in 1999 I earned a Ph.D. in sociology from the Graduate School and University Center of the City University of New York. Upon graduation, I began working as an assistant professor of sociology and a research associate at the Gastón Institute for Latino Community Development and Public Policy at the University of Massachusetts Boston. Currently I hold a tenure-track posi-tion as an assistant professor of sociology at the University of New Mexico in Albuquerque. Given that my parents had not even been able to complete ele-mentary school, did not speak English, worked in the garment industry, and eventually separated, a question remains: How did I, a low-income, bilingual, racially stigmatized, second-generation Dominican woman, who was raised in New York City public housing projects by a single mother of five, beat the odds?

Two narratives can be used to explain my educational trajectory. First, a hegemonic, "commonsense" perspective would focus mainly on my individual-level characteristics, such as my parents' "family values," my intelligence, my self-esteem, and my willingness to work hard and raise myself "by my bootstraps." As a sociologist I turn to a more holistic analysis, which examines historical forces, social movements, institutions, and larger processes. A second and more substantial explanation of the educational attainment of an entire category of students would be one involving not just students' individual characteristics or their families, but rather larger social structures, such as the school system itself, race, gender, and class stratification. A counterhegemonic, critical perspective would explain my educational attainment as being due in large part to my serendipitous birth during the peak of the Civil Rights Movement and the women's movement and the expansion of educational opportunity programs for low-income, racially stigmatized students.

One afternoon, I was given an opportunity that few of my peers received. A counselor from the Double Discovery Center (DDC) housed at Columbia University invited my honors Regents English class to participate in a program designed to link low-income, first-generation college-bound students with a college enrichment program. The DDC program opened a whole new chapter in my life. Although Columbia University was only a short train ride way from my downtown high school, it was a world apart from any of the resources that I or the vast majority of low-income students in New York City public schools had ever had access to, namely a college library, computers, guidance counselors, workshops on applying to college, meaningful work experiences, funding to visit other colleges, and seminars on writing a successful college admissions essay. Given that none of these resources were available at my high school, I took advantage of DDC, and all of my college admissions, scholarships, and financial aid applications were typed in their computer labs. Most importantly, DDC also provided me with workshops on racism, homophobia, and sexism—critical dialogue seldom nurtured at my former high school.

President Clinton's Initiative on Race showcased DDC as a wonderful example of a program designed to reduce the achievement gap among racial minority groups. At its 35-year anniversary, DDC celebrated it success in sending 96% of its participating students to college. Considering that the high schools that most DDC students came from were like mine and graduated less than a third of their students, the accomplishments of DDC's programs are particularly impressive. In essence, educational opportunity programs that target low-income Latino and Black students can provide the missing link for students who attend schools that lack basic resources, books, quality curriculum, and support.

At UHS almost all of the students were low income, but the college office received only a limited number of fee waivers for the SAT and college applications. "There's money for scaffolding but not for the PSAT (Preliminary Scholastic Achievement Test). . . . Students wait too long to find out about college," lamented Ms. Sanchez as she ran off to her next period class, just as Mr. Matos walked in. Mr. Matos reflected on why he believed there were more young women graduating from UHS than men: "Young men don't do well in school because they do not want to. It's part of rebelling." Mr. Matos continued, "Girls are more compliant and reformist." Again, Mr. Matos reiterated the "commonsense" explanations for the race-gender gap—innate individual characteristics—leaving the structural and institutional origins of this phenomenon unquestioned.

In an effort to get a better sense of the experiences of ninth graders, all of whom were housed in the trailer classroom, I accepted Ms. Mastri's invitation to visit her "global studies" course.[6] While I stood outside the chain-link fence, waiting for the bell to ring, I chatted with Mr. Grant, an African American security guard in his thirties, who was stationed at the entrance. Mr. Grant shared his motivation for working with youth: "I hope to help these young men. I was once from the streets. I want to show them that there is a way out." Before Mr. Grant had a chance to finish his thoughts, Ms. Davidson, a White female teacher in her forties, came dashing toward us abruptly: "I need you to come into my classroom and explain who has control of the classroom!" Dejected by Ms. Davidson's urgency, Mr. Grant was summoned for backup and left to comply with what seemed to be a routine occurrence. "Riker's Island," the colloquial name given to the trailer classroom, suddenly seemed an appropriate description of the trailers. Fenced in with barbed wire and staffed by several security guards, the entrance to the trailer classroom resembled a juvenile facility.

Ms. Mastri, a White teacher in her twenties, had spent a summer abroad in South America learning Spanish, so whenever we chatted we spoke in Spanish. She had expressed an interest in my research project and had extended to me an open invitation to her class. My presence in the classroom caused quite a stir. Students were ecstatic because they automatically concluded that I was a substitute. After disappointing them, I queried them about their thoughts on the race-gender gap. Miguel quickly called out, "School is boring!" and the rest of the class laughed. Before I had an opportunity to talk to them about why they felt this way, Ms. Mastri whisked in and plopped a backpack full of papers on her desk and began feverishly writing the aim for the day on the blackboard: "How did the Buddhists act as a rebellion to the Hindu social system?" Analiza, the ninth-grade class president, took the opportunity to make an announcement about after-school tutoring services.

I could barely hear Ms. Mastri over the automatic flushing toilet located in the back of the classroom. Trailer classrooms were each equipped with one unisex automatically flushing toilet. For some unexplained reason the toilet was flushing by itself every ten minutes. Even after I got up and closed the door shut, I was still distracted by the noise. Despite the distraction, Ms. Mastri continued, comparing scheduled classes in India to affirmative action in the United States. Trying to link Indian social movements with students' everyday lives, Ms. Mastri asked, "How would you organize to protest a school rule you found to be unfair?" Before Ms. Mastri had a chance to call on any individual student, a chorus of students called out, "Get rid of the uniform rule!" At that point I scanned the room and noted that indeed every student, both young men and women, was wearing light blue shirts and beige pants.

Ms. Mastri pressed students to formulate a strategic plan. Ramfis, one of the young men in the classroom, joked, "We should just get rid of Ms. Bermatelli!" and the rest of the class cheered and clapped in approval, "Yeah!" On a previous occasion, I had had the opportunity to meet with Ms. Bermatelli, a middle-aged Latina veteran teacher and the assistant principal for ninth graders; I queried her about the existence of the uniform rule. "The uniform rule is necessary in order to instill order to the classroom." After we finished talking, Ms. Bermatelli took a disdainful look at my attire—T-shirt and jeans—and advised me to dress more formally so that I would not be mistaken for a "rebel student" protesting the uniform rule.

Analiza continued the discussion by suggesting: "We need to organize and form a mass protest where everyone wears regular clothes." Ms. Mastri gently reminded them that they should also analyze the consequences of any actions they take. Students discussed the possibilities, including losing their identification cards, having their lunchroom privileges revoked, and having their parents called. Throughout the discussions, I was struck by how physically and emotionally grown-up the young women appeared in comparison with their male counterparts, who appeared so infantile.

Toward the end of class, Ms. Mastri asked students to work quietly at their desks. Joel, a young man sitting in front of me, turned to me and whispered, "Miss, are we passing? Miss, are you going to chill with us?" Smiling, I nodded my head. Ms. Mastri approached my desk and asked for advice about whether or not she should tell the class that she was going to be absent the next day. Along with student absenteeism, teacher absenteeism was a common occurrence at UHS. After the bell rang, Analiza approached me and asked me about applying to the City University of New York. Although she was only a ninth grader, Analiza clearly had been thinking about her postsecondary studies. As I rushed off to Mr. Hunter's class, which was located in the main building, I bumped into a group of young men in the courtyard of the trailer complex who cheered, "No uniforms!"

Mr. Hunter's Class

I barely had enough time to make it to Mr. Hunter's tenth-grade global history, which was located on the fourth floor of the main building. Mr. Hunter, a White man in his mid-twenties, usually opened his class by saying, "Guys, you have to do work; let's get going." Familiar "Do Now" on the chalkboard read: "Why did the United States enter W.W.I? Define Neutral, Proclamation, Isolation, Read Page 435." I was always careful to avoid the seats by the window because the ceiling near the windows was visibly patched up—evidence of the collapsed ceiling problems that plagued UHS. Today, I was pleased to see an uncommon sight: textbooks. To my dismay, while distributing the books, Mr. Hunter added, "These are just for class, guys. You don't have to take them home."

Mr. Hunter called on Gustavo to read a passage from the book, but I noticed that he was having trouble pronouncing some of the words. Yocasta, one of the most active participants in the class, who always sat in the front row, interrupted, "I'll read!" Upon finishing the passage Yocasta boasted, "I'm doing my homework because I want to get a 99 in class. I'll do a report if that's what it takes to get a 99." Mr. Hunter then called on several young men who were talking, and they all declined. Next, Sandra volunteered but warned, "I am going to read, but no one else is going to interrupt me. I'm not going to read if there is constant chitchatting." Young women always appeared more preoccupied with their learning than did young men.

Before the end of class, Mr. Hernandez, a Latino security guard in his twenties, stopped by warning students who were disobeying the hat rule: "Listen up. . . . Whoever is wearing a hat should take it off, all right? You don't want to make your teacher look bad. There was a memorandum passed around." Interestingly, the same plainclothes security aides who regularly interrupted classes to enforce the hat rule always wore their baseball caps as they patrolled the hallways with their walkie-talkies strapped to their hips. In general young men complied by removing their hats during class, however, as soon as they darted out the door for their next class they always put their hats back on. Mr. Hernandez then summoned Yocasta. As Yocasta packed up her things, a group of young men that always sat by the window teased, "You're in trouble!" Grinning, Mr. Hernandez assured them: "Don't worry; it's just to get her glasses." Vindicated Yocasta just smiled back at the young men. Yocasta's interaction with security personnel stood out in stark contrast to the demeaning encounters many of her male counterparts endured with security guards.

The next day the aim listed on the board read: "What did Mr. Hunter teach me about W.W.I?" As the young men entered, several of them were wearing major league baseball gear, including baseball caps. I overheard Felipe talking about almost being recruited into the major leagues. Ricky, an older looking tenth grader who was also dressed in baseball attire, greeted his friends by slapping hands. Mr. Hunter began by whining, "Guys, why am I seeing more and more hats? You know that you are not allowed to wear them." I noticed that five young men had their baseball caps on. Yocasta retorted, "You know girls are allowed to wear them." Previously, I had asked Mr. Castellanos, the head of security, about the double standard regarding the prohibition of hats on the school premises; he reiterated the official regulations, which stipulated that no student, male or female, may wear a hat on the school premises.

Since young men continued chatting, Mr. Hunter urged, "Ricky, I like it when you sit up here." While Mr. Hunter passed out a handout on the rise of nationalism in Germany, he complained about someone taking his lollipop. Mr. Hunter called on some of the young men who sat in the back of the classroom, but they shook their heads and refused to participate. Mr. Hunter warned, "Sosa, if you don't stop talking you're going to have to leave. It's rude." Yocasta commanded, "Separate them." Yocasta indulged in numerous disruptions of class, but she was never disciplined.

Mr. Hunter finally began a class discussion on the causes of World War I. He apologized: "Guys, I made a mistake yesterday so erase yesterday's notes." Disappointed, students remarked, "What!" Since the classroom was located in a corner that connected two major corridors, a security guard was permanently stationed in a makeshift desk, just outside the classroom. More often than not there was more noise coming from the security guards' walkie-talkie than from inside of the classroom. A few unfamiliar young men strolled in late and said that they were supposed to be in English class but the teacher was not there. In an effort to quiet his students down, Mr. Hunter yelled, "Excuse me, I'm working here. Guys, does this make sense? When you think of economy, you think of? Everything bad is Germany. If Germany wasn't communist, what were they? You guys with me so far? How am I doing, guys?" After the class settled down, Mr. Hunter probed students on World War I with yes or no questions. I noticed that Luis, a young man sitting beside me who wore a row of corn braids in his hair, was doing his homework during class, and Mr. H, as he was colloquially known, never said a word.

Mr. Hunter continued, "Guys, we have a test tomorrow. The 'Do Now' is going to be on tomorrow's test; multiple choice, cause and effect, short answers, and pick one of two essays. Mad fun!" he added sarcastically. Mr. Hunter mentioned that the test would actually be the day after tomorrow because tomorrow was "teacher's day stuff," a professional development day when teachers would discuss the implementation of new standards for graduation and the Regents examinations.

Interruptions were a regular occurrence in Mr. Hunter's class. It seemed like twenty minutes went by before any academic work was done in class. Mr. Hunter finally began his explanation of the causes of World War I. "Austria is hungry for war." Before Mr. Hunter could finish his sentence, we had yet another disruption. Ms. Jones, a White teacher in her twenties, came by to show Mr. Hunter pictures of her last vacation to the Caribbean. To my surprise Mr. Hunter suspended class and started giggling with Ms. Jones over the pictures. Seemingly annoyed by the disruption, Yocasta began distributing announcements for ASPIRA, an educational opportunity program for Latino students that provided tutoring and other academic support. Yocasta then demanded, "Mr. H, why don't we start?" Annoyed by Yocasta's insistence, Mr. Hunter shot back: "Why don't you come up to the front of the class and teach the material if you know it so well?" Up for the challenge, Yocasta darted to the front of the classroom, while Mr. Hunter grudgingly took a seat next to me in the back of the classroom and Ms. Jones left. Yocasta lectured adroitly, at times referring to the map while explaining the background and immediate causes of World War I. Throughout Yocasta's presentation, Mr. Hunter seemed distracted, constantly looking at his watch. Upon finishing her talk, Yocasta took her seat unscathed. Mr. Hunter ended class early, collected the books, and, before the bell rang, made informal chitchat with students.

On the day of the exam, Mr. Hunter quickly announced, "All my tests are from the Regents and the Final is cumulative. I made a mistake on number 4; there is no right answer." José walked in late and flashed the peace sign at Mr. Hunter. During the exam, I noted that while several young women left their seats to consult the map, none of the young men had done so. Before the end of the class period, Yocasta called out, "Mr. H, come here. I'm finished!" Mr. Hunter grabbed her test, eyed it, and jokingly declared: "You failed!" Yocasta retorted, "I studied my ass off!"

The next day the aim for the day was "How well did I do on the exam?" Urging the class to quiet down, Mr. Hunter looked glum as he distributed the exam. "Alright, guys; have a seat, people. Guys, I'm not happy." Mr. Hunter gave Ricky his exam, which he had failed, and then Ricky started

teasing one of the girls in the class. Upon receiving her exam, Yocasta gleefully bragged, "I got a 100!" Dampening her celebratory mood, a group of
young men who always sat beside the window retorted in unison: "You
cheated!" Yocasta rejoined: "I took my Regents and everyone cheated off of
me!" I noticed that Elias, a young man who sat just in front of my seat in the
back, had scored a 94. However, he was not vocalizing his joy as several of
the women in class did. Most importantly, Yocasta and Sandra were always
calling out in class, but they were not sanctioned as harshly as the young
men who engaged in the same behavior.

Although Mr. Hunter did not speak Spanish, he went over the exam in a
comical tone. "Okay Guys. Preguntas on número uno." (Questions on number one.) Since no one raised a question, Mr. Hunter continued. "Bueno."
(Good.) Instead of concentrating on the exam, students were quite distracted by the dense March fog that was hovering outside the window. Although we were only on the fourth floor, I could barely see the bright orange
trailer classrooms that dotted the baseball field below. A group of young
men who always sat in the front of the classroom near the window continued
chatting about sports and "girls." Since Mr. Hunter's door was not locked,
Ms. Hernandez, a twenty-something Latina teacher, rushed in and sat in
the back of the classroom, grading her papers and preparing for her next
class. Just as I thought the class was settling down, there was yet another in-
terruption. Marisol, a young woman who was not in the class, came by, displaying a pigeon she had found flying around in the school. It was
disheartening to see that the unsanitary and decrepit conditions at UHS had
become so pervasive that pigeons flying around UHS through broken windows were considered a normal occurrence. Most importantly, the entire
time Marisol stood at the front of the class with the bird, she was not disciplined. I wondered if a young man doing the same thing would have been
treated the same way.

After the distraction, Mr. Hunter once again ended class early and put
away the textbooks. While he waited for the bell to ring, Mr. Hunter chatted with young men who were sports aficionados: "When are you going to
Chapel Hill?" Felix responded, "We are all going on Saturday night. . . .
Don King will give us money so that he can give something back to the
community." The young men in the classroom all seemed to have nylon
sports outfits on. Sandra interrupted, "Mr. H., you know we only have
eight more weeks of school. When are we going to have the review? What
are we going to do tomorrow? This again?" "Yes." answered Mr. Hunter.
"Alright. We will finish tomorrow!" declared Sandra as she marched off

to her next class. Women always seemed more concerned about their learning than men.

The day after the review, Mr. Hunter's class welcomed an invited guest, Ms. Penner, a White woman in her fifties who was the health educator from the HIV Prevention Programs Clinic. "Are we protected against the HIV when we use any kind of birth control?" Jokingly Mr. Hunter declared, "It's too late; many of you are already having sex." Ms. Penner rejoined, "Thirty percent of teens are not having sex. The 100% way of never getting HIV or getting pregnant is abstinence." When queried about the different methods of birth control, young women clearly knew more methods than young men. While the young men were busy fooling around and not taking the class seriously, young women were the first to mention condoms as a means of preventing the spread of the HIV virus.

Although the young men in Mr. Hunter's class outnumbered the young women, it was the young women who were the leaders in this class. When Mr. Hunter asked for volunteers, it was the young women who read, often demanding silence before they continued. Women also handed in homework more consistently than men, and they were among the most active participants in the classroom, sometimes volunteering to co-teach classes. It appeared that women were not interested in doing enough just to pass their classes. They strove for academic excellence, and they were proud to verbalize their efforts to study and earn good grades.[7] Moreover, in response to the low-curriculum tracks they were subjected to, women demanded an education more often than men did.

Teachers' Staff Development Day

At UHS, teachers' uneasiness over the introduction of the new Regents requirements for graduation was palpable during the day-long staff development workshop. I walked into the morning plenary at 9 AM, and already about 300 teachers, counselors, and administrators were gathered, talking incessantly. It took a while for the facilitator, Ms. Bloomberg, a White woman in her sixties, to quiet down the teachers, who were noisier than students. Ms. Bloomberg began her discussion by affirming, "We need to speak English because students need to pass the English Regents. Students treat English as if it were an elective. They don't take it seriously. I have a new student who is dying to learn English. We can start a dinner club to promote English. English must be learned!" Meanwhile, pigeons were flying overhead through the broken auditorium windows.

Harping on hegemonic understandings of the aptitudes of English Language Learners, Ms. Bloomberg added her own commentary:

> I personally feel that the English Regents is not appropriate for "our students." Albany has ears; our students can write letters; LEP [limited English Proficient] students are taking this test! They are not hearing us!

No one even questions the fact that these students are given a substandard education long before they enter high school. Instead, Ms. Bloomberg intimated that her students are not capable of doing advanced coursework because they possessed a deficient culture. The question remains: Were not these examinations appropriate for her own children? "The problem we have right now is a non-reading culture. If you change the expectation you will bring about a cultural change. We are teaching a new way of approaching the material." Absent from teachers' critique was the acknowledgment that curriculum tracking and unequal resource allocations were some of the mechanisms by which educational inequalities were manufactured, even before students entered through the school doors at UHS. Cultural explanation abounded. Not once was the lack of books and other basic teaching supplies mentioned as part of the problem.

Mr. Hilton, a White middle-aged teacher sitting in the front row, stood up and faced the auditorium, asserting, "I am confident that we can bring our students up to meet the new standards." At that point, Mr. Kaufman, a middle-aged White teacher, stood up and bursted out screaming, "I'm already working hard! I'm already working hard! Don't play me and say that I'm not working hard!" Sharing his frustrations, a number of the teachers in the audience applauded him. Calmly Mr. Hilton rejoined, "Thank you for that anger. We are not saying that you are not working hard. We are just asking you to do some changes. Schools are communities of learners. We are going to ask you to work together more through the use of reading groups and focus groups."

In the political assault on public schools, students and teachers have become scapegoats for larger structural inequalities. Beginning in the fall of 1998, all incoming New York City public school students were required to pass the statewide Regents examinations in English to graduate; however, private and parochial schools were exempted from the requirement. Not surprisingly, then, the implementation of "tougher" standards for graduation has been met by systemwide resistance from many teachers. Interestingly, while many of the teachers who had been in the system for decades were visibly defensive, younger teachers did not appear to feel personally attacked by the imposition of these new standards.

Freed from the usual constraints of the regular 40-minute class periods on the staff development day, teachers had the rare privilege of actually leaving UHS for lunch. I joined a group of mostly Latino teachers, as well as Ms. Mastri, at one of the Dominican restaurants near UHS. We had a family-style meal where Ms. Gutierrez, Ms. Sanchez and several other teachers shared the Dominican *bandera: arroz blanco, habichuelas guisadas, pollo al horno, and tostones* (white rice, pinto beans, baked chicken, and fried green plantains) and finished it off with a steaming cup of *café con leche* (expresso coffee with milk). Most of the White teachers ate at the cafeteria adjacent to UHS.

Upon returning from lunch, we were all assigned to small discussion groups that met in different classrooms on the second floor. My group consisted of Mr. Foner, a white male in his thirties who taught art; Ms. Crane, a White science teacher in her twenties; Ms. Dhingra, an Asian woman in her twenties who taught science; and Ms. Espinal, a Latina in her twenties who taught social studies. Our discussion topic was the analysis versus the application of constitutional rights. Mr. Foner and Ms. Espinal argued for quite some time. "The Constitution is a document that can simply be applied," Mr. Foner asserted. Ms. Espinal begged to differ: "You have to understand that the Constitution is a document that requires analysis. The rights that are represented in the Constitution do not apply to everyone equally." Ms. Espinal pointed to the legacy of racial and gender discrimination that has historically been sanctioned and encoded in law.

After the break we regrouped into discipline-based small groups. At the social studies small group discussions, teachers from racially stigmatized groups shared critical views of mainstream education reform. When asked for suggestions about the implementation of the new standards, Ms. Gutierrez offered, "Change the whole curriculum. Eliminate the dumb-down books." Mr. Valdez, a Latino man in his twenties concurred: "We must drop the textbooks and start using monographs." "I wish I had double periods," sighed Ms. Espinal. Regrettably, the social critique emanating from teachers who spoke from the margins was not heeded by school administrators and policymakers who designed educational reforms.

Institutional Engagement and Marginalization

Overall young women were more institutionally involved in extracurricular activities and vocational programs than were their male counterparts. The CO-OP Program, a high school work-study program, where students attended high school classes one week and worked for designated employers the next, has been one of the funnels for vocational schools. An advertisement for the CO-OP Program beckoned, "Join CO-OP today. It pays!" The CO-OP program operated in forty-five schools across the city, with the participation of 2200 students. To enter the CO-OP program, juniors and seniors had to be in good academic standing, with an average higher than 80. Students worked in both the private and public sectors, performing low-skilled clerical work, such as typing, filing, and photocopying. Students were paid from $6 to $8 an hour and earned a grade from their employer. More often than not, these pink-collar vocational classes prepared young women for work only at the lowest levels of the service sector.

When asked about the gender breakdown of the program, Ms. Smith, a middle-aged White woman, veteran teacher of over twenty years, and the CO-OP coordinator, exclaimed, "Of course, there are more girls than young men! The girls are much better workers!" Ms. Smith remarked that 90% of her CO-OP students received summer jobs upon finishing the semester. Ms. Smith even boasted that one of her students was placed with one of the most prestigious financial firms on Wall Street and for someone with only a high school education commanded an impressive salary of $30,000 a year. However, she later admitted that most students worked in low-level clerical positions, and some students actually earned CO-OP credit for working in fast-food establishments. Ms. Smith lamented that the mostly female program was changing gradually because Mr. Perez, the school principal, was informally restructuring the program to serve as a safety net for students deemed "at risk" of dropping out, most of whom were young men.

Not once did I see college recruiters on the school premises. Instead, in the spring the hallways were swarming with uniformed recruiters from the U.S. armed forces, who visited all of the senior classes. Darting from classroom to classroom, recruiters enticed graduating seniors with the prospect of a career in the military. One bright spring morning, two army recruiters visited Mr. Green's third-period class. Private Robles, a Puerto Rican woman in her twenties, wore army fatigues, and Sergeant Rosario, a Dominican man in his thirties, wore a more formal blue uniform. Before beginning Private Robles inquired, "Is this bilingual?" In spite of the fact that most of his students were indeed Spanish speakers, Mr. Green assured her, "No. It's monolingual." Continuing in English, Private Robles explained that she was training to become a linguist over a one and a half year period at the Internet Center:

> Before that I had to do seven months of basic training. It's not bad. You can sign for a four-year enlistment and listen to the radio and become a voice interceptor. It's a lot of fun. You get $40,000 for college if you make it. Every month we send you a check with benefits. For the first 12 months $400 will be deducted from your check.

Women were generally more skeptical about the many "benefits" promised by the army recruiters than were their male counterparts. Rosie interrupted, "My question is that you are saying all the good stuff. Why don't you describe a day in basic training?" Private Robles answered, "You get dressed in two minutes. It's not bad; you get used to it." Monica, a West Indian student in the class, asked, "Why did they move my friend against her will? What if you leave AWOL?" Private Robles answered: "You will go to jail. You sign a contract. They will bring you back in handcuffs."

Quickly changing the subject, Sergeant Rosario boasted that in a few years he will retire at the age of 41:

> We have a tuition assistance program where 75% of your tuition is paid. The Army is a job. So you can get an education while in the Army. You have the Montgomery GI bill where you are guaranteed $15,000 together. The College Fund gives you $40,000. You get free medical and dental benefits and 30 days of paid vacation. Not only that but you get military discounts; travel benefits, military flights; life insurance.

Viscaino remarked: "My uncle is in the army. What kinds of jobs are you trained for?" Sergeant Rosario answered, "Business administration, computer training, and fire fighters." Before leaving, Private Robles and Sergeant Rosario distributed information cards requesting the addresses and phone numbers of students and asked, "How many of you would consider joining the army?" I looked around the room and noticed that only a handful of the young men raised their hands. Not a single young woman in the class indicated an interest.[8]

During the last week of classes, Mr. Green had his class observed by Mr. Perez, the principal, and Ms. Rivera, the assistant principal for social studies. Mr. Green began his fourth-period class by asking students to comment on a timely article in the *New York Times* that dealt with controversial plans to eliminate remediation at the City University of New York. The aim on the board asked students to write in their journals: "What is the main point of the article? Why do some critics say that the changes will penalize Blacks and Hispanics disproportionately?" As Mr. Green walked around the room checking students' articles, Josefina admitted, "Mr. Green, I didn't bring the article," and he responded, "Okay. I'll give you something else to work on in the meantime." I noticed that this response was totally different from the interaction he had had with young men who had not brought their articles to the previous class. When Viscaino from the previous class had not brought his article, Mr. Green berated him publicly: "Students should learn how to take notes. Take out your article and I will supervise your note taking. If you didn't do it I will give some article but I will take off points. Don't tell me that you were not here. Absence is no excuse."

Mr. Green continued the lesson for the day by connecting the processes of note taking with writing a research paper. However, Cindy had other concerns on her mind: "How will the ending of remediation affect financial aid? I want to graduate from college. I just want to graduate from college." Mr. Perez, the school principal, answered for Mr. Green: "It's important because it will affect you personally." Felipe asserted, "It won't affect this year's graduating class." Cindy repeated, "I just want to graduate from college."

Conclusion

In this chapter we focused on young women's experiences at UHS. Although men and women were members of the same ethnic group, attended the same high schools, and came from the same socioeconomic background, they had fundamentally different cumulative experiences of the intersection of race and gender processes in the school setting. Differing race–gender experiences in the school setting were significant because they eventually framed outlooks toward education and social mobility. Since young women were not seen as threatening, they were not disciplined as harshly as young men, even when they engaged in the same type of infractions of school rules. Women were also more active in extracurricular activities than men. Women took pride in their academic excellence and actively strove to achieve their academic goals. In response to the low-curriculum tracking they were exposed to, time and time again young women were the ones who were the most vociferous in demanding an education. What is important here is that both men and women were subjected to substandard education: dilapidated facilities, lack of books, and inadequate resources. However, young women resisted their racial oppression by actively voicing their desire to achieve academically and demanding an education.

In the aftermath of the women's movement, schools have been one social space where feminist ideologies have been circulated and practiced.[9] Against the backdrop of demands for racial, gender, and sexual preference equality, a critical mass of women teachers have imparted a gender identity that is inextricably linked to feminist practices, namely pursuing an education as a means of achieving independence. Moreover, the presence of large numbers of female teachers in the state system provides a space for feminist ideologies to be embodied and enacted. Teachers such as Ms. Gutierrez left a lasting impression on their students, particularly young women, many of whom looked to her as yet another example of a strong and independent woman. In these safe spaces, women carved feminist discourses on education, financial independence, and motherhood as coexisting rather than contradictory.

In the next chapter we enter the homes of the second generation, exploring the issue of changing gender roles and family life transition. As we will see, these lived experiences of gendering within family life also left a substantive imprint on the outlooks of the second generation toward education.

CHAPTER 6

Homegrown:
How the Family Does Gender

In a relationship, the man has to work as equally hard as the woman does in order for it to work. And that's the way I see it. Because there is no man on this earth that's going to tell me, "Go, get up and cook dinner for me, woman!" I'd be like, "Please!" Because whoever my husband was going to be, I'm not cooking for him. If he wants food, let him go cook! Because of the type of career that I'm going to be in, I'm not going to have time to go make some gourmet dish for some man who's sitting down doing nothing! I want to finish school. I want to be financially stable.

Nicole, 18-year-old West Indian woman

Introduction

Although Nicole was only 18 years old and still in high school, she articulated a biting feminist critique that was rooted in the lived experiences of her mother. Nicole's visceral commitment to her independence as a woman was a lesson learned from her mother, who had emigrated to the United States from Jamaica when she separated from her husband, whom she described as "lazy." The fact that Nicole's mother left Nicole with her grandmother in Jamaica, emigrated by herself to the United States, found a job as a home attendant, and then brought Nicole to the United States as the head of her household left a lasting impression on Nicole about what it means to be a woman. Independence from men was the lesson second-generation women gleaned from their mothers' experiences.

In this chapter I explored the ways in which women and men fashion their gender identities and how these identities are tied to their understanding of the role of education in their lives. Feminist articulations among second-generation women were part and parcel of gender role transformations that are occurring across the globe, including Latin American and Caribbean nations.[1] The emergence of a feminist critique among second-generation Caribbean women was linked to the historical development of feminism among Caribbean women, which resulted from the increased labor-force participation of Caribbean women, both in their home countries and in the United States. Second-generation women created their gender identities against the backdrop of their immigrant mothers' struggles. The gendered division of labor in immigrant households played an important role in shaping men and women's outlooks toward education. In due course women fashioned feminist outlooks and practices, which led them to define education as the route to independence.

Conversely, men's exemption from the adult responsibilities imposed on their female counterparts left them deprived of the emotional supports readily available to women. Men actually occupied rather precarious positions within the family structure. Most second-generation men spent much of their leisure time outside of the home or engaged in sports. Men seemed preoccupied with establishing a firm gender identity. Men did not necessarily perceive their masculinity as their education. Men established their sense of manhood by becoming preoccupied with asserting their masculinity through work, dating, and distancing themselves from home life. The first part of the chapter details the distinct *lived experiences* of women, and the next section highlights men's gendering processes.

Women's Gender(ing)

Working Mothers = Adult Girls

The globalization of the economy has brought about striking changes in traditional gender roles and family structures.[2] As more and more women have entered the paid work force, men are no longer necessarily the breadwinners in their households.[3] The restructuring of labor markets and concomitant changes in gender and family ideologies have resulted in a large increase in the number of female-headed households across the globe.[4] Women constitute the majority of immigrants from the Caribbean. In a quest to establish financial independence and provide a better future for their families, many Caribbean mothers emigrated to the United States, with or without their spouses and families. During the 1960s and 1970s, as many as 70% of Anglophone Caribbean and 54% of Dominican and Haitian immigrants were women.[5] Since women were often the first to migrate, Caribbean families were reconfigured with mothers as the sole economic providers for their families. In New York City women headed 50% percent of Dominican households, 44% percent of Trinidadian households, and over 33% of Haitian households.[6] These patterns were mirrored in our survey sample: 45% of the women and 54% of the men had grown up in households headed by women. Since the 1960s, Caribbean immigrant women have been concentrated into the lowest echelons of the declining sectors of manufacturing, especially in the garment industry, and in low-level service sector jobs, such as home attendant and nurse's aide.[7] Thirty-three percent of Dominicans, 21% of Haitians, and 11% of Jamaicans in the United States lived in poverty.[8]

Caribbean mothers' entry into the paid labor force had a palpable effect on the lives of their daughters. While their mothers worked, women served as surrogate mothers to their siblings at a very young age. Marie, a 19-year-old Haitian woman who had grown up in Crown Heights, Brooklyn, was attending a community college. Over her kitchen table, Marie giggled as she reflected on the adult responsibilities she juggled when she was just a girl:

> I was nine and my brothers were eight. We used to stay home by ourselves because my mother had to go to work and she didn't have any money for a babysitter. My obligation was to make sure that all my brothers and sisters met in front of the school and waited for each other. Then we used to walk home. My mother was very strict. She would tell us that she was going to call us to make sure that we were home safe. And then I would get dinner started, clean the house and that was how it was.

Like many other Caribbean women, Marie's mother worked long hours as a nurse's assistant and was seldom home. Because gender role expectations assigned women to the domestic sphere, Marie, who was only a year older than her twin brothers, was made responsible for household chores and child rearing.[9] Indeed, during interviews, women were usually busy preparing meals, washing dishes, or feeding and diapering younger siblings. One lesson the gender-biased division of labor at home taught women was that homemaking is hard work.

A fundamental difference between the immigrant mothers of the second generation and European American mothers was their relationship to power structures. European American mothers have spouses who earn "family" wages.[10] However, regardless of whether or not there is a working spouse present in the household, working-class women who are members of racially stigmatized groups have always had to work in the paid labor force to provide for their families.[11] Ironically, many Caribbean women and other racially stigmatized low-income mothers toil as childcare providers and housekeepers for affluent families, most of whom are European American, yet they may be labeled "bad" mothers because they cannot afford childcare for their own children.[12] Middle-class European American mothers enjoy the luxury of choosing whether to remain at home with their children.

Katia, a 19-year-old Dominican woman who had grown up in Flatbush and Canarsie, Brooklyn, was attending a community college in the Bronx. Katia laughed when discussing the differences she noticed between Dominican families in the United States and other American families:

> For Dominican girls, by the age of twelve, you know how to cook, clean and wash by hand. We had no washing machine, back then. It seems to me that in an American [White] home, a typical one, the mother does everything, while the daughter is out shopping at the mall after school. And she has her own car and everything.

As Katia pointed out, working-class Caribbean young women cannot count on middle-class luxuries, such as washing machines, cars, credit cards, and stay-at-home mothers. Although Katia's mother and father both worked—her mother in the garment industry and her father as a repairman—their household income with two workers was only $10,000. As members of the working class, women clearly differentiated their home experiences from those of middle-class European Americans, who did not have to worry about their livelihood, as they were not expected to be the breadwinners of their households.

Because women's gender roles scripted them to assume adult responsibilities at an early age, they were also more likely than men to have served as institutional brokers for their families.[13] Ofelia, a 20-year-old Dominican woman who had been raised by her aunt in Corona, Queens, after her mother had passed away, spoke at length about translating for her family:

> When my aunt went to unemployment, anything that she needed, I read the letters that came through the mail and stuff like that. For me it was a source of pride because she used to say, my niece reads in English, look she knows. I felt bad and proud at the same time because she would compare me to my brothers and she would ask them while they watched television what are they saying, and my brothers couldn't tell her. Yeah. I felt like an adult. That is one thing but I wasn't embarrassed about it. As a matter of fact, we did it so much that my Mom [aunt] would not go out by herself. Even if they spoke

Spanish, you were not allowed to go out. One of us had to go with my Mom all the time.

At an early age women learned how to navigate a maze of institutions that were unfamiliar to their parents.[14]

Familism, a sense of affinity, obligation, and closeness to the family, permeated the narratives of the women. Cassandra, a 27-year-old Dominican woman who had grown up in Washington Heights, Manhattan, and earned a BA in psychology, echoed women's sentiments:

> Translating for my parents made me feel like an English-speaking brain. It felt good to know that I knew a lot of English. . . . Whenever my mom had to go to any office or hospital, I just had to go because if I didn't go they're going to treat my Mom differently. They are going to make her wait and if I went they're were going to take care of her right away.

Although both men and women viewed translating for their parents as an obligation, gender differences emerged in relation to their feelings about it. Women reported not only feeling proud of these responsibilities; they felt a deep sense of respect for their mothers in particular. These types of experiences were significant not only because they helped women enhance and maintain their bilingual skills, but also because they helped them foster a sense of competence and efficacy in the outside world. In due course, women matured more quickly than their male counterparts and simultaneously cultivated a sense of pride and appreciation for the struggles of their immigrant families, particularly those of their mothers.

Dual Frame of Reference

Women narrated stories that depicted their mothers as the most important figure in their lives and spoke about their own growth process, occurring against the backdrop of their mothers' experiences.[15] Maryse, a 21-year-old Haitian woman, had grown up in a mother-headed household in Crown Heights, Brooklyn, and was attending a vocational training school for computer programming. Maryse voiced the dual frame of reference experienced by women:

> In Haiti, you didn't have that much education. I mean, the education there was not as much as over here. Therefore, my mother's goal was for us to get all the education there was out there. . . . I would never disrespect my mother because I know how hard she works for us. There were times when she would break her back for us.

Maryse's deep respect for her mother, who labored as a home attendant to provide for her family, had a strong impact on her views about the role of education in her life. Maryse viewed education as a way of showing respect to her mother and bringing honor to her family.

Yvelise was a 24-year-old Dominican woman who had grown up in Washington Heights, Manhattan, and had dropped out of high school but had eventually earned a GED and attended postsecondary vocational training in computer technology. When asked about what kinds of things she was proud of in her life, Yvelise did not hesitate:

> My mother. She has been there. She understands. She is my best friend. My mother. I call her for everything. [So you can always count on her?]

> Yes. I have a mother. Some people don't have a mother.

> [Besides your family, are there any other important people or events that have influenced you either in a positive or a negative way?]

> Definitely, my grandmother, in a positive way, because when I have a problem, she tells me not to feel bad and she talks to me a lot. She supports me a lot. And she was the one who pushed me to "Go to church." So she pushed me into going to church and I feel better. I see her weekly. Every week. When you go to church, when you're Catholic and you go to church, you feel better about yourself. You will get more strength to want to do anything. If you don't go to church, you don't anything, just lay around. You don't want to do anything. I go every week.

Yvelise beamed as she described how her relationships with her mother and her grandmother were fountains of emotional support for her during difficult times. The significance of these "home spaces" is that they may provide women with support to succeed in spite of daunting obstacles. Pastor et al. (1996) posit that "home spaces" that provide emotional support are not limited to homes, but may include other social spaces found in schools and churches. Growing evidence suggests that spirituality is yet another space in which women cultivate webs of social support.[16]

Yvelise connected her deep commitment to her mother to the importance of pursuing a college education:

> I want to go, not really for myself but for my mother. I really want to finish for my mother, maybe become a teacher or something for my mother because she would feel proud of me. She would say, my

daughter, the one who finished college, she's a teacher, she's this, she's that, whatever.

Expressing a deep feeling of love and respect for her mother, Cassandra, a 27-year-old Dominican woman who had grown up in Washington Heights, Manhattan, explained what propelled her to pursue her education:

> I see my mother. She always wanted to get a better job, but she didn't speak English. She couldn't read. She couldn't write. So, to me, that was a push for me. I have to do better than that. Not that I didn't want to become my mother, because to me, my mother was the most wonderful person. But, because I didn't want to go through all the obstacles she went through. Right now, I am definitely planning to go back for my master's degree.

Women consistently assessed their educational and employment aspirations against the backdrop of the hardships their mothers had endured because they had not had opportunities to further their education.

Yvonne, a 22-year-old Dominican woman who had grown up in Williamsburg and Bushwick, Brooklyn, and was attending a community college in Manhattan, recalled that her outlook on education crystallized when she learned about her mother's past hardships:

> What really influenced me was my mother. She was the oldest of the eight children who came to the United States. She was 16 and all the other ones were much younger, so they went through elementary school and high school here; so they basically grew up knowing more English than Spanish. Then my grandmother and grandfather were working, so it was basically upon my mother to come home, cook, clean and help with the raising of the children. My aunts they got more of an advantage than my mother did and my aunts and uncles have very good jobs today. My aunts have very good jobs. They've gone to college. They've had more opportunities than my mother did. I remember being very young and my aunts would take me to their jobs and I would love the offices. The truth was that's what motivated me.

Women's decisions about their futures were etched against the backdrop of a self-sacrificing mother, as well as other women in their families. Through assessing their mothers' situations, women were able to evaluate their options regarding marriage, education, family, and career plans. Women's views about the role of education in their lives were intimately tied to their status as women. Suarez-Orozco (1987) found that Salvadoran youth maintained a dual frame of reference in which they contrasted their present situation with that which their parents had left in the home country. An intense feeling of guilt and obligation toward a sacrificing mother, along with the dream of ending family hardship, led these young people to emphasize academic success as a means of bringing honor to their families.[17]

Familism and Social Support

Janet, a 26-year-old Dominican woman who had grown up in Washington Heights, Manhattan, had earned a BA in psychology. Janet explained nostalgically the nurturing she received in her family:

> In some ways, I think, Hispanics, in general, tend to be a little bit more on top of their children than white Americans. White Americans tend to be more individualistic. I don't see them having the heart-to-heart talks. In Hispanic families and in my family, if one of us did something, immediately someone would be calling an aunt to tell her. It didn't matter if it was just a bad report card; everybody knew your business. Whereas, I find that in white American families it was a little different. I think there was probably a little bit more affection in Dominican families. We were more touchy, feely—you get hugged a lot more. But I think you also get a lot more sheltering sometimes and you feel caught between two worlds. You have that very strong Dominican heritage and that family influence, but then there was also this very independent, be-on-your-own mentality.

Janet's assertions that Caribbean families are "touchy, feely [spaces] were you get hugged" pointed to the high levels of familism present in these homes. "Home" was a place where women felt the strong hand of social control and bore the brunt of a gender-biased division of labor, but it was also a "safe space" in which women sought support through woman-centered social relations.[18]

Family gatherings provided another space in which women wove close ties to their family members, particularly other female kin. Marie recalled the gendering processes that took place during family get-togethers:

> When we used to go out to a family party, my brothers would just run away and start playing with each other, or they would start playing ball and they did not really talk to the grown-ups. So my brothers were really shoddy when it comes to speaking Haitian Creole. They try, but they don't speak it because they always avoided family

members. Meanwhile, we [the sisters] were always talking with the grown-ups.

Research has shown that second-generation women are more likely to be bilingual than men.[19] Second-generation women literally spend more time in their homes, interacting with older adult relatives who may not speak English.[20] In part because gender roles prescribed women to interact more regularly with their extended kin by helping their mothers prepare meals and entertain family members during special occasions, women were more likely to forge relationships with these women and thereby have more opportunity to retain their mother tongue.

Aunts, godmothers, grandmothers, and mothers were the nodes in the woman-centered webs of emotional support that second-generation Caribbean women were able to draw upon during difficult times. During moments of family crisis, Caribbean women took the lead in solving problems. Marie reminisced about the special relationship she had had with her godmother:

> When we lived in Crown Heights, I remember my godmother. She was my second mother. My godmother would come over, she had five children of her own, and every weekend she would come with a big bag of clothes for us. Of course they were hand-me-downs, but they were already washed so we just picked out the clothes we could wear. Sometimes on our birthday we would get some money. I just love my godmother!

Marie explained that she had a very close relationship with her godmother, such that she felt comfortable talking to her about sex and other personal issues. Marie, who planned to pursue a career in the health industry, also spoke fondly of an aunt whom she admired because she had struggled in college to become a registered nurse. For women, talking with older family members often grew into close familial bonds and lasting relationships.

On Cloistering and Sexual Policing

One common thread in women's stories about their childhood was that they grew up sequestered in their homes. Despite the familism that permeated their narratives, women spoke about the cloistering and sexual policing they were subjected to in family life. Cassandra, the 27-year-old Dominican woman had grown up in Washington Heights, Manhattan, explained that while her brothers were allowed to go to baseball games, she was not given the same liberties:

I had to come home straight from school. Some of my friends were in young adults clubs, but my mother didn't believe in that. Oh, no! Like my brother was allowed to go out to the movies, go outside. I was not allowed. Even in high school I wasn't allowed to go out. It was not fair. My brother was allowed to go out with his friends and party. My brother went to the prom. I didn't because I was a girl. My mother didn't trust the school. I didn't go. I remember that night. I cried so much. I was so embarrassed. And I bragged to everybody that I went. "Where are the pictures?" "Oh, I didn't take pictures." . . .

* * *

I don't think it was fair that my brother could use the phone. If somebody called me on the phone, "Who is that?" "My girlfriend." "Oh, she called yesterday, too. What are you guys talking about so much?" But we always had girls calling my house for my brother and his friends used to come over and my girlfriends, if they come over, "How could you come over? Your mother lets you outside like that?" So, automatically she'd assume they were bad girls because they came out by themselves.

Young daughters were sometimes not even allowed to visit their friends' homes. Maryse, a 21-year-old Haitian woman who had grown up in Crown Heights, Brooklyn, recalled:

We didn't have friends growing up. Not even on the phone could we speak to a classmate. We had to stay out of people's business. After school, we had to hurry up and get home. We couldn't stay for an after-school program or latchkey programs. If my sisters did, I would have to go and pick them up so that we could hurry home. That's how we grew up.

When asked to describe their childhood activities in the street, women responded with bewilderment: "We tried to stay off of the streets." In effect, the gendered social control of women in second-generation Caribbean households resulted in the cloistering of young women from the outside world. Diana, an 18-year-old Dominican woman, lived a couple of blocks from my Inwood apartment in Manhattan; however, she insisted that the interview take place elsewhere because her mother was working during the daytime and she did not allow strangers in her home when she was home alone. In contrast, many of the young men interviewed expressed shock and concern that I, a woman in her mid-twenties, had entered a stranger's home, especially a man's home, unaccompanied. One young man even warned me about calling from my home phone number when scheduling appointments because caller identification devices listed my number.

Jahaira, a 30-year-old Dominican woman who had grown up in Bushwick, Brooklyn, did not appear to be resentful of the cloistering she was subjected to during her childhood:

> Even though we grew up here, we weren't really engulfed in all the elements and all the trends and all these things that make you an American. I was in my early teens, like 14. We couldn't hang out with the kids. We couldn't go to Bobby's house for dinner. We didn't do any of that stuff. No camping. My Mom had us so tight that we didn't know anything. If we went to a party, it was a Dominican party; one of her friends; and our friends were her friends' kids. And that's how it was. I don't know if that's good or bad.

In a study of second-generation Vietnamese students' social adaptation to the United States, Zhou and Bankston (1998) found that young women, unlike young men, were subjected to strict social control, and they were responsible for more household work than their male counterparts. However, they concluded that strict social control of young women had a positive influence on their education, in that it actually propelled them into academic achievements.[21] Young women growing up in such controlled social environments may come to view schools as the only way to achieve some degree of independence. Zhou and Bankston concluded that traditional Vietnamese culture may have been conservative in intent, however, in practice, it had a positive effect on the education of young women in these communities.

Parents further "protected" their daughters by limiting the amount of time they could spend socializing outside the home in the company of young men. Mothers and fathers often warned their daughters that they needed to pursue their education because of their subordinate gender position. Margaret, a 21-year-old West Indian woman of Antiguan ancestry who had grown up in Springfield Gardens, Queens, and had earned a bachelor of arts degree in psychology, reflected on her parents' advice:

> My parents would tell me, "You have to work twice as hard because you are Black and you have it even worse because you are a woman." And, I guess it kind of made me want to be one of those women that can be independent without depending on somebody.

Mothers, in particular, warned their daughters about the perils of depending upon a man for economic support.[22] Rosy, a 19-year-old West Indian college student of Trinidadian ancestry, who had grown up in Flatbush and Bedford Stuyvesant, Brooklyn, remarked that neither of her parents approved of her dating during high school:

> My father personally doesn't want any guys around me because he knows how he was when he was younger and he thinks that every male was like that. And my mother, she doesn't want me to get tied down because of what happened to her when she was younger. She doesn't want me to go through the same thing. She had her first child when she was fifteen and married when she was twenty-something. So she didn't get a chance to do anything. So she was putting all of that on me.

Interestingly, Rosy's mother's fundamental concern was for her daughter's long-term independence and happiness, whereas her father was more interested in Rosy's immediate safety and in protecting her from the sexual advances of young men. Nonetheless, Rosy took her mother's advice and planned to pursue a Ph.D. in psychology.

Avoiding premature childbearing was a theme that emerged in the narratives of women in this study, but not in those of men. Women spoke about deliberately avoiding sexual activity and self-policing their sexual desires to ensure that they achieved their educational goals.[23] Nicole, the 18-year-old West Indian woman of Jamaican ancestry, quoted in the introduction, aspired to become a medical doctor. While we sat at her kitchen table Nicole prepared food, cleaned the kitchen, and played intermittently with her baby sister, Lisa, who marveled over my tape recorder and occasionally approached Nicole to play with the microphone pinned on her shirt. Although Lisa was a toddler, Nicole boasted that she had taught her the alphabet, as well as addition and subtraction. When queried about her plans for marriage and children, Nicole asserted passionately that she did not plan to get married any time soon: "I have no intentions of letting men screw up my life! I have to finish school. Definitely. Once I'm through with school, I'll be in my thirties. Then, I can think about having a child." Among women, the intention to delay marriage and child rearing was always discursively linked to the stigmatization of their sexuality and the importance of acquiring educational credentials for dismantling these stereotypes. Although Nicole was still enrolled in high school, she had an A average. When asked about her grades Nicole insisted that she was not going to become another "teenage mother statistic." These findings contrast sharply with other studies that suggest that upon reaching adolescence women lose self-esteem and become embedded in a culture of romance.[24]

Complicating this dynamic was the larger issue of the traditional role of men as economic providers and women as homemakers. Lidia, a 20-year-old Dominican community college student, had grown up in Inwood, Manhattan. Lidia explained why she planned to delay childbearing:

> I don't think I'm ready to have kids. I don't think it's the time for me to have kids. I think I'm too young. I should wait until I graduate from college and have a degree because my child will depend on me. I want to have something to give my child while it was growing up.

Lidia was an unusual case in that she grew up in a single-parent household that was headed by her dad. When Lidia was a young girl her mother passed away, leaving Lidia as the primary mother figure to her younger brother. Although her father raised her, implicit in Lidia's comments was an acknowledgment that women cannot depend on a man for their family's economic stability. A few women said that they did not want to have any children, and a number admitted that they had never thought about raising children until I posed the question to them.

"Homegrown" Feminism

While women spoke appreciatively of their mothers' sacrifices and courageous efforts to provide for their families in the face of daunting obstacles, they also criticized the double standard that marked the difference between acceptable behavior for men and women. Marie, a 19-year-old Haitian woman, had some sharp comments about her mother's gender-biased child-rearing practices:

> Of course, the guys could get away with it. They didn't want to do their homework, they didn't want to do the dishes and they could get away with it. But let me and my sisters decide one day that we didn't want to do it, she will talk to us all night long. My mother would say: "You'll not get married and no man was going to want you." I remember one time my sister didn't do the dishes. It was 2:00 in the morning! My mother went and woke her up! She said: "Get up and go do the dishes!" My sister was dead sleeping and she had to get up and do the dishes.

When asked to describe how she felt about this double standard Marie elaborated:

> In one way, it was kind of unfair because my brothers always got
> away with stuff, but in another instance, I can't really blame my
> mother because I see where she grew up.

Women often empathized with their mother's struggles. Although Marie
criticized her mother's double standard regarding household duties, she
still expressed a deep respect for her mother and did not blame her for her
gender-biased child-rearing practices.

How can second-generation women critique the double standard in
their homes, while at the same time remaining firmly committed to their
families and their communities? In *The Color of Privilege: Three Blasphemies
on Race and Feminism*, Aida Hurtado (1996) sheds light on this apparently
contradictory phenomenon. According to Hurtado blasphemy involves
confronting unpleasant, unvoiced, and often ignored social relations that
have been suspended for the sake of group survival. The Chicano movement during the 1960s took on the progressive political agenda of promoting voter registration, prison reform, and the unionization of farm workers,
yet it had not confronted the issue of sexism within the Chicano community. Hurtado explained that in bringing attention to issues of sexism,
Chicanas sought to dismantle gender oppression in their homes by embrac-
ing their families and cultural heritage, not by divorcing themselves from
the men in their communities.[25] Hurtado argued that these efforts were
not condoning male domination, but rather served as bridges in bringing
about the important work of community-building and social change.[26]
In this light, the effervescent feminist critique among second-generation
Caribbean women is blasphemous because it grows out of a deep love and
respect for their community.

Some scholars have suggested that the development of a feminist consciousness among Caribbean immigrant women is a simple by-product of
assimilation into the American mainstream.[27] However, the development
of feminist practices among second-generation Caribbean women in the
United States is a messy and complex process with historical origins
and cannot be explained solely as a function of assimilation. Multiple
generations of Caribbean women have historically engaged in feminist
practices that have challenged male domination. Feminist rumblings are
rooted in global structural changes in the economy, family structures, and
culture.[28]

Jahaira, a 30-year-old Dominican woman who had grown up in Bushwick, Brooklyn, and earned a B.A. in public administration, talked about
how she learned her feminist practices:

We didn't grow up with that big a male dominance. My mom was always the person that you asked permission to and the person who said whether you can go or not. Or you can have this or not. Even though my father was there at times, she was always the steady person there so she was the one who said what to do and when to go. In my family we're strange because we tend, now in our relationships, to be dominant.

Jahaira, clearly did not envision being taken care of by a man. Divorced and raising two children, Jahaira was in no rush to marry the father of her children:

You mean like get married? No. I'm not rushing to do it because a lot of marriages are failing. I don't see these children's father and I being the perfect, ideal couple that will last untold years. So, if we get married that's okay. But it's not something I have to do. I am self-sufficient. A lot of people get married and it is out of love and stuff but sometimes it is convenient and it is economically sane to do. I take care of myself.

Given that many second-generation Caribbean women had mothers who were the first in their families to emigrate, it was not surprising that they articulated a homegrown feminist discourse rooted in their mother's actions. Multiple generations of strong women who headed their households both in the Caribbean and in the Diaspora were inspirations to second-generation women.

Cassandra, who had grown up in a two-parent household, remembered that as a child she was extremely critical of her father's authoritarian behavior in the family:

My father never learned how to cook. My father doesn't even know how to boil an egg! He was so demanding! "The food was too hot! It's too cold! My clothes were wrinkled!" I would say to myself, "Why can't you do it? You're a person too." We were always upset about it. I remember when he used to come from work, oh my God! We had to have his sandals waiting for him. All he had to do was give us the look.

Cassandra's reaction to her home life was imbued with anxiety, anger, fear, and love. Although she resented her father's behavior as a *caudillo* (the strongman of the household), Cassandra also noted that her mother, despite her wifely submissiveness, resisted her husband's social control and was not completely dependent on him for financial support:

My mother always used to put in an equal share of the household money because even though she was at home raising us, she never sat down in the house. She was never home waiting for my father to bring the check. My mother was making more money than my Dad. We used to go out and clean apartments together and we used to baby-sit. I used to go and help her out. She was always doing something. She used to bring in more money than he did. My father never even knew how much.

Cassandra's mother probably did not view herself as a "feminist"; however, her behavior can be described as feminist because it was aimed at producing some degree of self-determination.[29] It was her mother's resistance to male domination that provided Cassandra with the vantage point from which she made decisions regarding marriage, work, education, and career. Among many working-class and third-world women, adherence to a feminist identity is not a prerequisite for feminist practices. Even in patriarchal homes, women carved out their own autonomy.

Cassandra divorced because she found her husband to be too domineering. When I asked her if she was considering remarrying, Cassandra remarked:

I'm just waiting for the right thing to happen. I'm not in a rush, but at the same time I haven't found the adequate partner for me, somebody who has gone to school, like me. Somebody that has gone through school; that's what I want because I'm not just going to pick any guy from the street just to know that I have a man. No. I can take care of my child. My child and I, we're doing fine. It's rough being a single parent, especially since I grew up with my mom and my dad, they married for so many years, that for me it is very hard to put myself in this situation. But I'm not just going to take anybody. No way! To me, success means having stability financially, having a house, being self-sufficient.

Women's commitment to independence and egalitarian gender roles was always defined with reference to their mothers' hardships. In due course, women wove a "homegrown" feminist standpoint that was anchored in the lessons they had gleaned from their mothers' perseverance in the face of daunting obstacles.[30] In a study of Mexican immigrants in California, Hondagneu-Sotelo (1994) posited that "it is not feminist ideology but structural rearrangements that promote social change in spousal relations."[31] Likewise, in a study of women's labor-market participation in the Dominican Republic, Puerto Rico, and Cuba, Safa (1995) found that women's entry into the paid labor force has translated into greater autonomy within the household. However, she also cautioned that the micro-level gains in terms of gender equality at the household level were undermined at the macro level. This was due to the fact that Dominican, Puerto Rican, and Cuban women toiled in low-wage manufacturing industries that were infamous for their labor abuses and exploitative wages. Thus, while women's entry into the labor force has allowed them more freedom to challenge male hegemony within their homes, it has not automatically translated into an improved living standard for women at the macro level.

Diana, an 18-year-old Dominican woman who was attending a vocational program at a community college, recalled that her mother explicitly warned her about the pitfall of depending on men:

> My mother used to say, "Don't depend on men. Your husband may just leave you and have everything in his name; but, if you get an education, then you'll have something to fall back on because you will have graduated and you'll have a good job and you'll do O.K." My mother would have wanted it to be that way for her, but now she can't do anything about it because she already has kids. She can't work now. She doesn't know English. She didn't have a chance to go to school. But she tells me that equality was the way it's got to be; that it's got to be fifty-fifty. She tells me that I cannot be the way that she is now because she's not living the way that she wanted it to be. She's depending on my father and she doesn't like that.

Diana described the emergence of her feminist consciousness in terms of her mother's actions, supporting the view of Hondagneu-Sotelo (1994:195) that changes in gender relations result from experiences in the home rather than from a "modernizing" Anglo influence or the acculturation process. Caribbean mothers' life choices and experiences and their ability to communicate their feelings about those choices to their daughters have an important impact on the kinds of decisions their daughters eventually make for themselves. What is important here is that mothers and daughters pinned their independence to the importance of attaining an education.

When asked about her views on family, marriage, and gender roles, Janet, a 26-year-old Dominican woman who had grown up in Washington Heights, explained:

> I just have no desire to be married. I think I have a lot more to accomplish and kind of follow through on before I commit myself

to somebody. . . . My sister was very career-oriented and actually we get that from my mother. My mother married in part to get out of the house and kind of gave up her dream career to be married. If a woman comes from a strong Dominican family and her family was a big influence on her, she has two choices: either get married, or go to college and get a degree, become something. Guys come in and out whenever they want, they can do whatever they want. You'll find that women want to get as independent as they possibly can, otherwise you will have to stay in the house for the rest of your life!

These feminist patterns are also evident in the home country. The development of a feminist consciousness among third-world women is echoed in the growing literature of the Caribbean Diaspora.[32] In *Breath, Eyes, Memories*, a novel by Edwidge Danticat (1994), we meet several generations of independent Haitian women, many of whom have never left the island. Facing the ravages of poverty and political oppression, these women expressed an unwavering sense of hope and maintained high aspirations.[33] Far from being the passive victims of a male-dominated society, they dream of becoming doctors and engineers. Sophie, the main protagonist, who was born in Haiti but grew up in New York City, embodied how Caribbean women have maintained a long legacy of self-determination and insubordination to male domination. Likewise, in *How the Garcia Girls Lost Their Accents* (1991), *In the Time of Butterflies* (1994), and *Yo!* (1997), Julia Alvarez depicts how the development of a feminist consciousness is rooted in a legacy of island-born and -bred Dominican women.

The gender-differentiated experiences that young women had in their homes provided them with a unique standpoint from which to evaluate their options regarding their futures and work. These changes in the economy are not limited to the United States, but are occurring globally. According to Arnot, "from the 1950s onward, the majority of girls growing up in new 'Elizabethan England' witnessed their mothers working and struggling with family relationships in highly constrained circumstances—a reality which was to have a considerable effect . . . on their own aspirations."[34] These changes are not limited to Europe and the United States but resonate in the Caribbean, where increasingly women are the breadwinners of their households.

Critical feminist theorists argue that minority women actively resist their marginal status in the larger society through their *positionality*—the emergence of knowledge from their particular social locations as gender, racial, ethnic, and class minorities.[35] In *The Color of Privilege: Three Blasphemies on Race and Feminism*, Hurtado (1996) argues that the gender oppression faced by women of color was fundamentally different from that faced by White women. These differences produced qualitatively distinct experiences. Hurtado posited that the differences in the feminism of White women and that of women of color stemmed from their differing relationships with White men; White women were *seduced* into compliance because they were needed to "reproduce" the next generation, while women of color experience racial, gender, and class oppression through *rejection* because their labor is used to maintain the status quo.[36] Thus, the *experiential differences* between White women and women of color stem from their distinct relationships to power structures.

Women from racially stigmatized groups have remained optimistic about the future, and they have actively pursued education as a way of rebuilding their families.[37] In a study of poor and working-class young adults in the Northeast, Fine and Weis (1998) found that Latina and African American women were engaged in a quiet revolution, whereby they were pursuing education even more vehemently than men did.

Men's Gender(ing)

The Absence of a Dual Frame

Men were absolved from the adult responsibilities imposed on their female counterparts. When asked about his household responsibilities while growing up, Andrés, a 24-year-old Dominican man who had grown up in Corona, Queens, and who was enrolled in the police academy, explained that he was not responsible for housework while growing up:

> We were boys. We didn't have to do many chores around the house. My mother used to take care of the house and do the cooking. When my mother was working she used to have a neighbor come over and stay with us until she returned.

As Andrés explained, in a household where there were no girls, in the mother's absence, another woman, usually a relative or friend, assumed the domestic chores. Regardless of their age, men were rarely expected to assume childcare responsibilities, perform domestic duties, or assume other family obligations. This pattern differed from the conclusions in Valenzuela's (1999) study of the role children played in the settlement of Mexican immigrants living in California. He found that while daughters were often expected to play a more active role in helping the family, the eldest regardless of sex had to assume these chores.

Since men were absolved from chores, they did not compare their present situation with that of their parents, even when their fathers were present. John, a 25-year-old Dominican man who had grown up in Washington Heights, Manhattan, and had dropped out of school but eventually earned a GED, chuckled when recalling the gendered division of housework in his family: "I never washed dishes. I was never expected to wash dishes. But my sisters, my mother showed them to cook. She showed them how to clean the house." Because mothers excused their sons from the responsibilities automatically assigned to their daughters, young men growing up in these households did not personally identify with their mothers' struggles as parents who were often the heads of their households. In essence, men's lived experiences with the gendered division of labor in Caribbean households did not provide them with a dual frame of reference from which to evaluate their choices about marriage, education, and career, as it did for women.

The gender(ing) that took place within Caribbean homes reinforced men's traditional views on gender roles and family ideologies. Rodrigo was a 23-year-old Dominican man who had grown up with both of his parents on the Lower East Side of Manhattan. Rodrigo had dropped out of high school in the tenth grade, but he had eventually earned a GED. When asked about the differences between how boys and girls were raised, Rodrigo justified his lack of participation in household responsibilities: "My sisters had to clean the house and stuff like that. Me, I just had to stay and watch TV. I didn't really have that much responsibility. I'm not good at housework." Not surprisingly, Rodrigo smirked when I asked him about his views on gender roles and family ideologies. While he agreed that in a marriage the husband and wife should work and contribute to the household expenses, he still felt that childcare responsibilities were primarily the responsibility of the wife. Rodrigo's sentiments were echoed in a survey: twice as many men as women indicated that in a marriage housework and childcare were primarily the woman's responsibility.[38]

Men also did not serve as institutional brokers for their families. Indeed, several men mentioned that during the few times they translated for their parents, they felt somewhat embarrassed. Rodrigo remarked:

> Translating? Well, when I was growing up that was usually my sisters. That was usually their forté. Now that I'm the only one at home, if they have a phone call or anything that they needed me to

help them out with, then I do it. . . . It feels OK. But, I mean, they've been here for so many years; I wish they would have learned English by now.

The meanings men assigned to the task of translating for their families contrasted sharply with women's affirmations that they felt "smart" and "proud" that they were able to help their parents. Moreover, another consequence of men's lack of responsibilities in the family was that men did not maintain close relationships with their family members.

Streetboys

In spite of the brisk March breezes, Rodrigo, who shared a one-bedroom dilapidated Lower East Side tenement apartment with his mother, father, and sister, insisted that we conduct the interview outside, saying "I hate being upstairs cramped up with my parents. I'd rather conduct the interview downstairs in the park." So we headed downstairs to a park bench not far from his home. While we spoke Rodrigo kept an eye on his motorcycle and greeted his neighborhood friends as they walked by. While most of the interviews with women took place in their homes, I often conducted interviews with men outside of the home: in parks, in fast-food restaurants, on the street, or on the run in a car.

Despite parental efforts to protect both daughters and sons from the vices of the street, in practice men were given more liberties. Another case in point was Denzel; he was an 18-year-old West Indian man who was born in Trinidad and Tobago, but whose parents were from Grenada. He had grown up in Flatbush, Brooklyn. Denzel had a C average in high school and was still enrolled in the eleventh grade. As with the other men in the study, scheduling an interview with Denzel was a challenge, as he was never home. According to Serena, his 15-year-old sister, who always answered the phone, Denzel was outdoors playing basketball and only returned home in the late evening. When asked whether concerns about crime ever kept him from going out, Denzel instead described his family's efforts to safeguard his teenage sister:

My mom tries to keep her safe. Told her she shouldn't talk to boys. My mom makes sure that if a boy calls and my sister stays on the phone too long, my mom tells her: "Get off my phone and do your work because I don't want you talking to boys who can screw up your life." So my sister is protected from "the boys element." When I see her talking to a boy, I say: "Let me talk to you for a minute. I think you were talking to a bad person." She might give you a hard time but afterwards she leaves him alone and goes about her business. [So your mom was basically very protective of your sisters, more than with the boys?] Yeah, because she knows we can take care of ourselves. But with her, she makes sure my sister doesn't get caught up with the boys. My sister, she goes to my high school and has a 93 something average, so right now she can get into any college she wants.

Serena attended the same high school as Denzel, but unlike her brother she was an exemplary student who was on the honor roll. Before dashing off to his game, Denzel proceeded to tease his younger sister, Serena, for being a feminist. Serena shared a poem she had written for her English class, which essentially spoke about how men were "dogs" and women could not count on men these days—a lesson she had learned from her mother, who was head of the household with four children. Freed from the onerous domestic tasks required of their sisters, men had much more leisure time on their hands. At the end of the interview, Denzel and his older brother were off to play basketball with the makeshift milk-crate hoops that lined the neighborhood streets. Meanwhile, Serena was confined to the home, playing the role of surrogate mother, taking care of their baby sister, cleaning, and cooking.

Unlike women's narratives about having close relationships with their families, men's childhood stories were peppered with episodes of spending time "in the streets," playing basketball, and "hanging out," usually with other young men. Men justified their preference for the street by pointing to their overcrowded apartments. Severe overcrowding in many working-class and poor Caribbean homes was often resolved by transforming the living room into a substitute bedroom. In accordance with the principle of maintaining the privacy of the women in the home, the sole bedroom in the apartment often became a de facto woman's space, while the more public living room quarters were designated a male space. Young men growing up in overcrowded homes may not want to stay home all day because they lacked any private space—their bedrooms were public spaces during the daytime. This was the case in the homes of Peter, Joaquín, Richard, Perry, and Denzel. Denzel and his older teenage brother shared a sofa bed in the living room, while his mother and two sisters shared the only bedroom in the apartment. In spite of the greater freedom men enjoyed in comparison with their sisters, they occupied rather marginal spaces within their families.

One unifying thread in the narratives of men was their fixation on sports. The makeshift basketball courts that lined the streets of the Caribbean homes visited attested to the fact that sports have become a metaphor for masculinity and freedom. Mark, a 24-year-old West Indian man whose mother was born in Jamaica and whose father was born in St. Vincent and St. Grenadine, had grown up in Crown Heights and Brownsville, Brooklyn, in a de facto segregated housing project. Mark reminisced about how sports became one of the most important social spaces for him as an adolescent:

> We didn't have gangs. Our housing project just doesn't tolerate gangs. Everybody in our society would stay in touch. My housing project was a close neighborhood, you know, everybody knew everybody, you know. And it was a huge housing project, about 37 buildings or something like that. Everyone knows everybody. There was no purpose for gangs in our neighborhood. Everybody in our project was just oriented to playing basketball. We just liked playing basketball.

When queried about the drug economy and violence, Mark explained that a young man's fame as a good basketball player preempted him from involvement in drugs. Indeed, Mark reminisced about how his neighborhood community banded together to protect aspiring basketball stars from the ravages of drugs:

> If some one was good in basketball it was like, "Well, he's going make it; I know he's going to make it; he's going to represent our neighborhood." So, they would take care of him and make sure that he stayed out of drugs and all that. You see, some of the guys in the neighborhood smoked weed. But that's one thing. I never had the peer pressure. When guys smoked weed, they never smoked it around me. Let's say after a game they want to smoke weed or something, they'd go somewhere else with that.

Mark's description of his public housing project suggested that while young men tended to spend more time "hanging out" in the streets than their female counterparts, they did not necessarily use illicit drugs or engage in other criminal activities. In a study of New York City public housing projects, Williams and Kornblum (1994) found that housing projects are far from the violence-ridden and dysfunctional communities depicted in the mass media. Instead, youths living in public housing projects created spaces where they fashioned dreams and hopes for a better life. These findings echoed my own experiences growing up in a housing project on the Lower East Side of Manhattan, where my mother as well as the majority of single mothers raised children who were not involved in drugs.

Becoming a Man

Steven, a 23-year-old West Indian man, had grown up in a two-parent household in East Flatbush, Brooklyn; his mother was from St. Vincent and his father was from Grenada. Steven, who was enrolled in CUNY and had a D+ average, described why he had looked forward to work after school throughout his high school years:

> I didn't want to be home. I didn't want to be there cramped inside the house. That's one of the reasons I always worked. I didn't want to be there with my mom. I wanted to be out! Being at work was like freedom, even though you had to take crap. That's why I always worked.

As described by Steven one aspect of men's quest to fashion a gender identity was actively distancing themselves from their mothers. The quest to establish a firm sense of gender identity—a deep-seated sense of self as "masculine" or "feminine"—became a project that occupied much of men's free time.[39] Regardless of whether their fathers were present, young men had a more formidable task before them than their female counterparts.

Deren, an 18-year-old West Indian man of Guyanese ancestry, had grown up with both parents, dropped out of high school in the eleventh grade, but eventually earned a GED and was attending a community college in Queens. When asked why he liked to hang out, Deren smirked as he remembered what it was like growing up in Corona, Queens:

> Well, that's personal; you know what I'm saying. Street life is very different. I can't explain it. Like us guys, we can't stay home like all day. Like if you stay home, what if they call you mama's boy if you stay home and all that. I want to be outside, I don't want to be home. I don't want to be with my TV at home; I want to be outside, playing basketball, doing something, anything but staying inside, and watching TV.

Men recalled that while they were growing up, being at home with their mothers was problematic. Partly because of the gendered division of space in the home and young men's quest to establish their sense of masculinity, the street became a space where most men spent their free time. Young men boasted that they made every effort to spend as little time as possible at home because the street served as a space in which they were able to construct a sense of masculinity. Men's experience of hanging out in the streets contrasted sharply with women's stories about growing up cloistered within their homes.

Another aspect of proving one's "manhood" was engaging in fights. Men narrated many instances of "testing," particularly in junior high school, where young men were compelled to prove their manliness by physically defending themselves. Denzel, an 18-year-old West Indian man, described some of the male hazing rituals he underwent during his preadolescent years:

> It was rough! Because in junior high school kids try to play hard rocks. They try to act like big men and do bad and stuff. The first day I was in that school, this kid I knew said something that got him in trouble and I tried to stick up for him and he put the whole thing on me so then I had to fight five guys.

Of course episodes in which men had to demonstrate their virility by engaging in fights often translated into problems at school. Haitian men, in particular, recalled many violent incidents at school. Perry, an 18-year-old Haitian man who had grown up in Prospect Heights, Brooklyn, was still enrolled in high school, with a C average. Perry's sense of manhood was intimately tied to defending his blemished ethnic identity:

> The thing I didn't like was why some Haitians would lie and say they're Jamaican. I'd look at them and say that's your country, why were you putting yourself down because people call you names? It's important for me to let people know that I'm Haitian. I don't care if they don't want to be my friend.

Men saw ethnic teasing as a direct assault on their masculinity and responded by engaging in fights. Fine and Weis (1998) used Benamayor's (1992:72) concept of cultural citizenship to explain how Puerto Rican men's sense of ethnic pride was intimately tied to their notions of what it means to be a man who defends his race. Cultural citizenship is a process through which an oppressed people arrive at a common identity and establish solidarity. In this light, men's attempts to defend their ethnicity can also be understood as intimately tied to notions of hegemonic masculinity.

Instead of focusing on postsecondary education, men sometimes turned to a time-honored bastion of maleness—the military—to establish their sense of manhood. Reynaldo was an 18-year-old Dominican man who was born and raised in Inwood, Manhattan, and had grown up with both parents. Reynaldo, who was still enrolled in high school with a C average, mentioned that he did not plan to go to college:

> I'm going to the military to see if I can make a man of myself because I like to chill too much. I don't like school that much. I barely made it through high school because I like chilling too much. You know, like hanging out with your friends playing basketball and stuff.

For Reynaldo, joining the military was the first step in becoming a man and feeling like an adult. It was striking that several men mentioned joining the armed service as a career path, but none of the women did so. While, at an early age, women already felt like women because they had assumed many adult responsibilities in the home, men struggled to achieve a secure sense of gender identity. In the end, men had to actively seek spaces where they could establish their sense of manhood, such as sports, the workplace, or the military.

Yet another space in which men attempted to construct their masculinity was romantic relationships with women. Men's narratives were peppered with references to many episodes of "chasing girls" throughout their adolescence.[40] When asked about the most important aspect of high school, many of the men, especially those who had not done well in school, responded with "Chilling, talking to the girls." Steven, a 23-year-old West Indian, joked about how he decided to attend college: "I was following a girl. . . . Do not let my name be known that I went to college to follow a girl. Everyone knew this. All my friends, they knew this because they knew the girl." Now that Steven was older, in retrospect he came to the conclusion that "it was stupid" to attend college because he wanted to chase after one particular woman.

Some of the men indicated that they sometimes skipped classes during high school to follow "girls." Sam, a 26-year-old Haitian man who had grown up in Flushing, Queens, admitted that his biggest flaw in life was that he was only interested in women and openly bragged that he was a "ladies' man." Sam remembered that he had actually transferred to a high school that offered a nursing program because he wanted to attend a high school that had more girls. In a study of African Americans enrolled in a public high school in Washington, DC, Fordham (1996) found that low-achieving men were also preoccupied with their masculinity. These young men measured their manhood in terms of having sexual freedom and not committing themselves to any particular women. In contrast, high-achieving men tended to have only one serious girlfriend.

When queried about why they thought that more women in their communities graduated high school than men, José, a 25-year-old Dominican man, chuckled:

> We were *tigueres* [tigers]. We were chilling in the street all the time. You won't see girls in the corner, especially in Dominican families. They lock down. Then, the only thing the girls can do is open a book and read.

In Dominican culture, a *tiguere* is a male cultural form. A *tiguere*, like a tiger, is a man who is quick on his feet and is usually hanging out in the street; he is witty, can fend for himself against insurmountable odds, and is deemed to be a maverick in the art of persuasion. The *tiguere* is also known for his sexual prowess.

Men felt that women's higher educational attainment was related to the different ways in which men and women evaluated their futures. Deren, an 18-year-old West Indian who had grown up in Corona, Queens, explained:

> Girls are more serious than guys are. Guys, we just want to hang out and do other things, but girls are more studious. Girls mature faster than guys do. When guys still want to play around, girls are already mature. They want to go to school more. They want to learn and they have the idea to look in the future.

Although Deren did not explain why "girls are more serious" about their education than young men, seemingly home life is an important part of the reason. Whereas women were expected to be serious and responsible in family affairs at a very early age, men were not. In essence, the gender-biased division of labor in family life contributed to the different ways in which men and women were gendered and evaluated their futures.

Men even defended the double standard, boasting that they took an active role in keeping their sisters away from the "boys element." Otherwise, according to Denzel, your sisters might come home "with a belly right in front of you." While men reported that their parents warned them about "getting a girl pregnant," they did not share any of these worries themselves.[41] Since men did not see themselves as responsible for childcare, they expressed little concern about becoming parents. Unlike women, who did not want men "screwing up" their lives, men did not talk about delaying sexual activities as a way of securing their future educational opportunities.

Conclusion

This chapter began with the question of how changing gender roles influence the outlooks of women and men toward the role of education in their lives. I found that gender-biased child-rearing practices within the home setting have an important influence. At a young age, second-generation women assumed adult responsibilities and in some cases become surrogate mothers to their younger siblings. This led them to have closer ties to the family and develop a strong gender identity as women. In spite of the social supports available to women in their homes, they were also subjected to stricter social control than their male counterparts. Women also became institutional brokers for their families and felt pride in being able to assist their parents in this capacity. In due course, women developed a dual frame of reference in which they contrasted their own situation with that of their mothers. Women's narratives were marked by the assumption that they would assume full responsibility for the well-being of their families. These experiences provided women with an important vantage point from which to evaluate their decisions regarding their futures, leading them to reject early childbearing and to define education as a way of achieving independence. The challenges of the gender-biased division of labor in the household provided women with a critical consciousness from which to understand the role of education in their lives.[42]

The feminist outlooks and practices articulated by women were not simply by-products of assimilation into U.S. society; they were part and parcel of the lived feminist legacies of strong foremothers, including mothers, grandmothers, and great-grandmothers.[43] Notwithstanding the fact that the legacy of the women's movement has left an indelible imprint on the outlooks of young women growing up in the United States, women's dreams of an education and financial independence were also an extension of the lived experiences of their immigrant mothers. Rather, they represented the historical legacy of Caribbean women who have headed their households both in their home countries as well as in the Diaspora and could be described as manifesting *transnational feminism(s)* that originated in the sending society and was rearticulated in the Caribbean Diaspora.[44]

For several reasons, men did not articulate a dual frame of reference. First of all, gender-biased childrearing practices generally absolved men from many of the adult responsibilities imposed on their sisters. Men also spent much of their time during their childhood and adolescent years outside their homes, usually playing sports. This led them to have very weak ties to their extended kin. In short, the webs of family ties that women maintained with other family members provided them with emotional supports that perhaps were unavailable to the men. At the same time, it was clear that for men achieving gender identity was fraught with problems. While women's narratives tied notions of womanhood and independence to education, men discursively linked their feelings of independence and masculinity to hanging out, working, and establishing romantic relationships with women. Whereas women expressed deep concern about the consequences of premature childbearing, men did not articulate any of these worries. In the next chapter we turn to the race-gender experiences the second-generation encountered in the workplace.

CHAPTER 7

After Graduation:
Race and Gender in the Workplace

In a way I agree with my mom about the importance of an education, but when I see people who can't get jobs, I kind of gave up on that, but then again, it was good to go to school and get a degree and let it sit there. At least you know you have it, you don't have to go back and do it over. It was good to let it sit there and when opportunities open you can go for it. Eventually, you can be the lucky one.

Richard, 24-year-old Haitian man

Reflecting on his experiences during the job search and while on the job, Richard expressed reservations about the value of a college education for him as a racially stigmatized man. However, Richard did not hold an oppositional stance toward schooling. Eventually Richard would like to finish college and become a physical therapist.

This chapter examines how the race-gender experiences men and women had during their job search and in the workplace influenced their outlooks on the role of education. My guiding questions were: How did the second generation fare in the postindustrial economy? How did the work trajectories of men and women differ, if at all? And how did their experiences shape their views about education and social mobility?

The first part of the chapter explores men's *marginalization* within the workforce and the way in which their job experiences contributed to their worried outlooks about social mobility and education. The second section focuses on women's *ghettoization* in the labor market, showing that although women were networked into pink-collar jobs and faced racial-gender subordination, they maintained optimistic outlooks about their future prospects for employment through obtaining an education.

Men's Marginalization

Color(ing) and Gender(ing) Job Searches

Richard, the 24-year-old Haitian man quoted in the introduction, had grown up in Prospect Heights, Brooklyn, and had worked in an assortment of odd jobs, including as a stock boy at a retail store, as a maintenance man at a school cafeteria, and reading meters for a gas company. However, most of these jobs were part-time or temporary jobs. At the time of the interview Richard had been looking for work but had not been successful:

> Employers tell you, "Oh yes, we were hiring last week. We're not hiring anymore. We'll keep your application on file. When we have an opening, we'll let you know." Yeah, right! I've thought about this and I've spoken to a few people about this. You go to certain job interviews and they turn you down. After you get turned down six or seven times, everywhere you go, all you hear is, "Oh yeah, we'll keep your application on file." Some people get so frustrated they don't even want to go back out there to deal with this BS!

Richard acknowledged that he had more employment opportunities in the United States than in Haiti. However, he believed that times were hard for members of racially stigmatized groups. Even when applying for minimum-wage, entry-level jobs, Richard felt that he was discriminated against.

One morning Peter, a 23-year-old Dominican who had grown up in Washington Heights and Inwood, Manhattan, went downtown to apply for work, and he was promptly reminded that his color was always seen as a source of suspicion:

> I will never forget. I went to the Department of Labor and there was a white man who was helping me. And he looked at me and really quickly asked me, "Can I see your green card? Can I see your green card?" And I looked at him and I said, "I was born in the United States." And then he didn't apologize or anything and I didn't like that.

Peter was asked for his immigration status because the Immigration Reform and Control Act of 1986 had established requirements to prove work eligibility before starting a job and created sanctions for employers knowingly hiring undocumented immigrants. Since the national narrative has scripted the "color" of undocumented immigrants as dark, second-generation Caribbean youth were automatically assumed to be foreigners or undocumented immigrants when applying for work solely because they were dark-skinned. These incidents were not merely inconvenient; they left a lasting impression on the second generation. Repeated episodes of discrimination during job searches led men to doubt that opportunities were open to them, as their dark skin preempted them from ever "looking American," regardless of their place of birth or ethnic identification. This would not have been the case if they had been of European phenotype.

Peter had had a very checkered work history. Previously, Peter had worked as a stock boy in a bookstore, a hardware store, and a supermarket; he had also worked in the informal economy, unloading trucks of a wholesaler and as an assistant at a gas station, as well as a dishwasher. After continuing to experience numerous problems in securing white-collar employment, Peter expressed worries about his future:

> I think that if I'm applying for a job and there's a white person, the job would be given to him because he's white. And that has happened to me in a job that I applied for. It was a job in a lawyer's office. I remember that I applied and then I just kept calling them and calling them and calling them, until one day, I they told me the job was taken. And I knew something was up. They sounded kind of fishy to me. I know it probably had to do with my race because they looked at me funny.

In Peter's case, his mother was Dominican and his father was European; however, Peter was dark-skinned. Peter's parents had separated when he was a boy, and he had grown up with his mother. Notwithstanding the discrimination faced by all immigrants and people who are not of European phenotype, there is an internal hierarchy with respect to people of color. People of any discernible African phenotype are generally ranked lower in the U.S. racial pyramid than Asians or lighter skinned Latinos.

Peter also commented that his friend, another Dominican man, had not been able to find employment commensurate with his education:

> Well my friend, he's about the same age as me, and he graduated from a technical college and he was supposed to work as a computer

technician and he ended up working as a mechanic where his father works at. They laid him off. I still think that that wasn't right.

Peter had attended a four-year college but had been demoted to a community college because he had not been able to remain on good academic standing. Nevertheless, Peter planned to return and finish an associate's degree in computer programming someday; however, when asked about whether he agreed with his mother's advice about the importance of education, Peter expressed some degree of ambivalence:

> First of all, let me say that I agree, but to a certain point. Because if you try, try and try and you don't succeed, then you're not going to make it. It's just not going to be. You can only make it to a certain point. And then you cannot do anything about it. But, sometimes you can get somewhere.

Peter had been working part-time as a customer service representative for a cellular phone company, but at the time of the interview he was in crutches convalescing from a car accident, in which he had lost his mother and sister. Since he could no longer pay the rent for his mother's apartment, Peter was sleeping in his aunt's living room and hoped he would still have a job when he recuperated. When queried about the advice he would give his future children about how to "make it" and become successful in this country, Peter replied, with some resignation in his voice, "as time passes by I will give them advice, depending on the experience that I will go through." Against the backdrop of a restructured urban economy, men spoke at length about their vulnerability as stigmatized racial minorities.

Experiencing the "Hoodlum" Narrative at Work

Men experienced the "hoodlum" narrative, not only through the difficulties they encountered while looking for work, but also while on the job. José, a 25-year-old Dominican man who had grown up in Washington Heights, Manhattan, had held an assortment of jobs, including working as a security guard, a maintenance man, in fast food, and in the city's Summer Youth Employment Program (SYEP). José painfully recalled the negative interactions he experienced while working as a temporary stock boy for a major electronics store in midtown Manhattan:

> When I go to work everybody's white; everybody's white. There's only one Hispanic and two black guys, but everybody else is white. Three days ago, I went to the main store at the electronic franchise

where I work to get something for my boss because he needed a piece for a television set and as soon as I entered, the employees at the main store did not know I was from the same store, so everybody just came up to me looking at me strange, looking at me like I was going to steal something! I was so upset that I yelled: "Excuse me but I work for this store! I came to get a piece for my boss!"

José remarked that he wished he were a lawyer so that he could sue employers that discriminated against Latinos and Blacks.

Although José had initially dropped out of high school, with the encouragement of his mother and sister, he eventually earned a GED. When asked about his beliefs about the value of an education, José affirmed that he agreed with his mother's advice that education was the key to his future, and he asserted that he would tell his son to go to school. However, José did not plan to continue his education, saying that there were jobs in the service sector that paid relatively well and did not require educational credentials: "I know some people that they don't have their diploma and they are still making like $16 an hour. They showed me their paycheck and I be like, 'What?!!!' They were elevator men and stuff like that." José planned believed that his chances for employment in blue-collar public-sector work were better than in the private sector, so he applied for work in the sanitation department.

During high school, Steven, a Brooklyn-born, 23-year-old West Indian man, whose mother was born in St. Vincent and father was born in Grenada, had worked off the books at an Italian-owned ice cream parlor. Steven painfully recalled that his boss sometimes hurled racial epithets at him: "One time I didn't put enough sugar in the ice machine and that's the main ingredient and my boss screamed at me and called me all types of words. They always call you the Negro, nigger word." Blatant discriminatory experiences such as these reminded men of their stigmatized status in the White/Black racial pyramid. Most importantly, these episodes deeply affected men's thinking about the "color" of social mobility in contemporary U.S. society.

Men had very checkered work histories, in low-level blue-collar jobs that were not only unstable, but hazardous. Since racially stigmatized men were placed at the end of the hiring queue, they were largely confined to the most exploitative jobs. Joaquín, a 20-year-old Dominican man who had grown up in Inwood, Manhattan, had worked as a jack of all trades at an elite social club in midtown Manhattan. When asked why he left, Joaquín grimaced:

I got back spasms and I figured out that anybody was going to get back spasms lifting 200-pound folding tables by himself, while working without a carry belt. One day I fell down and I hurt my back. I couldn't pay the ambulance. My boss didn't want to call an ambulance, so I had to call my cousin to pick me up. That's why I left. I don't know how I didn't get a hernia!

Without health insurance or disability coverage, Joaquín was forced to leave his job because the unsafe working conditions left him maimed. Previously, Joaquín had tried to obtain unionized blue-collar work in sanitation and construction, but union jobs, which provided a steady source of employment for early poor and working-class European immigrants, have withered in the new economic landscape.[1]

In many ways, the labor market experiences of second-generation Caribbean men echoed those of their parents, many of whom were locked into the most exploitative dead-end jobs in the lowest echelons of the labor market. The proliferation of income-generating activities outside the sphere of public regulation is an integral part of the postindustrial city. During the 1980s, the real wages of the average worker declined by 10% while poverty rates continued to climb.[2] Subcontracting, part-time work, and personal services and working "under the table" were the linchpins of restructured urban labor markets. Low-wage service workers, such as messengers and part-time clerical workers, are the sweatshop employees of the late twentieth century.

Social Critique and Worried Outlooks

Men felt a general sense of vulnerability in the newly restructured postindustrial labor market. When asked whether he felt it had been easier for his parents to find work than it was for him, Mark, a 24-year-old West Indian man of Jamaican ancestry, echoed the sentiments of the men: "I'd say times were harder. I'd say it's gotten worse. It's not like back in the eighties. People just had more money, period. They were just better off. Now, most jobs don't pay that much." To support himself during college, Mark had to piece together multiple part-time jobs, working mostly as a stock boy in supermarkets. After seven years, Mark had not yet been able to earn a bachelor of arts degree, and he admitted that at times he wondered if college might be a waste of time. Mark mentioned that some of his friends who had earned college degrees were unable to find employment commensurate with their credentials.

Part-time, temporary jobs, such as helping out with a move, handing out flyers, unloading trucks, busboy, packing groceries, and making deliveries for grocery stores for "pocket money," were often the only kinds of job men were able to obtain. Paul, an 18-year-old Haitian man who had grown up in Crown Heights, Brooklyn had been looking for work for over a year and had applied for entry-level work in fast-food establishments, pharmacies, and supermarkets without much success. Although Paul had held a job as a newspaper representative who promoted home subscriptions, that did not last:

> When I was working for the newspaper, I wasn't getting paid by the hour. It was by commission. If you don't work, you don't get paid. If you get only one order a day—each order was $3.00. Let's say you did five orders a week. Then when they called the person, if they didn't want it anymore, you didn't get paid for that order. At the end of the week you might end up with a check for $3.00.

When asked about the lowest wage he would accept, Paul's reflections reverberated with the sentiments of men: "It doesn't matter to me because I really want to get a job. As long as I am getting paid, I'll accept any kind of job." It has been widely argued that second-generation Caribbean youth will experience "second-generation decline" because they have adopted a "native minority oppositional" antischool attitude and lack the work ethic needed to sustain steady employment.[3] Allegedly, unlike their parents, who accepted exploitative jobs, second-generation youths are expected to reject minimum-wage menial jobs and lack the skills to pursue professional jobs.[4] Rather than express contempt for servile work, the men in this study said they would accept any job that paid the minimum wage.

Men who are racially stigmatized have born the brunt of economic restructuring and continued racial discrimination. Increasingly, they have comprised a reserve labor force that is not able to find stable employment. In a study of poor and working-class fast-food workers in Harlem, Newman and Ellis (1999) also found that Black and Latino youth did not disdain low-status jobs. The more prevalent problem for racially stigmatized youth, particularly men, is that it is hard for them to secure any kind of paid work. Discrimination continues to play a role in the employment problems experienced by men who are racialized as Black, as they are still underrepresented even in unskilled jobs.[5] It is the temporary nature of the jobs being created in the newly restructured economy and racial discrimination, not the quality of the employees or their work ethic, that accounts for the employment troubles of the men.

Despite the gains in education, the employment of Black men has worsened, especially among the younger cohorts. During the 1980s, the unemployment rate for Blacks, aged 16 to 19 years old, was 36%, while the rate for Hispanics was 33%.[6] In contrast, the unemployment rate for Whites was less than half that for Blacks and Hispanics. These figures leave out the unknown number of discouraged workers who have traditionally been excluded from the calculation of unemployment rates. The decline of the wage-labor economy has translated into the outright deproletarianization of a growing segment of the urban poor.[7] This population of peripheral workers increasingly comprises racially stigmatized youth, especially young men.[8] Marginalization, or the pushing of groups to the edges of the labor force, leaving them redundant or confining them to the worst jobs, results from a combination of factors, including technological change, racial discrimination, and government inaction.[9]

Rodrigo, a 23-year-old Dominican man who had grown up on the Lower East Side of Manhattan, recalled that one of his male friends had earned a bachelor of arts degree in computer technology, but he was unable to find work, so he resorted to working as a mechanic with his father. Not surprisingly, Rodrigo had developed concerns about his prospects for employment:

> I think that in this day and age, you need people in high places. Because imagine, the people from Yale, Princeton, Columbia, all those rich people! They had their mom and dad pay for their education and they had contacts with people in the business world. All the parents had to do was say, "Do me a favor" and they're set. And us, for us, it will be much harder. You have to have people in high places in order to get the connections.

Rodrigo had dropped out of high school in the tenth grade but planned to return to college someday. Although Rodrigo aspired to become a computer programmer, he was working in maintenance at a luxury building in midtown and worried about his ability to obtain secure, steady employment.

Paven, a 19-year-old West Indian man of Guyanese ancestry who had grown up in Bushwick, Brooklyn, fretted that he might face the same difficulties his older cousin encountered:

> My cousin, who has a B.A. in accounting, was working as an intern for the number two firm in the city, but out of the ten interns, two were already chosen. Right now he's not working. He quit a job at some bank because they had him photocopying and that really

pissed him off. He jokes about it, but I know that deep down inside he feels angry. He tells me, "You know what I think about school? What's my philosophy on school now?" I was like, "Forget school because what has it gotten you in four years? Look what you're doing. You're doing nothing!" That's the answer to it!

While Paven was ambivalent about the payoff a college education would have for him in the future, he was still pursuing an associate's degree at a community college. Paven dreams about becoming a corporate executive officer for a major footwear company, but he did not believe that he had much chance, and he did not know what he would do instead.

Isidro, a 23-year-old Dominican man who had grown up in Flushing, Queens, first entered the labor market as a cashier at a fast-food establishment through his uncle who worked there. Then while in college, Isidro obtained a job packaging thermometers at a manufacturing company in Queens. Since Isidro was majoring in economics, he applied for his first white-collar position as a bank teller at a local bank and was offered a job. However, Isidro quickly found the work environment hostile to racially stigmatized employees: "I worked mostly with whites. There were only a few Dominicans working there. I didn't like it at all. I'm a professional, you know, and there were some managers who used to treat us bad. They used to curse at us. It was a racial thing. That's basically why I left." Upon earning a bachelor of arts degree in economics, Isidro hoped to pursue a graduate degree and become a financial analyst. However, Isidro did not plan to seek employment in a corporate headquarters. Instead, Isidro wanted to open his own business so that he could circumvent the discrimination he had experienced in the labor market.

The legacy of racism has meant that historically education has had less of a payoff for members of racially stigmatized groups than for Whites. During the 1990s, Black men with college degrees earned $798 for every $1000 earned by White men.[10] Moreover, Black and Latino men who entered semiprofessional careers were concentrated in the lowest rungs of their career ladders.[11] In light of these trends, Feagin and Sikes (1994) have concluded that whereas Whites have careers, Blacks and Latinos have jobs.

Steven, a 23-year-old West Indian man whose parents were from St. Vincent and Grenada, had grown up in East Flatbush, Brooklyn. Steven interrupted his undergraduate studies because of academic troubles as well as financial hardships, but when I pressed him about his future career goals he expressed doubts about returning to earn a bachelor of arts:

I know I have to go back to school . . . so that I can get my college education. You get a little more respect when you have that paper—
the college diploma. You use your mind when you get the paper.
But, it's just a bragging right. That's all it is. I think that there will
always be discrimination.

Steven did not oppose education, but he worried that regardless of the level
of education he reached, he would be discriminated against in the workplace. Men's outlooks diverged sharply from those found by MacLeod's
(1995) ethnographic study of White, Black, and Latino young men living in
a New York City public housing project. MacLeod found that Black and
Latino young men believed racial minorities were advantaged vis-à-vis
Whites through affirmative action programs, which worked to prevented
discrimination in the workplace.[12] In contrast, the men in this study felt that
their race was a liability in the job market.[13]

Some researchers have speculated about the ability of second-generation
youths to tap into the job networks of their immigrant parents.[14] Segmented
assimilation theorists have posited that second-generation youth who suffer
discrimination in the mainstream economy may be able to seek refuge in ethnically oriented small business.[15] However, second-generation Caribbean
youth did not appear to be working in the ethnic economy or within an ethnic
niche. Although there is a small concentration of first-generation Haitian and
West Indian women in the health industry, it is unlikely that their children
will be able to obtain professional positions within the health industry, given
the deficient academic preparation that they are subjected to.[16]

Sam, a 26-year-old Haitian man who had grown up in Flushing,
Queens, was the only person in the study to have opened his own business.
Sam passionately recounted how his negative race-gender experiences pro-
pelled him to circumvent racial discrimination by opening his own business:

One cannot make it in this country working for someone else because this is a white man's world. And any racism or discrimination,
I'm going to try to break through that glass ceiling. I'll do anything
that I have to do. I am my own business owner. I'm 26 years old and
I have a house. The first thing that I did was made sure I was going
to have a place to live. I opened up a business and I'm going to put
all I can into it to make sure that it is successful.

With the help of his family, Sam pooled resources and opened a Caribbean
restaurant in Queens.

Although many of the men in this study expressed an interest in opening their own businesses, the reality was that they often lacked the capital to do so. Among the few Dominican men who had worked as stockboys in Dominican-owned *bodegas* (grocery stores), none wanted to pursue this type of work in the future. Reynaldo, an 18-year-old Dominican man who had grown up in Inwood, Manhattan, chuckled when he explained why working in his father's grocery store would not provide him with a safety net:

> We're not rich. My father owns the bodega just to maintain ourselves, just to keep us going in life. I used to work with my father in the bodega, but I didn't like it because he cheats on me too much! He's always saying that he's giving me a lot of things during the week. Yeah, right! So, when I was working with him at the end of the week, he was like, "Here's your money." Like, $50 or something and I'm like, "Man, I'm working, give me my money!"

Reynaldo humorously pointed out that many of the jobs that were being generated in the ethnic economy were exploitative, paying far below the minimum wage, and in some cases were dangerous.[17] Reynaldo eventually found a minimum-wage job in the fast-food industry, where he was at least assured a minimum wage.

Besides small business, another historical refuge for racially stigmatized groups has been the public sector. Given that in the private sector men were hired for the least secure and most exploitative jobs, they spoke about pursuing public-sector work in traditionally male-dominated fields, such as law enforcement and the military, because they felt that they would have a better chance of finding long-term employment with benefits. Alejandro, a 23-year-old Dominican man raised in Corona, Queens, smirked while explaining why so many of his college peers sought employment in the rapidly expanding prison-industrial complex[18]:

> You see right now a lot of college people are applying for jobs in the police department. But they are not applying because they want to be there, but because that's the job market that was open right now. So, that's where you're going to apply.

Previously Alejandro had worked part-time in the shipping department for a retail store, and as a security guard, but these jobs did not last. With a C average at the public university, Alejandro was pursuing a bachelor of arts degree in criminal justice, and he planned to enter the police academy upon graduating. In the meantime, he hoped to find stable employment working as a Spanish-English translator, again in the criminal justice system.[19]

Although public-sector jobs have traditionally provided stigmatized minorities with an alternative route into the middle class, these jobs have been difficult for parents to pass on to their children because they are largely controlled through certification and civil service examinations. Sullivan's (1989) study of three Brooklyn neighborhoods in the 1980s found that social networks accounted for the differences in the labor market and crime patterns of three groups of men from diverse racial communities. Sullivan (1989) found that social networks helped Whites get jobs over their Black and Latino peers, even if the racially stigmatized applicants had higher educational credentials.[20]

In a race-conscious society such as the United States, entire categories of people have been ordered into hiring queues by race and gender, with skill-relevant characteristics serving as additional weights.[21] Employers draw sharp distinctions between female and male employees, especially among those from stigmatized minority communities.[22] One respondent in Kirchenman's (1997) Chicago-based study of employer discrimination offered his explanation of why the experience of racially stigmatized women in their search for work has been different from that of their male counterparts:

> Whites are not afraid of Black women because Black women have been part of their households for a long time—as the white man's mistress, as the mother of his children, as domestics, as cooks in restaurants and as office cleaners.[23]

In the United States, the symbolic taint attached to men of dark skin casts them as unstable, uncooperative, dishonest, uneducated, and generally unreliable workers, while their female counterparts are viewed as more exploitable.[24] In the end, whereas potential employers might fear hiring racially stigmatized men because they have been racialized as problematic workers, they might not have the same reservations about racially stigmatized women.[25]

The rejection of dark-skinned men in the labor market appears to be a global phenomenon. Model's (1997) cross-national study of West Indian immigrants living in the United States, Canada, and England found that Caribbean men had lower occupational status than women. Hurtado et al. (1992) also found the same dynamic affected Latino communities. Census data show that Latino male employment and earnings were lower than those of White males with the same education. However, the racial gap is less pronounced between White women and Latina women, as well as between Black and White women.[26]

Women's Ghettoization

Networked into Pink-Collar Work

Women reported fewer difficulties in finding employment than did men because they had better networks for potential job opportunities.[27] When asked about how they found their work, women cited community-based organizations, churches, and family members. Cassandra, a 27-year-old Dominican woman who had earned a bachelor of arts degree, had grown up in Washington Heights, Manhattan. Cassandra nostalgically remembered obtaining her first formal job through the SYEP:

> I still have my Summer Youth Employment cards. I remember going down there to get my medical records and get the little green card so we can work. I worked daycare in summer youth programs in Inwood, Manhattan. I remember my first summer youth employment job; I got paid $95 for a whole month. For me, that was a lot of money and I had a lot of fun. When I was in daycare, we used to go to a lot of places that I'd never been to. That was the first time I went to the Great Adventure theme park. So, to me, it was more like a fun thing, too.

A quarter of the women surveyed had entered the labor market through SYEP, compared with only 8% of the men. This may be due in part to the fact that the types of jobs offered through this program were traditionally pink-collar jobs, such as childcare and administrative assistant. Women reported that sometimes SYEP jobs translated into part-time work during the academic year. Cassandra remembered that while she was working in the SYEP, her brother worked making deliveries for a *bodega* or as a mechanic.

Good relationships with teachers sometimes materialized into employment opportunities for women. Janet, a 26-year-old Dominican woman who had grown up in Washington Heights, Manhattan, and earned a bachelor of arts degree in psychology, reminisced:

> I got my current job as the director of fund raising at my former Catholic high school through my principal, who happened to be my eighth grade teacher and thought I was capable. The job that I had prior to this, actually all the jobs that I've ever held have been

through people who know me and know that I was probably capable
of it—my first job being with my aunt. Then, one of my roommates,
when I lived on Long Island, got me the job at the college, in the
bursar's office and now this job. So for me, that's how it has been.

Rosenbaum et al. (1995) found that women were far more likely than men to
have established supportive relationships with people, such as teachers, who
were networked to job opportunities. In a study of high school-to-work links
in Chicago, Illinois, Rosenbaum and Binder (1997:79) concluded that teachers
"provide a good channel of access for students, and in inner city schools, these
students' best chance of getting a job is through their teachers."

Family members, particularly other women, such as aunts, sisters, and
cousins, were also important in providing women entry into growing sectors
of the economy. Yvonne, a 23-year-old Dominican woman who had grown
up in Williamsburg, Brooklyn, credited her aunts with giving her a valuable
"jump start" in the labor market:

> I started working as a research assistant at an investment firm be-
> cause my aunt worked there. She actually spoke for me. My aunt
> once told me, "You know what, the first job you get, try it for it to be
> a good job and something that can take you somewhere." I never
> really thought about it, but it's true. My first job was at the broker-
> age firm and my friend's job was at our local supermarket. My friend
> is still at the supermarket! We're the same age, went to the same
> high school and college, had the same upbringing and she's still a
> cashier at that supermarket! I'm sure that if my aunts didn't have
> those kinds of jobs I would have been a cashier too, because I didn't
> know where to start or where to go.

Yvonne planned to become an investment banker in part because her experiences as a research assistant at an investment firm gave her a panoramic
view of potential career trajectories in a growing sector of the economy—an
experience many of the men lacked. Although Yvonne entered work in a
low-level pink-collar job, she, like many other women, "got her foot in the
door" to an expanding economic sector.

Maryse, a 23-year-old Haitian woman who had grown up in Crown
Heights, Brooklyn, had an employment trajectory that mirrored that of
women:

> It was an internship program through the school. . . . It was basically
> administrative work like typing and filing. It was a great experience

for me, definitely a learning experience. I was working for an architect. My boss actually constructed my school. I really enjoyed working there . . .

During high school I worked in the summer for three years. It was administrative work. It was a program through my mother's union that they constructed for the summer for kids whose parents were working through the union. I also worked as a childcare provider through the Summer Youth Employment Program.

Although Maryse was looking for work at the time of the interview, she was confident that her office skills and references would help her find administrative work. Through their job experiences in the service sector, women acquired many "soft skills," such as familiarity with professional demeanor and dress. Hence, by the time they graduated from high school, men and women had accumulated resumes, references, work experiences, and contacts that were quite different.

Color(ing) and Gender(ing) the Glass Ceiling

Despite women's entry into the expanding sectors of the economy, they still faced a colored and gendered glass ceiling. Jahaira, a 30-year-old Dominican woman who had grown up in Bushwick, Brooklyn, worked as a research assistant at an investment firm in downtown Manhattan. Jahaira explained that her race and gender put her at a disadvantage at her workplace:

They expect you to do much more work than your white counterpart. Same exact job but they expect you to do so much more for less money. I didn't think that existed but it does. It really, really does. I was getting paid . . . $23,000 a year and this white woman who just started, came in with the same credentials. I'm a college graduate. The only thing that she had that I didn't have was something called a Series 7, which you have to get to be a broker. It's a licensing thing. Okay, so that's why she was making $35,000 already. So, when I heard her talking on the phone she was making $40,000 a year. I raised hell and I got a lot of raises quickly!

Instead of being discouraged by the racial and gender discrimination she experienced at work, Jahaira fought back by "raising hell" and not accepting her ghettoization. Jahaira aspired to become an investment manager and planned to obtain a master's degree in business administration:

> Education is something that people cannot take from you. At my place of work, if I wouldn't have had the college degree, they could have thrown that in my face. "Well, you don't have a college degree—she does." The only thing they threw in my face was that she has a license and you don't. So, what did I say, "Okay, what do I do to get one?" And I got it. So, when someone says it doesn't matter how much education you have, that's an ignorant person.

Jahaira also knew other women who had not been able to find work commensurate with their educational credentials; however, she was still committed to the value of an education:

> I know there are a lot of lawyers, like my sister's friends, who are lawyers who graduated and passed the bar and can't find work. One is a Dominican girl. But out of ten people, maybe one person is like that, or maybe two. What are your odds if you don't go to school? For sure you're going to be in that fast food restaurant, working the cash register. So, that's what I say to people like that. I say, "Yeah, but you're more likely . . . if you have an education at least you can try."

The feminization of the work force has had mixed results for Black and Latina women. Occupational shifts have produced vacancies in white–collar work for Black and Latina women who were formerly confined to domestic services and factory work; however, women continue to work in ghettoized jobs and do not receive a salary commensurate with their educational credentials.[28] Even "Black women with four years of college who work full time, on average, earn the equivalent of a white male high school dropout who works full time. 'Equal' education does not translate across racial/ethnic and gender into equal 'income.' Despite these harsh realities women remained hopeful."[29]

Cassandra, a 27-year-old Dominican woman who had grown up in Washington Heights, Manhattan, also had a social critique of the race-gender stratification she experienced at work. Cassandra explained that she experienced a multifaceted glass ceiling while working at a major commercial bank:

> I started with the bank as a teller and I worked myself up. Within six months I became a customer service representative. Then I did sales. I worked in the mortgage department. Then I went to personal banking. I was authorized to sign any documents in the name of the bank, which is a big thing—a big step for you to have, but then I was never given the title of Assistant Treasurer and I was doing the job

already. And I waited and waited for it. "Oh, maybe they don't see me. Hello."

* * *

I worked in corporate America for six years and believe me, yes it was very good when you're bilingual, but they use it against you when it comes to promotion time. Oh yeah, they love to have a bilingual person. I had a Spanish-speaking clientele that was from Argentina and Israel and they wouldn't ask for anybody else but me. But when it comes to being an assistant manager, which I was already doing the job and I knew everything, somehow it never got to me. I was always the next in line, but they always skipped the line to the next White person.

Cassandra's experience was not simply the addition of gender, racial, class, or language discrimination, but a complex entanglement and interaction of all of these processes at once. After her negative experiences in the private sector, Cassandra sought employment in the public sector and obtained work in housing management for the city government.

A more insidious form of discrimination in the workplace was episodes of racialized sexual harassment. Racialized sexual harassment is "a particular set of injuries resulting from the unique complex of power relations facing . . . women of color in the workplace."[30] Cassandra recalled how she also grappled with the "mamasita" stereotype at work:

It's a very shocking thing. It's a constant. They have a stereotype of Dominican and Latina women as mamasitas. I have even had guys ask me, "Are Dominican women as hot as they say they are?" And I say, "Why don't you do me a favor. Take a hot pepper and stick it up yours and see how hot it is!"

Cassandra added that at times her male co-workers, regardless of race, insisted they knew that Dominican "ladies" liked to be called "mamasita."

It pissed me off. It's a stereotype. I worked during the transition period between working for the bank and then moved on to a city agency. Then I moved to work for a very small clinic, a Jewish organization. And I remember I used to direct meetings with job coaches and most of them were blacks and Hispanics. One of them, that always says, every time he had a question, he used to call me, "Mamasita, Mamasita." I said, "Never call me that." I hate that word because that's not my name. "Oh, but Dominican ladies always love to be called Mamasita. I had this Dominican girl who never let me off my bed." I said, "Well, then she had a problem."

The stereotype of Latina women as "mamasitas"—sexually available, immoral, and "cheap" women—is akin to the jezebel stereotype of African American women. This narrative is part of the race-gender-sexual exoticization and symbolic taint of the urban ghetto and its inhabitants. Hill-Collins (1990) explains that these "controlling images" are used to justify the exploitation of women who are deemed racially inferior.

Jahaira, who also worked in finance, recalled a White male colleague, who she described as a "WASP" (White Anglo-Saxon Protestant), who always wanted to know where she was "really" from:

> He was annoying. Every clique that could possibly be about any one nationality, he would ask you if he thought you were. He thought I was Haitian. I said, "No, but I could be because they are the same island." I probably have Haitian blood, more than likely. He said, "Oh, you know they're coming in the boats trying to cross the water. So many got killed last week." Or whatever. I said, "Yeah, it's a shame. To come here and find nothing."

Even at the company Christmas party, Jahaira's White co-workers asked her if she was feeling okay because she was not dancing or talking loudly. In their view, all women from the Caribbean were naturally wild and colorful partygoers. These racial(ized) and gender(ed) stereotypes are rooted in the historically unequal power relations, military interventions, and exploitation in the third world.

Optimistic Outlooks

In spite of the negative race-gender experiences women were subjected to at work, they consistently remained optimistic about their future prospects. Jahaira and Cassandra both spoke about the importance of pursuing graduate studies to combat racial discrimination. Ironically, the painful incidents women had had with discrimination reminded them about the importance of pursuing education. Research indicates that Black women are considerably more likely than White women to believe that they need to pursue postgraduate work to advance their careers. A study by Higginbotham and Weber (1999) of Black and White professional women found that while

White women were content with their work situations, Black women anticipated moving to a new firm to move up the career ladder.

Women pointed to examples of other women who had become successful by pursuing an education. Marie, a 19-year-old Haitian woman who had grown up in Crown Heights, Brooklyn, was struggling with academic problems in college, but she was still firmly committed to education:

> I think that if you work hard in school it will pay off. I truly think that. Like my aunt, right now; she wanted to be a registered nurse so bad. She was a nurse's aide. She went to school; she just studied; she was in the library every day and she went back to college. Now she's a registered nurse and she's really happy.

Even those women who were ghettoized into the lowest service sector jobs and those who were temporary workers maintained an optimistic outlook about the importance of education.

Tina, a 21-year-old West Indian woman whose parents were from Antigua, had grown up in South Ozone Park, Queens. Although Tina worked as a nurse's assistant while attending college, she had high aspirations:

> Education is very, very important. I see people stuck. . . . I'm not going to stay there. But, for them that's their family support. . . . In my opinion, people can make it by getting a good education and then finding a good job. It takes a while to get where you're going. But, eventually you get there. It's better than just sitting home and staying stagnant and not doing anything. Even if you get your bachelor's, from there you go on, you do another two or three years, or four years for a doctorate degree. But you still get there.

It was shocking that while many of the women knew about a Ph.D., none of the men mentioned this as a possibility. Tina expected to earn a graduate degree and become a child psychologist. Whereas men struggled to name a specific career they wanted to pursue, women articulated clear career goals, such as psychologist, teacher, investment manager, or registered nurse. This was due in part to the fact that women saw possibilities for work in these expanding sectors of the economy, while men, lacking this type of work experience, did not even have a clear sense of where they fit in the new postindustrial economy.

Women always discursively linked the importance of obtaining an education to their status as women. Maryse, the 21-year-old Haitian woman who had grown up in Crown Heights, Brooklyn, was attending postsecondary training for paralegal studies. However, Maryse planned to become a lawyer: "You can be successful through education, hard work, and persistence. That's how you can make it in the business world. You have to be educated because you are competing against men." Although women expressed interest in traditionally female-dominated fields, such as nursing and teaching, it is significant that they aspired to professional jobs within those fields.[31] These findings contrast sharply with Weis' (1990) study of the effect of deindustrialization among White working-class youth, where women articulated career goals that were pinned to traditional pink-collar ghettoized work, such as secretarial work.

The dramatic loss of manufacturing jobs, traditionally a mobility ladder for less skilled men, and the simultaneous expansion of low-level white-collar jobs, which increasingly employ women, have important implications for the way men and women regard education. "Of the ten occupations that will require the largest number of new workers, two—registered nurses and primary school teachers—require college degrees. All of the others—janitors, cashiers, truck drivers, and the like—involve skills that can be picked up on the job with little if any schoolroom knowledge."[32] Moreover, the jobs that require college degrees are occupations that were traditionally considered women's work, while those that required minimal training were typically considered men's work.

Growing industries such as finance and law rely heavily on a peripheral support staff composed mostly of women. To be exact, in the 1980s, four out of five people who worked in offices and processed information for businesses and government were women.[33] However, despite women's continued entry into traditionally male-dominated work, the sex segregation of occupations has continued. Eighty percent of clerical workers were female in 1980, compared with 60% in 1950.[34]

Although women maintained a social critique of racial and gender discrimination in the labor market, they also remained hopeful about the role of education in contesting negative stereotypes about them as "mamasitas."[35] This was due in part to the fact that they have had more work experiences in the formal labor market, which has allowed them to see the relevance of educational credentials in a postindustrial economy. Women who had obtained jobs as administrative assistants at law firms or social service agencies learned about white-collar professional positions, such as social work, law, and education. In a study of racial identity among second-generation Haitian and West Indian youth, Waters (1996) found that women believed there were more work opportunities for them than for men. Similarly, Dunn (1988) also found that African American women completed higher levels of education because they believed there were more jobs for them than for their male counterparts. A study by Fine and Weis (1998) of the social critique emanating from poor and working-class White, Black, and Latino communities also found that men were generally concerned that educational credentials would not pay off in the future. Fine and Weis (1998:234) understand this ambivalence as "an accurate portrayal of the economic prospects of poor and working class young adults in America in the 1990s." However, they also found that whereas men may experience ambivalence, women appear more hopeful about their occupational prospects.

Conclusion

Men and women both experienced discrimination in the labor market, however, their experiences were distinctly different. Men had great difficulty in finding work and were *marginalized* in the least secure, temporary, low-wage jobs, usually within the informal economy. Although men acknowledged that they had more employment opportunities in the United States than in their parents' home countries, they also believed that times were harder for them because as racial minorities, they faced discrimination even when they applied for minimum-wage, entry-level jobs. Since men's job experiences were often limited to the lowest level of service-sector work, such as working in grocery stores or as messengers, they did not have access to potential career paths in the growth sectors of the economy.

Continually encountering negative experiences during their job searches and while at work, men increasingly perceived a *job ceiling* working against them. In due course, men formulated *worried outlooks* about their employment possibilities. It is important to note that men did not oppose education as a route for social mobility. Men expressed doubts that education would protect them from the virulent racial discrimination they encountered even when looking for entry-level work. The multiple problems men experienced in the labor market were not due to any "oppositional identity" they harbored, but rather reflected the reality that they are continually placed at the bottom of the hiring queue.

Women generally reported fewer difficulties in finding work than men. They tended to be employed in traditional sex-typed work, such as secretarial work and nursing. Although these positions were often in pink-collar ghettos, they did provide women with a window to potential professional career paths into the growth sectors of the economy, such as education, health, and finance. Since many of these positions required educational credentials, women came to link social mobility with education. Despite the negative race, gender, and sexual incidents they confronted in the workplace, women formulated optimistic outlooks about the importance of education for them as women who are defined as racial minorities. Men and women's disparate outlooks related to the distinct and cumulative race-gender experiences they were subjected to in their everyday lived experiences during their youth and young adulthood.

CHAPTER 8

Education as a Way Out: The Future of Latino and Black Education

I really want to go back to school. I tell my daughter, the one that is going to school now, go to school. That's all you do. That's your problem, and that shouldn't be a problem to you. . . . I think if you had an education, you would be able to do anything you wanted.

Yvelise, 24-year-old with a GED

Yvelise's hopeful outlook points to why women attain higher levels of education than men, particularly in racially stigmatized communities. Taking a new approach to the issue of race and gender disparities in urban education, I explored the ways in which *race and gender processes* intersected and influenced the ways in men and women were treated across several social domains. My guiding questions were: How did racialized and gendered experiences in public spaces mold outlooks toward education? How did racial(izing) and gender(ing) processes intersect within the school setting? And, finally, how did changing gender roles influence the outlooks of men and women toward education? How have men and women experienced work within the postindustrial economy?

To answer these questions I investigated the intersection of race and gender as *lived experience* among the largest new immigrant group in New York City—the children of Caribbean immigrants from the Dominican Republic, Haiti, and the Anglophone West Indies. I conducted focus groups, life history interviews, and participant observation in a neighborhood public high school. I found that because men and women encountered distinctly different experiences across four key social spheres, including public spaces, schools, work, and family life, they responded to stigmatizing race-gender experiences in very different ways.[1] Women maintained optimistic outlooks, while men were worried about their futures. The differing outlooks of men and women were not innate, but rather were the outgrowth of their distinct race-gender experiences. *Experiential differences* with racial(ing) and gender(ing) processes in a variety of social realms shaped the life perspectives of the second generation. It is important to underscore that men did not openly reject the importance of an education in achieving upward mobility. Instead, men's worries can be understood as a consequence of their mistreatment in society, rather than as the cause of their educational problems.[2]

Toward a Race-Gender Experience Framework

Most of the existing literature on the second generation has rested squarely on the heels of the ethnicity paradigm, which makes the assimilation process the centerpiece of its inquiry. Reducing race and gender to elements of the assimilation process is problematic because it deflects attention from "the ubiquity of racial [and gender] meanings and dynamics" in everyday life experiences as well as institutional practices.[3] Given that the very networks and resources that are open to the second generation were structured along racial and gender lines, it is important that future studies of the second generation place race and gender processes at the forefront of the analysis.

Drawing on central concepts from racial formation theory, which examines race as a synthesis of racial projects that occur both at the macro level of large-scale institutions as well as the micro level of lived experiences, and critical race feminist theory, which examines race and gender as overlapping processes and seeks to derive theory from experiential differences, I utilized a race-gender experience framework. A guiding premise of this framework is that gender and race oppressions are socially constructed and intertwined.

Two major conceptual tools, *race-gender experiences* and *race-gender outlooks*, were at the heart of the race-gender experience framework. *Race-gender experiences* were the social interactions in which men and women underwent racial(izing) and gender(ing) processes in a variety of social spheres, such as public spaces, schools, family life, and the workplace. Over time, repeated *race-gender experiences* had a cumulative effect on outlooks. *Race-gender outlooks* were life perspectives on education and social mobility. They were an outgrowth of the different experiences men and women have with racializ(ing) and gender(ing) processes. The race-gender experience theory emphasizes that there are no "essential" differences between men and women. Rather, differing race-gender outlooks arose because of differences in experiences, not biology. Experiential differences with race-gender were the outcome of social interactions and structural relationships.

The strength of the race-gender experience framework is that it examines how youth and young adults were assigned racial meanings that were gendered, and how these definitions became "naturalized" and institutionalized throughout society such that they produced qualitatively distinct *life experiences* for second-generation Caribbean men and women. Race-gender experiences, not ethnic identity, are the keys to unraveling the schooling trajectories of youth. Although I used the race-gender framework to investigate how race and gender processes intersected in public spaces, schools, the workplace, and family life, there are countless other social spaces in which we can unravel race and gender oppression, including peer groups, community organizations, religious institutions, sports, and popular culture.[4] It remains to be seen if the race-gender conceptual framework can "travel" and be useful for understanding the educational trajectories of young adults from various race, gender, and class positions in the United States, as well as abroad.[5] Many more studies are needed.

Unveiling the social processes that create the power differentials among groups that are racialized as "White," "Black," "Hispanic," and "minorities" represents a first step in debunking the "naturalness" of these taxonomies. Some questions that are a step in that direction include: How can oppressive race(ing) and gender(ing) processes be revealed, interrupted, rearticulated, and dismantled to eliminate race and gender disparities? How can public spaces be de-gendered and de-raced? How can schools take inventory of the informal and formal macro- and micro-level practices that contribute to the race-gender gap within school walls? How can we re-create the gender(ing) that takes place in family life? How can we re-envision alternative workplace arrangements, which dismantle occupational race and gender hierarchies? The answers to these questions have important implications for practitioners, families, communities, and youths who are interested in eliminating race and gender disparities in education.

De-rac(ing) and De-gender(ing) Public Spaces

Race continues to be a fundamental organizing principle in the United States.[6] Racial hierarchies permeate social structures at all levels, such that individuals and groups who are defined as "White" comprise the top of the racial pyramid, while those who are defined as having one drop of African blood are relegated to the bottom. Other groups, such as Asians, fall somewhere in the middle of the bipolar White/Black continuum. Given that the majority of Caribbean immigrants in the United States could trace their ancestry to populations that originated in Africa, upon arrival or birth in the United States the overwhelming majority of children of Caribbean immigrants fall to the bottom of the White/Black racial pyramid.

Although Dominican, West Indian, and Haitian immigrants are indeed different ethnic groups originating from Caribbean countries with different languages and cultural backgrounds, they were subjected to similar racialization and stigmatization processes on U.S. soil. However, their racialization differed by gender. Men painstakingly described numerous incidents in which strangers and storeowners cast them as muggers, women automatically assumed that they were rapists, and taxi drivers refused them service. The hegemonic images of dark-skinned men as potential criminals was so powerful that men reported many instances in which they were treated as "suspects," not only by members of the dominant group, but also by their own communities. In part because Caribbean neighborhoods have been symbolically tainted as undesirable communities, the constant threat of police brutality came up in the narratives of men.[7] Men spoke about being stopped and questioned by the police about crimes simply because they fit the profile of a suspect. Not surprisingly, men's repeated negative experiences in public spaces left them with many doubts about the openness of mobility structures in the United States.

The racialization of women in public arenas took on a different tone. Women's racialization stemmed from stigmatized notions of them as exotic, sexual objects. The disapproving looks that women were subjected to in the public area occurred largely when strangers automatically assumed that they were teenage mothers. Through these social interactions, women learned that they were viewed as "welfare queens" and sexually promiscuous "mamasitas."[8] However, in an attempt to contest these negative images, women defined education as imperative.[9]

Second-generation Caribbean men and women all pointed to the media, which created and circulated negative images of their communities. These misrepresentations went beyond simple stereotypes to the realm of public policies, which ultimately circumscribed the lives of youth, thereby reproducing racial, gender, and class oppression.[10] The racial stigmatization of dark-skinned young men in the media as potential criminals or "suspects" has been used to fuel the justifications for the rapid expansion of the prison-industrial complex, the passing of anti-immigration legislation, as well as the dismantling of open admissions and affirmative action programs. Images of dark-skinned "welfare queens" who live high on the hog with dozens of children out of wedlock have been used to dismantle public assistance to low-income mothers and their families. The mass media must be held accountable for the dissemination of cultural representations that demonize men of African phenotype and exoticize their female counterparts.

Rewriting Gender School Lessons

Schools as institutions are also not impervious to the racial constructions that occur in the wider society. The gendered racial stigma that second-generation Caribbean youths encountered in public spaces followed them through school doors.[11] Through their institutional practices many school policies "framed" working-class minority young men as problematic students and potential juvenile delinquents who must be controlled and contained.[12]

Informally some teachers, administrators, and security guards treated racially stigmatized youths, particularly men, as "statistics"—that is, "at-risk youths" who will not amount to anything. Aware that they were being warehoused in low-level curriculum tracks and that little is expected of them, men responded with "willful laziness," expressing their resentment by making no effort to achieve good grades. Men admitted that they did not study hard and that they frequently cut class. As a result, a disproportionate number of them are placed in special education classes, and they have higher expulsion and dropout rates than female students.[13] Special education classes have become warehouses for misbehaving boys, especially those from racially stigmatized communities.[14] At Urban High School, 6% of students, most of whom were young men, were placed in self-contained special education classes. Since racially stigmatized young men were cast as potential troublemakers, they tended to have poor relationships with school officials, which often led to suspensions. Institutional expulsion characterized the experiences of the men.

Although women attended the same schools, they had experiences that were qualitatively different from those of their male peers. Women remembered being exhorted to behave like "young ladies," that is, to remain silent and obedient. At the same time, teachers were less threatened by young women and were more lenient toward them when they transgressed against school rules. Moreover, as schools became more overcrowded, "feminine traits" such as passivity, silence, and obedience were rewarded. Conversely, women who misbehaved were not sanctioned as harshly as men. Not surprisingly, women spoke about having favorable relationships with their teachers throughout their academic careers.

In spite of women's congenial relationships with their teachers, they were still tracked into low-level curricula during high school. Vocational classes, such as pink-collar training programs in secretarial studies, left many women woefully underprepared for college. Although low-level sex-typed curriculum tracking may be viewed as being in the best interest of working-class youth, in the long run, these programs undermined their prospects for social mobility.[15] Regardless of intentions, tracking reinforces racial and gender disparities among students.[16]

Women were institutionally engaged with their schools and maintained high aspirations. They were active participants in the classroom and school activities, taking lead in organizing many of the school activities, such as senior proms, cultural festivities, dances, etc. Although women were subjected to low-curriculum tracks, they were institutionally engaged in their school and came to see education as a way of achieving social mobility.

To address the problems that plague urban schools one major issue that must be addressed is the structural overcrowding and chronic underfunding of schools attended by racially stigmatized youths. Students in poor and immigrant neighborhoods, such as those enrolled at Urban High School, have had to contend with many infrastructure and hygiene hazards. State officials have responded to the systemic problems in the schools with erratic short-term solutions, such as recruiting teachers from abroad, providing provisional classroom spaces, and touting publicly financed school vouchers for use in private schools as the solution to the ills of urban public education. Regrettably, substitute teachers and trailer classrooms do not solve the fundamental problems of an inequitable educational system.

The call for the privatization of public education is perhaps the most worrisome trend in urban school reform. During the 1990s, the debate over educational reform centered on the use of publicly financed vouchers in private schools.[17] However, this political project is problematic on a number of grounds. First, it contributes to the notion that public education is a privilege, rather than a basic human right. Second, it also permits the state to shirk its responsibility to provide a quality public education to *all* members of society. Third, it depletes funding from already underfunded communities. And finally, it places the blame on individuals, namely teachers, students, and their families, who are allegedly not working hard enough and therefore must be forced to compete for an education. The more important question remains: why are school buildings crumbling and why are students crammed into overcrowded classrooms without textbooks and funneled into low-level curriculum tracks while metal detectors can be found in the school entrance?

Changes in classroom pedagogy would also play a pivotal role in eliminating the race-gender gap in education. According to traditional pedagogical practices, students are empty receptacles that should be ready for the educational "deposits" made by an authoritative teacher.[18] "Banking education," in which a student records, memorizes, and repeats information, without perceiving issues of relative power and contradictions, serves as an instrument of oppression.[19] Therefore, it is extremely important to examine the ways in which the social critique emanating from students is silenced or channeled to bring about social change.[20] Critical dialogue and praxis—action and reflection—pave the way to a more democratic learning environment.[21]

Ms. Gutierrez was one example of a teacher who strove to bring about social change; she was able to create an egalitarian classroom environment by validating the students' knowledge and promoting mutual respect. Ms. Gutierrez treated students as co-teachers and collaborators in the educational enterprise; she encouraged students to pursue their own intellectual interests and welcomed diverse interpretations of historical events. This often meant stepping outside of the "official" curriculum. Through promoting critical literacy—social empowerment and democratization—transformative teachers can promote a language of possibility for a more democratic society and inspire young men and women to participate in their education.[22] In this type of classroom environment, all students feel compelled to participate because they are genuine members of a community. To eliminate race and gender disparities in education, teachers, policymakers, and school personnel must always reflect on whether they are working to counteract or reproduce power relations between racially stigmatized youth and the dominant society.

Re-creating Homes

The gendered division of labor in the home setting provided men and women with very different sets of experiences and vantage points from which to evaluate their options regarding, work, education, and family. Female-led emigration from the Caribbean has resulted in high rates of female-headed households in the United States. While their mothers worked, second-generation Caribbean women assumed adult responsibilities from an early age, caring for children and performing household chores. Through identification with their mother's struggles as immigrants, racial minorities, and language minorities, women began to evaluate their futures in terms of a *dual frame of reference*, comparing their own situation with that of their mothers. Women described learning their feminism(s) by witnessing their mothers' resistance(s) to male domination; thus, their feminist articulations can be described as "homegrown."[23] While the home was a source of social support for women, it was also full of contradictions.[24] Women appreciated the help they received from their relatives, and they contested the double standard regarding the gendered division of labor in their homes. In due course, women fashioned a "blasphemous" feminist critique in which they criticized their mother's double standard at the same time that they respected their mothers and families.[25] Through this process, women identified education as a means of securing social independence and helping their families.

Men's experiences with gender(ing) processes at home contrasted sharply with those of their female counterparts, in that they rarely assumed adult responsibilities, such as cooking and caring for younger siblings. Instead, men spent much of their free time outside of their homes, usually playing basketball or other sports. Moreover, men also tended to have weak ties to their relatives and therefore lacked the social supports that their female counterparts thrived on. As a result of these gendering differences, men did not articulate a dual frame of reference or contrast their situation with that of their parents, even when the fathers were a part of the family life.

Another reason why men held ambivalent attitudes toward education was that for them, achieving a gender identity was fraught with problems. "Men, even more than women, are fettered to gender roles."[26] Second-generation men created their sense of manhood in a number of ways. First, men discursively distanced themselves from their mother's experiences. They openly bragged about preferring to work or hang out in the street, rather than staying at home with their mothers. Men also attempted to assert their masculinity through relationships and dating. Whereas women talked about not letting men "screw up" their lives, men did not express such concerns. Instead, they described countless episodes of chasing girls throughout their adolescence and young adulthood. Indeed, when asked why they had received only average grades in school, men offered two explanations: "I was lazy" and "I was there for the girls." It is important to note that men did not necessarily view education as a feminine pursuit, as some studies have argued.[27] However, establishing a sense of manhood was not discursively linked to obtaining an education.

Contrary to the prevailing assumptions of male hegemony in Caribbean households, men occupied marginal spatial locations within the home. Men's displays of masculinity were not necessarily tied to concrete forms of male domination in the home. Rather, they can be understood as "personally and collectively constructed performances of gender display and so should be distinguished from structurally constituted positions of power."[28]

At the micro level, the possibility of building a two-gendered community that is not defined in the opposition of the sexes to one another, but rather speaks to a collaborative effort to build community while working toward the elimination of gender oppression.[29] Parents have an important role to play in this process. A necessary first step in re-creating homes involves working toward the elimination of gender oppression in family life. Several questions remain: Are daughters given more adult responsibilities than sons? What kinds of relationships are being nurtured across the generations or with extended family members? What lessons are young men and women learning about what it means to be a man and what it means to be a woman? The answers to these questions will contribute to creating more egalitarian gender relations in family life.

Re-envisioning De-raced and De-gendered Workplaces

The experiences of men and women in the labor market were distinctly different and often propelled them into quite divergent employment trajectories. The jobs that men were able to obtain were usually concentrated in the most marginal service-sector jobs, such as working as a stock boy or messenger or in security or maintenance. Men experienced many difficulties in securing even entry-level employment. Men were often "between" jobs and frequently worked in the informal economy. Men recalled that they were treated as untrustworthy employees and that they were subjected to verbal abuse and physical exploitation.[30]

Through their interactions with supervisors, clients, and co-workers, men learned once again that they were viewed in a negative light; those who were able to obtain work had painful memories of negative *race-gender experiences* on the job, including racial slurs and the assumption that they were potential thieves.[31] Men added these experiences to their existing reservoir of knowledge about social mobility and concluded that they were disadvantaged in the labor market. Men frequently mentioned that they had friends and relatives who had earned college degrees but had to resort to working as managers in fast-food establishments because they were unable to secure work commensurate with their educational credentials. In response to these repeated negative race-gender experiences in the labor market, men formulated *worried outlooks* about their future prospects for social mobility.[32]

One reason why women experienced fewer difficulties in finding employment than their male counterparts was that they had wider social networks.[33] Since women generally had better relationships with teachers than did men, they were more likely to be recommended for internships or other resume-enhancing work experiences.[34] Another reason why women experienced fewer difficulties in finding work was that historically employers have had fewer reservations about hiring minority women than about hiring their male counterparts.[35] Whereas employers have tended to cast minority men as unreliable and untrustworthy, they have viewed minority women as the "manageable" minority.[36]

Since women tended to work in the growing sectors of the economy, they were provided with a window to potential careers. While men's work experience was largely confined to jobs in the informal economy, women's work took place in a more formal work environment, such as medical offices, law firms, and finance. Nevertheless, women were still largely confined to ghettoized work in pink-collar jobs in offices. Women spoke about being subjected to racialized sexual harassment from their co-workers, bosses, and clients and experiencing a "colored" glass ceiling at work. However, women responded to these negative race-gender experiences by articulating a firm commitment to education as a means of attaining social mobility. Women consistently cited examples of other women they knew who had pursued an education and had been successful. Over time, women developed *optimistic outlooks* about the importance of an education for them as racially stigmatized women. The outlooks of men and women on social mobility were anchored to their concrete experiences in the world of work.

If the goal of policymakers is to reduce the level of race and sex segregation in the labor market, school-based internships and employment programs have an important role to play. Do these programs counteract or reproduce race and gender stratification in the labor market? Are school internships preparing women to be secretaries and men to be maintenance service workers? Policymakers should evaluate programs such as the Summer Youth Employment Program and the Cooperative Education Program in terms of their success in providing both men and women with substantive work experiences that enhance their skills and spark their career interests.

Given that the demonization of men of African phenotype as undesirable workers has been well documented in numerous studies, a question remains: How can we eliminate the racism racially stigmatized youth encounter in the labor market? Policymakers should explore ways to enforce antidiscrimination policies, such as affirmative action in the workplace. It is also imperative that particular attention be paid to the "color" of the sexual harassment in the workplace.[37] "The Law's current dichotomous categorization of racial discrimination and sexual harassment as separate spheres of injury is inadequate to respond to racialized sexual harassment."[38] In this regard, the sexual harassment that racially stigmatized people are exposed to must also be understood as intersecting with racial discrimination. Employers see and treat the second generation not as "genderless ethnics," but rather as racial(ized) and gender(ed) bodies.

Conclusion

One important step in disrupting the race(ing) and gender(ing) that takes place across domains of *lived experience* in the larger society is the notion that that racial, gender, and class oppression is socially constructed at the micro level of everyday social interaction, as well as at the macro level of institutional practices. To obliterate systems of oppression, we must *always* be aware of how we are race(ing) and gender(ing) others during the course of our micro-level social interactions, as well as in our macro-level institutional practices.[39] For instance, at my job I am constantly asking myself, how can I work toward eliminating race and gender disparities in education at my university and beyond? At the micro level, how can I work toward improving my pedagogy? How can I work with individual students to assist them in their educational endeavors? How can I work with administration to enact broad-based changes that enhance the educational outcomes of all students, particularly those who come from racially stigmatized groups, such as Native Americans, Latinos, Asians, and African Americans? Everyone has a role to play.

Despite claims of objectivity and neutrality, for better or for worse, social science plays an important role in the oppressive race(ing) and gender(ing) that takes place in the larger society. As long as poverty, schooling tracking, residential segregation, overcrowding, and racial and gender segregation in the labor market are rendered as "natural" and acceptable social phenomena, social scientists, myself included, will continue to measure and describe them and thereby normalize their existence. Alternatively, social scientists can try to uncover how social processes of subordination are created, deployed, and resisted. In this manner, we can engage in the important work of demystifying the "naturalness" of race, gender, and class subordination and domination in society.

Most studies of race and education, including my own, are fixated on studying the "other"; however, racial and gender disparities in education are far from a problem caused by racially stigmatized groups. Unraveling the race and gender disparities in education also requires a simultaneous examination of "whiteness as a race, as privilege, as social construction."[40] Hegemonic ideologies, such as the belief that the United States is a meritocratic society where anyone regardless of race, class, and gender oppression can "make it" and become successful through individual hard work, render whiteness as objective, normal, *and* yet invisible in U.S. society.[41] Future studies on educational disparities would benefit from unpacking whiteness processes and their impact on race and gender disparities in education.

There were many "dangers" in pursuing a research project on why women attained higher levels of education than men in racially stigmatized communities. First, this research question may contribute to an essentialist discourse, which is premised on the myth that women are "naturally" better students. Second, the examination of gender disparities in educational attainment in racially stigmatized communities may also be used to perpetuate the misperception of competition between men and women. Third, it may detract from the achievement gap by race.

The gender gap in educational attainment between minority men and women was not just the result of "natural" differences between men and women who are in competition with one another. Rather, these differences reflected the oppressive reality that racially stigmatized men and women have been treated and racialized quite differently. Racialized and gendered patterns in educational attainment speak more about the type of society that minorities and immigrants reside in than they do about the behavior of the individual racially stigmatized men and women involved. Nor are men and women in competition; they are members of the same communities who both believe in the value of an education.[42] Finally, while it is true that in racially stigmatized communities women attain higher levels of education, it is also the case that the overwhelming majority of men and women in these communities have the lowest educational attainment of any groups, even when we control for class background.

The micropolitics of day-to-day practices contain the seeds for social change that is intended to eliminate social oppression along race, class, and gender lines. It is my hope that this study will generate new questions and enhance the existing theoretical frameworks, which seek to eliminate race and gender disparities in education. The question that remains is whether or not we want to disrupt the race(ing) and gender(ing) processes and other systems of oppression that have been rendered a "normal" part of our personal lives and institutions.

> How is domination a puzzle that can be understood in order to be dismantled, and how were we all players *in relationship* to one another, with different access to power, much of it contextually based and some of it ever present? Our social existence is intertwined, for better or worse, and, whether we live next to one another or not, we influence one another's lives. To be conscious of this *all* the time and to act in relationship to this *all* the time is what will be required to understand fully domination and oppression and to conceive of and construct a world in which race, sexual orientation and gender will not matter and in which we will not know the meaning of class.[43]

Appendix A: Description of Second-Generation Caribbean Women Interviewed, Ages 18–30

Jahaira, 30, was born in the Dominican Republic and came to New York City at the age of seven. She grew up in Bushwick, Brooklyn, and now lives with her partner and child in Flushing, Queens. She earned a BA in economics at a public university and works full-time as a research assistant at an investment bank. Jahaira would like to finish a graduate degree and work as an investment manager.

Janet, 26, was born in New York City. Her mother is from the Dominican Republic and her father is from Cuba. Janet grew up in Washington Heights, Manhattan, and now lives with a roommate in Inwood, Manhattan. She earned a BA in psychology from a private university and now works full-time as a director of school administration at her former high school. She expects to finish her graduate degree and become a psychologist.

Cassandra, 27, was born in the Dominican Republic and came to New York City at the age of seven. She grew up in Washington Heights, Manhattan, is divorced and now lives with her child in Inwood, Manhattan. She earned a BA in psychology and works full-time in city management for the housing department. Cassandra expects to finish a graduate degree in psychology.

Margaret, 21, was born in Antigua and came to New York at the age of six. She grew up in Springfield Gardens, Queens, and still lives there with her parents. She earned a BA in psychology from a private university. Although she is unemployed, she formerly worked as a library assistant. She would like to finish a graduate degree in psychology.

Diana, 18, was born in New York City and still lives with her parents in her childhood neighborhood of Inwood, Manhattan. She is attending an associate's degree program at a vocational business school. Although she is unemployed, Diana formerly worked as an office assistant. She expects to earn an AA and work in business administration.

Yvonne, 22, was born in New York City and grew up in Williamsburg, Brooklyn. She now lives in Inwood, Manhattan, with her husband. Yvonne is attending a public community college part-time while she works full-time as a sales research coordinator for an investment firm. She would like to obtain a graduate degree and work in investment banking and financial services.

Katia, 18, was born in New York City and grew up in Flatbush and Canarsie, Brooklyn. She now lives with her parents in Inwood, Manhattan. She is attending a public community college, pursuing a degree in nursing. Although she is unemployed, she formerly worked in clerical work. Katia expects to finish college and become a registered pediatric nurse.

Crimelda, 28, was born in New York City. She grew up in the South Bronx and still lives there with her partner and two children. Before becoming a full-time homemaker, Crimelda worked in retail sales. Formerly, she attended a public community college for business administration and expects to finish a graduate degree.

Orfelia, 20, was born in the Dominican Republic and came to New York City at the age of six. Her mother died at birth and her father died when she was ten. An aunt in Corona, Queens, raised her. She still lives in Corona with her husband and child. Before becoming a full-time homemaker, Orfelia worked as a teacher's aide. Formerly, she attended a public university and expects to finish her college degree in social work.

Yvelise, 24, was born in New York City and grew up in Washington Heights, Manhattan. She now lives with her partner and two children in Inwood, Manhattan. Before becoming a full-time homemaker, Yvelise worked as a receptionist in the medical industry. After obtaining a general equivalency diploma, Yvelise earned a certificate in secretarial studies from a vocational training school. She wants to finish college and work as an administrative assistant.

Lidia, 20, was born in New York City and grew up in Inwood, Manhattan. She still lives there with her father. Her mother died when she was a child and both her father and an aunt raised her. Lidia is working part-time as a clerical worker while she attends a general equivalency diploma program at a private community college. She expects to finish college and become an office manager.

Dorca, 18, was born in New York City and grew up in Corona, Queens, where she still lives with her parents. She is still enrolled in high school and works part-time as a cashier. Dorca expects to finish college and would like to become a forensic psychologist.

Tina, 21, was born in Antigua and came to New York City at the age of six. She grew up in South Ozone Park, Queens. She now lives with her parents in Springfield Gardens, Queens. She is attending a private university pursuing liberal studies. She is working part-time as a nursing assistant and expects to finish a graduate degree and become a child psychologist.

Thelma, 23, was born in Barbados and came to New York City at the age of six. She grew up in Crown Heights, Brooklyn, and now lives with her mother in Kingston Village, Brooklyn. She is attending public university and would like to finish a graduate degree and become a clergywoman.

Rosy, 19, was born in Trinidad and Tobago and came to New York City at the age of ten. She grew up in Flatbush and Bedford-Stuyvesant, Brooklyn, and now lives with her parents in Flatlands, Brooklyn. She works part-time as a salesperson at a department store while she pursues a psychology degree at a public university. Eventually, Rosy would like to finish a graduate degree in psychology.

Nicole, 18, was born in Jamaica and joined her mother in New York at the age of twelve. She lived in Jamaica, Queens, and now lives with her mother in St. Albans, Queens. She is still enrolled in high school and would like to pursue a medical degree and become a neurosurgeon.

Rhina, 19, was born in Trinidad and Tobago and came to Miami, Florida, at the age of five. She grew up in Flatbush, Brooklyn, and was raised by her grandmother because her mother is mentally challenged. Rhina is also mentally challenged but was still enrolled in a general equivalency program for mentally and psychically challenged youth, where she also worked as a clerical worker. Rhina hopes to finish college.

Marie, 19, was born in New York City and her parents were born in Haiti. She grew up in Crown Heights, Brooklyn, and now lives with her mother in the Flatlands, Brooklyn. She is attending a public community college, pursuing a degree in nursing. She is unemployed, but formerly worked part-time as a nurse's assistant. She would like to finish college and become a registered nurse.

Sedare, 19, was born in Haiti and came to New York at the age of six. She lives with her parents in her childhood neighborhood of Bushwick, Brooklyn. Although Sedare was looking for work, she is attending a paralegal vocational training program. Formerly, she worked as a salesperson in retail. She would like to finish a graduate degree and become a paralegal.

Maryse, 21, was born in Haiti and came to New York City at the age of three. She grew up in Crown Heights, Brooklyn, and now lives there with her husband. She is currently unemployed, but formerly worked as a salesperson for a department store. She is attending a vocational training school for a computer specialist certificate. She would like to finish graduate school and become a corporate executive officer.

Appendix B: Description of Second-Generation Caribbean Men Interviewed, Ages 18-30

Isidro, 21, was born in the Dominican Republic and came to New York City at the age of eleven. He grew up in Flushing, Queens, and still lives there with his parents. He works part-time as a bank teller while he pursues a degree in accounting and economics at a public university. Isidro want to finish graduate school and become a financial analyst.

Alejandro, 23, was born in the Dominican Republic and came to New York City at the age of one. He grew up in East New York, Brooklyn, but now lives with his parents in Corona, Queens. He is unemployed but formerly worked in shipping. He is attending a public university pursuing a degree in criminal justice and eventually wants to finish graduate school and become a probation officer.

Alfredo, 19, was born in New York City. He grew up in Corona and Elmhurst, Queens, and still lives there with his mother. He tutors students while attend a public state university. He expects to finish a graduate degree and become a computer network engineer.

Andres, 24, was born in New York City and grew up in Corona, Queens. He lives with his partner in Elmhurst, Queens. He is a full-time police recruit who is attending the police academy. He does not plan to continue his education and wants to become a full-time police officer.

Peter, 23, was born in New York City and raised by his mother in Washington Heights and Inwood, Manhattan. Peter is temporarily disabled due to a motor vehicle accident where he lost his mother and sister. Formerly, he worked part-time as a customer service representative for a mobile phone company. Previously he attended a public community college and would like to finish college and become a computer programmer.

Rodrigo, 23, was born in the Dominican Republic and came to New York City at the age of two. He grew up in my childhood neighborhood of the Lower East Side of Manhattan and still lives there with his parents. Rodrigo works full-time as a security guard. Formerly, he dropped out of high school in the tenth grade, but eventually earned a general equivalency diploma and was enrolled at a public university. Rodrigo wants to return to school someday and finish his college degree and eventually become a computer programmer.

Reynaldo, 18, was born in New York City. He grew up in Inwood, Manhattan, and still lives there with his parents. Reynaldo works part-time in retail. He is still enrolled in high school and would like to finish a law degree, but if not will enlist in the military.

Joaquin, 20, was born in New York City. He grew up on the Upper West Side of Manhattan and now lives with his mother in Inwood, Manhattan. Although Reynaldo was unemployed he had worked in maintenance. He is attending a general equivalency diploma program at a public community college and expects to finish college and become a video game programmer.

José, 25, was born in the United States and grew up in Inwood, Manhattan, where he still lives with his mother. He has one child that does not live with him. He works as a stockroom attendant at an electronic retail store. José dropped out of high school in the eleventh grade, but eventually obtained a general equivalency diploma. Previously he had hoped to become an architect, but now does not want to continue his education and expects to work as a laborer.

Mark, 24, was born in New York City. His mother is from Jamaica and his father is from St. Vincent and St. Grenadine. Mark grew up in Crown Heights and Brownsville, Brooklyn. Now he lives with his partner and child in Bedford-Stuyvesant, Brooklyn. He works part-time as a stockroom attendant for a grocery store while attending a public university pursuing a degree in business management. Mark expects to finish a graduate degree, but does not know what he wants to do ten years from now.

Owen, 18, was born in New York City and his parents are from Guyana. He grew up in Canarsie, Brooklyn, and still lives there with his mother. He is looking for work, but is attending a public university. He expects to finish a graduate degree and would like to become an electrical technician.

Steven, 23, was born in New York City. His mother is from St. Vincent and his father is from Grenada. Steven grew up in East Flatbush, Brooklyn, and still lives there with his parents. Steven works full-time as a computer systems analyst while he attends a public university. He would like to finish his college degree and become a bioengineer.

Paven, 18, was born in Guyana and came to New York City at the age of one. He grew up in Bushwick, Brooklyn, were he still lives with his parents. He works part-time in packing and clerical work for a warehouse while he attends a public university. Paven does not want to continue his education, but would like to become a corporate executive officer for a footwear company.

Deren, 18, was born in Guyana and came to New York City at the age of five. He grew up in Corona, Queens, where he still lives with his parents. He works part-time in customer service for a retail store while he attends a public community college. Formerly, he had dropped out of high school in the eleventh grade, but eventually obtained his general equivalency diploma. Deren would like to finish college and obtain and office job.

Denzel, 18, was born in Trinidad and Tobago and came to New York City at the age of ten. He grew up in Flatbush and Brownsville, Brooklyn and now lives with his mother in Crown Heights, Brooklyn. He is looking for work and formerly handed out flyers for a retail store. He is still enrolled in high school, but would like to finish college and play in a major basketball league.

Shawn, 25, was born in Haiti and came to New York City at the age of ten. He grew up in Prospect Heights, Brooklyn, and still lives there with his mother. He works full-time as an electrical technician for the cable company, while he attends a public university pursuing a degree in computer science. Shawn would like to finish a graduate degree in computer science or mathematics and run his own software business.

Richard, 24, was born in Haiti and came to New York City at the age of eight. He grew up in Prospect Heights, Brooklyn, and still lives there with his mother. He is looking for work and formerly worked in a school cafeteria. Formerly, Richard was enrolled at a public community college pursuing a degree in physical therapy. He would like to go back to finish college and become a physical therapist.

Sam, 26, was born in New York City and his parents are from Haiti. He grew up in Flushing, Queens, and now lives with his partner and child in Long Island, New York. Two of his children do not live with him. Sam is a restaurant entrepreneur. He graduated from high school but would like to finish a graduate degree and own a chain of restaurants.

Perry, 18, was born in Haiti and came to New York City at the age of ten. He worked as a dishwasher at a restaurant but was looking for work. He was still enrolled in high school, but would like to finish college and become a medical doctor.

Paul, 18, was born in New York City. His parents are from Haiti. Paul grew up in East Flatbush, Brooklyn, and now lives with his mother in Crown Heights, Brooklyn. Paul worked delivering newspapers and was looking for work. He would like to finish college and become an agronomist.

Appendix C:
Summary of Focus Group Participants

All of the participants in the focus groups attended the City University of New York (CUNY). Unless otherwise noted, all participants attended four-year colleges. The focus groups were conducted in a CUNY classroom during December 1995. They were tape-recorded and transcribed and generally lasted over two hours.

Dominicans

Men

1. Carlos is nineteen years old and he was born in the United States. He is majoring in liberal arts.
2. Guillermo is twenty years old and came to the United States at the age of five. He is studying business administration.

Women

1. Anivelca is twenty-one years old and was born in the Dominican Republic, but was brought to the United States when she was a few weeks old. She is majoring in political science and sociology.
2. Neyda is twenty-years old and was born in the Dominican Republic. She came to the United States at the age of ten. She is majoring in media.
3. Oneida is twenty-seven years old, was born in the Dominican Republic, and came to the United States at the age of three. She is a graduate student.
4. Cindy is twenty-eight years old and was born in the Dominican Republic. She came to the United States as a teenager. Cindy was attending a community college.

West Indian and Haitian Focus Group

Men

1. Adolf is nineteen years old and was born in the United States. His parents are from Belize.
2. Kevin is twenty years old and was born in the United States. His parents are from Guyana.

Women

1. Hazel is twenty-two years old and was born in the United States. She is majoring in pre-law. She lived in her parent's homeland between the ages of three and eight.
2. Evelyn is thirty years old and was born in Haiti. She came to the United States at the age of five. She is a graduate student.

Notes

Chapter 1

1. Urban High School is a pseudonym used to protect the anonymity of the school. All of the names of participants in this study were also changed.
2. In 1999 87% of 18- to 24-year-old women had completed high school compared with 85% of men. National Center for Education Statistics, *Dropout Rates in the United States: 1999* (Washington, DC: U.S. Department of Education, Office of Educational Research and Improvement, NCES 2001–2002), 19.
3. This figure includes public, private, and religiously affiliated two- and four-year postsecondary institutions. See Lewin (1998a).
4. U.S. Census Bureau (1998).
5. Kleinfeld (1998).
6. See Lewin (1998a).
7. Dunn (1998), Hawkins (1996), United Negro College Fund (1997).
8. Sum et al. (1999).
9. Among Whites it was 77% compared with 66% of men; for Asians it was 73% women and 62% men; and for American Indians it was 57% of women and only 40% of men. Excel Table provided by Ann Wolfe, Director, Assessment and Accountability, New York City Board of Education.
10. "Second generation" refers to the U.S.-born children of immigrants or foreign-born children who come after the age of 12. See Portes (1996).
11. Rumbaut (1995, 1998), Portes (1996).
12. Zhou and Bankston (1998), Matute-Bianchi (1991), Valenzuela (1999).
13. The principal investigators for the "Immigrant Second Generation in Metropolitan New York" project conducted by the Center for Urban Research at the Graduate School and University Center of the City University of New York were Professors John Mollenkopf, Philip Kasinitz, and Mary Waters. See Mollenkopf et al. (1998).
14. In 1996, women comprised 67% of Black and 63% percent of Hispanic undergraduates and 70% of Black and Hispanic graduate students at the City University of New York. See City University of New York (1996).

15. Quoted in Lewin (1998a).

16. The Dominican Republic yielded over half a million immigrants (580,225), followed by Cuba (456,997), Jamaica (417,652), Haiti (275,581), Guyana (179,627), and Trinidad and Tobago (129,618). See *Statistical Yearbook 1994* (Washington, DC: U.S. Government Printing Office), 28–31, quoted in Vincent Parillo, *Strangers to these Shores: Race and Ethnic Relations in the United States* (Boston: Allyn and Bacon, 1999), 426. See also Ramona Hernandez et al., *Dominican New Yorkers: A Socioeconomic Profile 1990* (New York: Dominican Studies Institute at the City University of New York, 1995).

17. Hernandez et al. (1995), Hernandez (2002), Hernandez and Rivera-Batiz (1997), Torres-Saillant and Hernandez (1998), Foner (1987), Kasinitz (1992), Pessar and Grasmuck (1991), Laguerre (1984).

18. Torres-Saillant (1995), Torres and Bonilla (1995), Grosfuguel and Georas (1996), Waters (1996).

19. Waters (2000), Zhou and Bankston (1998), Portes (1996).

20. See Waters (2000), Mollenkopf et al. (1998).

21. Gans (1992), Portes and Zhou (1993), Fernandez-Kelly and Schauffler (1994), Kao and Tienda (1995), Perlmann and Waldinger (1997), Portes and MacLeod (1996), Portes and Rumbaut (1990), Rumbaut (1995).

22. For Dominicans living in Washington, DC, assimilation into the larger Black community translated into upward mobility (Candelario, 2000).

23. See works in the bibliography by Michael Omi, Howard Winant, Joe Feagin, Melvin Sikes, Patricia Hill-Collins, Aida Hurtado, Ruth Frankenberg, Christine Sierra, Gloria Anzaldua, Michelle Fine, Lois Weis, Bell Hooks, Deborah Meier, Paul Willis, Paolo Freire, and Donaldo Macedo.

24. As explained by Hurtado (1996:124), "a cornerstone of a feminist paradigm is the importance of experience in the definition and acquisition of knowledge." See also Sierra (1986).

25. See Gilkes (1996), Hurtado (1996:26), Weis (1990a, b), Fine et al. (1997), Gibson (1988), Waters (1996), Hondagneu-Sotelo (1999), Haney-Lopez (1996), Omi and Winant (1994), Frankenberg (1993), Hill-Collins (1990, 1996), Roberts (1997), Landrine (1996), Leadbeater and Way (1996), Davis (1983), Fanon (1982), Lubiano (1992), Moraga and Anzaldua (1983).

26. The focus groups, surveys, and in-depth interviews utilized in this study were part of the Immigrant Second Generation in Metropolitan New York project conducted by the Center for Urban Research at the Graduate School and University Center of the City University of New York. The principal investigators for the project were Professors John Mollenkopf, Philip Kasinitz, and Mary Waters. Over a period of four years (1995–1999), as a research assistant for the project, I facilitated focus groups, participated in the design of the survey instrument, conducted and transcribed in-depth interviews, and conducted data analysis. The analyses that follow are solely my own. The

field work at Urban High School was not part of the second generation project.

27. Focus group participants were selected randomly from a phone list of enrolled second-generation CUNY students (n = 1537).

28. Massey and Denton (1994).

29. Fine and Weis (1998).

30. This percentage included college, vocational institutions, the military, and the police academy.

31. I conducted all but three of the in-depth interviews with Caribbean participants.

32. Interview quotes have not been edited unless it was absolutely essential for the sake of clarity.

33. Murguia and Telles (1996).

34. I did not observe bilingual classes because they would most likely contain recent arrivals, rather than second-generation students.

35. I asked Mr. Green why there was such a gender imbalance in his class, but he said that he did not know.

36. The majority of the teachers at Urban High School had been there for less than five years. The teacher "revolving door" phenomenon was increasingly common in overcrowded, undersupported neighborhood schools (López, 1998).

37. For example, MacLeod (1995) did not problematize the interviewee–interviewer dynamic in terms of race, gender, and class. In essence, he neglected to examine how his status as a researcher who was racialized as a White, middle-class man, "colored" and "classed" the conversations he had with the Brothers and the Hallway Hangers. As Royster (1996) explains, the Brothers' adherence to the achievement ideology may be understood as a form of resistance because, in proclaiming their belief in education, they dismantled widespread stereotypes that cast young urban minority men as anti-academic and oppositional to the larger society.

38. Kasinitz (1992), Vickerman (1999).

Chapter 2

1. Hacker (1992), Omi and Winant (1994), Sanjek and Gregory (1994).

2. Omi and Winant (1994).

3. Murray and Hernstein (1994).

4. Hurtado (1996), Oliver and Shapiro (1995), Massey and Denton (1994), Ogbu (1978), Wacquant (1997).

5. For a review of the ethnicity paradigm, see Omi and Winant (1994: Chap. 1). See also Gans (1962).

6. Perlmann (1988), Portes (1996), Park (1950), Gordon (1964), Gans (1962).

7. See Davis (1996) and Haney-Lopez (1996).

8. Roberts (1997), Omi and Winant (1994), Frankenberg (1993), Hurtado (1996), Mullings (1997), Hill-Collins (1990, 1996), Fine and Weis (1998).

9. Haney-Lopez (1996:14).

10. Haney-Lopez (1996).

11. See Omi and Winant (1994), Sanjek and Gregory (1994), Steinberg (1995).

12. Haney-Lopez (1996), Fordham (1996), Fine et al. (1997).

13. Steinberg (1981), Omi and Winant (1994), Waters (1990), Sanjek and Gregory (1994), Lieberson (1980), Blauner (1972), Ogbu (1974, 1978).

14. Massey and Denton (1994), Feagin and Sikes (1994), Steinberg (1981, 1995), Sanjek and Gregory (1994), Grosfuguel and Georas (1996), Candelario and Lopez (1995), Torres-Saillant (1995), Zephir (1996), Waters (1996), Haney-Lopez (1996).

15. Omi and Winant (1994:55).

16. Omi and Winant (1994).

17. Omi and Winant (1994:56).

18. Omi and Winant (1994).

19. Haney-Lopez (1996).

20. Lieberson (1980), Hacker (1992), Massey and Denton (1994), Feagin and Sikes (1994), Steinberg (1981, 1995) Sanjek and Gregory (1994), Wrigley (1999).

21. Kasinitz (1992:33).

22. Steinberg (1995), Omi and Winant (1994).

23. Omi and Winant (1994:68).

24. Although this study focuses on the intersection of race and gender, it does not discount the importance of class, sexuality, and age in constituting an individual's social location and lived experience.

25. Critical race theorists and feminist scholars have also examined how race and gender are social constructions that are experienced differently by men and women (Sierra, 1986; Hill-Collins, 1990; Hurtado, 1996; Fine and Weis, 1998; Frankenberg, 1993; Lubiano, 1992; Haney-Lopez, 1996; Crenshaw, 1996).

26. New York City Department of Planning (1999:2).

27. New York City Department of Planning (1999:6).

28. See Kasinitz (1992).

29. New York City Department of Planning (1999:31).

30. New York City Department of Planning (1999:29).

31. Torres-Saillant (1995), Rodriguez (1994), Grosfuguel and Georas (1996), Torres and Bonilla (1995), Eschbach and Gomez (1996), Parillo (1997), Candelario (2000).

32. Black (1986).

33. Herman and Brodhead (1984).

34. Massey and Denton (1994), Grosfuguel and Georas (1996), Robinson (1993), Blauner (1972), Flores (1997), Gilroy (1993), Klor (1997).

35. Rumbaut (1994), Nelson and Tienda (1985, 1997), Obler (1997), Romero (1997).

36. Hernandez (2002).

37. Hernandez and López (1997).

38. Hernandez et al. (1995), Hernandez (2002).

39. Foner (1987), Kasinitz (1992), Laguerre (1984), Waters (2000).

40. Robinson (1993:45).

41. See Kasinitz (1992). See also Vickerman (1999), Zephir (1996), Laguerre (1984), Waters (1994, 1996), Grosfuguel and Georas (1996), and Rodriguez (1994).

42. *New York Times*, May 16, 1998, p. B1.

43. *New York Times*, May 16, 1996, See also *New York Times* front-page articles on May 10 and 11, 1998, "Dominican Drug Traffickers Tighten Grip on the Northeast." See also Feagin and Sikes (1994:74).

44. Agger (1998:180).

45. It is significant that in the photo essays there were no images of Asian youths, thereby indicating that they are generally considered invisible in the U.S. racial landscape.

46. For a detailed analysis of prom nights as a space where narratives of race, class, gender, and sexuality are re-created, see Best (2000).

47. See Aroch et al. (1998:34).

48. *New York Times*, May 7, 1998. Halbfinger (1999), Rohter and Krauss (1998).

49. Roane (1999).

50. Anderson (1990).

51. Feagin and Sikes (1994).

52. See Waters (1994, 1996).

53. Wilgoren (1998).

54. "Police Training Manual Is Criticized," *New York Times*, March 17, 1999, p. B5.

55. Arnot (1999:90).

56. Feagin and Sikes (1994).

57. See Feagin and Sikes (1994).

58. Massey and Denton (1994).

59. Schill et al. (1988).

60. Mydral (1944), Massey and Denton (1994), Sanjek and Gregory (1994), Lieberson (1980).

61. Massey and Denton (1994).

62. Feagin (1995), Feagin and Sikes (1994), Waters (1999).

63. Feagin and Sikes (1994).

64. Feagin and Sikes (1994:105).

65. Candelario and López (1995), Roberts (1997), Lubiano (1992).

66. Murray (1984), Mead (1986).

67. Candelario and López (1995).
68. Sexton (1997), Stepick (1992), Katz (1989, 1993), Piven and Cloward (1993), Candelario and López (1995).
69. Candelario and López (1995).
70. Roberts (1997).
71. Fordham (1996).
72. Wacquant (1997), Roberts (1997).
73. Fine and Weis (1998).
74. Wacquant (1997).
75. Fine et al. (1997), Nelson and Tienda (1985), Massey and Denton (1994), Steinberg (1981, 1995), Takaki (1994), Ringer and Lawless (1989), Hacker (1992), Sanjek and Gregory (1994), Amott and Matthaei (1991), Williams and Kornblum (1994).
76. See also Waters (2000); Goffman (1964), Grosfuguel and Georas (1996), Fordham (1996), Kasinitz (1992), Feagin and Sikes (1994).
77. Anderson (1990), Waters (1994), Fine and Weis (1998).
78. Dovidio and Gaertner (1986).
79. Lubiano (1992), Mullings (1997), Roberts (1997), Espiritu (1997), Davis (1983), Hill-Collins (1990).
80. Leadbeater and Way (1996).
81. Leadbeater and Way (1996).

Chapter 3

1. Katz (1993), Wilson (1996, 1987), Fine (1994), Anyon (1997), Waters (1997).
2. See Steinberg (1995).
3. Kowal (2001:A05).
4. Kowal (2001).
5. Omi and Winant (1994:68).
6. Woody (1974:1).
7. Woodson (1972).
8. Ladson-Billings and Tate (1995).
9. Lewin (1998b).
10. Ladson-Billings and Tate (1995).
11. See Fine (1991:196).
12. Weis (1990a).
13. Fine (1991), Aronowitz and Giroux (1993).
14. Fordham and Ogbu (1986), Portes and Zhou (1993), Matute-Bianchi (1991).
15. Steele and Aronson (1995).
16. Ogbu (1995a, b), Fordham and Ogbu (1986).
17. Bourgois (1995), Fordham (1996), Willis (1981).
18. Arnot (1999).

19. Anti-intellectualism extends across racial and class lines, as evidenced by words such as "nerd" and "geek."
20. Solomon (1990).
21. Fordham (1996), Steele (1992), Steele and Aronson (1995), Ogbu (1995a, b), Willis (1981), MacLeod (1995).
22. Kleinfeld (1998).
23. Kleinfeld (1998).
24. Washington and Newman (1991).
25. None of the Haitians participants in this study said that they had been sent back to Haiti for their studies.
26. Quoted in *New York Times*, March 28, 1998, p. B1.
27. Sedlak et al. (1986).
28. See Anyon (1980), Fine (1991), Grant (1992).
29. Kleinfeld (1998, 1999), Rosenblum and Travis (1996:304).
30. Lee (1997), Meier and Stewart (1991), De Leon (1996), Attanasi (1994).
31. Grant (1992, 1994).
32. Hurtado (1996).
33. Fine (1991).
34. In a study of Punjabi Sikh students in California, Gibson (1988) also noted that young women were concentrated in vocational tracks.
35. Although religion and spirituality is not one of the social spaces that I explore in this book, it remains an important realm to investigate for a better understanding of men's and women's outlooks toward schooling. Women, for instance, spoke about the importance of spirituality and religion in their lives more often than men.
36. Waters (1997).
37. Stanton-Salazar (1997).
38. Ogbu (1978). In New York City public schools, Whites and Asians have graduation rates of 70% and 66%, respectively; Blacks and Latinos have the lowest graduation rates, 44% and 38% (Board of Education, 1995).
39. It is important to note that universal public education is not available to everyone in many Caribbean countries.
40. Feagin and Sikes (1994).
41. Reeves (2002).
42. Fine and Weis (1998).
43. Fordham (1996).
44. In *Closing the Gender Gap: Postwar Education and Social Change*, Arnot (1999) examines how the schooling of girls and boys growing up in Britain has changed since World War II.
45. Arnot (1999).
46. Orfield (1994), Massey and Denton (1994).
47. Kozol (1991, 1996).

48. Omi and Winant (1994: Chap. 5).
49. Oakes and Guiton (1995), López (1998), Oakes (1985), Anyon (1997), Bowles and Gintis (1976).
50. Washington and Newman (1991), Fine (1991).
51. Grant (1992).

Chapter 4

1. López (1998), Candelario and López (1995).
2. See Anyon (1997).
3. Not once during the course of fieldwork did I find a student smoking or doing drugs in the stairwells or in the bathroom.
4. While the majority of New York City public school students attend schools that are in the same deplorable conditions as UHS, new school buildings have been constructed for the elite public examination high schools in New York City, where there are few low-income students or Black and Latino students.
5. Kozol (1991).
6. Previously, I found that second-generation Dominicans expressed resistance to General Equivalency Diploma programs because they felt they would be stigmatized by potential employers and colleges (López, 1998). Therefore, many of them chose to remain enrolled beyond the traditional four years of high school.
7. López (1998).
8. Davis (1997).
9. See Davis (1997).
10. Fine (1991).
11. For a description of the fetish of "good intentions" see Fine (1991).
12. At a day-long teacher workshop at UHS, many teachers expressed their belief that students should only speak English while they were in school.
13. Gramsci (1971), Cummins (1993), Delgado (1992).
14. See also Gibson (1988).
15. See Gibson (1988).
16. Ybarra (2000), Valenzuela (1999).
17. See Fine (1991).
18. Ybarra (2000).
19. See Freire (1985, 1993), hooks (1994).
20. Gilbert and Gilbert (1998).
21. As previously mentioned, Mr. Green kept the door locked after the bell rang.
22. Kleinfeld (1998).
23. Kleinfeld (1998), Ginorio and Huston (2001).

Chapter 5

1. See Valenzuela (1999).
2. Religion is another space that must be investigated for a better understanding of the worlds of girls. In a preliminary study of three faith communities in Boston, Massachusetts, two of which have significant Caribbean communities I found that women are also the lay leaders in this context.
3. Rosie Perez is a New York City-born Puerto Rican actress who has starred in feature films such as *24-Hour Woman,* where she is presented as an independent and successful Latina woman.
4. Although I completed all of my schooling in New York City public schools, the first time I sat in a classroom with a student who was racialized as White was in college.
5. At my former high school, very few Regents classes were offered.
6. Although I would have liked to have regularly observed Ms. Mastri's class, shuttling between her trailer park classroom and the main building would have been a logistical nightmare.
7. Valenzuela (1999) also found that U.S. Mexican women who attend the same school and come from the same socioeconomic status have wider social networks and possess more social capital than their male counterparts.
8. On another occasion, Mr. Green asked students how many had been on job interviews, and one-third of the young women in the class raised their hands; only one young man did.
9. Arnot (1999:73).

Chapter 6

1. For a review of the literature documenting these patterns, see Tiano (2001), Safa (1995), and Hondagneu-Sotelo (1994, forthcoming).
2. Contrary to the popular perception that only women possess "gender," at any historical point, both men and women are gendered in relationship to one another (see Hondagneu-Sotelo, 1994, 1999).
3. Safa (1995).
4. Milkman (1987), Hondagneu-Sotelo (1994), Espiritu (1997), Mahler (1997), Lopez-Springfield (1997), Baca-Zinn and Thorton-Dill (1994), Safa (1995), Hernandez and Lopez (1997).
5. Hernandez et al. (1995), Kasinitz (1992), Zephir (1996), Laguerre (1984), Pessar (1987).
6. City University of New York (1995).
7. Kasinitz (1992), Pessar and Grasmuck (1991), Foner (1987).
8. Grasmuck and Grosfuguel (1997).
9. Valenzuela, Angela (1999).
10. Hurtado (1996), Ammot and Matthaei (1991).

11. In a study of childcare practices among elite White women in New York City and Los Angeles, Wrigley (1995) found that there is little pressure for high-quality government-monitored daycare because the privileged class has a choice. Wrigley (1992) warned that private solutions to larger public issues cannot solve social problems.
12. Wrigley (1995), Roberts (1997).
13. Valenzuela (1999).
14. Valenzuela, Abel (1999), hooks (1981), Pastor et al. (1996), Stanton-Salazar (1997).
15. See Hidalgo (2000), Rolón (2000).
16. Hurtado (1996), Fine and Weis (1998), Pastor et al. (1996).
17. Suarez-Orozco (1987) did not discuss gender differences, if any, between men and women's dual frame of reference. See Suarez-Orozco and Suarez-Orozco (1995).
18. Pastor et al. (1996), Zhou and Bankston (1998).
19. See Portes and Schauffler (1996).
20. Zhou and Bankston (1998), Perez (1996).
21. Zhou and Bankston (1998:184).
22. Washington and Newman (1991).
23. Tolman (1996).
24. Thorne (1993).
25. Hurtado (1996:79).
26. Anzaldua (1987).
27. Pessar and Grasmuck (1991), Georges (1990), Gil and Vasquez (1996).
28. Hernandez and López (1997).
29. Hondagneu-Sotelo (1994:196).
30. Momsen (1993), Senior (1991), Verene-Shepherd et al. (1995).
31. Hondagneu-Sotelo (1994:196).
32. Danticat (1994), Alvarez (1991, 1994, 1997).
33. De Leon (1996).
34. Arnot (1999:65).
35. Hill-Collins (1990), Zavella (1987), Hondagneu-Sotelo (1994), Hurtado (1996).
36. See also Ammott and Matthaei (1991), Roberts (1997).
37. Anzaldua (1987).
38. In the survey, 44% of the men compared with 21% of the women felt that in a marriage the wife should be primarily responsible for housework.
39. As explained by Anzaldua (1987:84), "men, even more than women, are fettered to gender roles."
40. Fordham (1996).
41. Vera et al. (1996).
42. Pastor (1996).
43. Paravisini-Gebert (1997), Lopez-Springfield (1997).

44. Hondagneu-Sotelo (1994), Baca-Zinn and Thorton-Dill (1994), Lopez-Spring-field (1997), Glick-Schiller et al. (1992), Moraga and Anzaldua (1983).

Chapter 7

1. Although in the 1990s some immigrant groups were able to make inroads into the construction industry, largely European immigrants and their co-ethnics continued to control it. See Waldinger (1996).
2. See Fine and Weis (1998:16).
3. See Ogbu and Simons (1998), Grasmuck and Pessar (1996).
4. Gans (1992), Grasmuck and Pessar (1996).
5. Kirchenman (1997:215).
6. See Griffins (1994).
7. Weis (1990a, b).
8. Mollenkopf and Castells (1991), Weis (1990a, b).
9. Katz (1993).
10. See Hacker (1992). Wealth disparities are even more blatant. Blacks with bachelors of arts degrees own twenty-three cents for every dollar owned by whites. See Oliver and Shapiro (1995:110).
11. See Robinson (1993:29–59).
12. MacLeod (1995:225)
13. Fine and Weis (1998).
14. Waldinger (1996), Pessar and Grasmuck (1991), Kim (1999).
15. Portes (1996), Waldinger (1996).
16. Foner (1987), Kasinitz (1992).
17. Kwong (1998).
18. See Davis (1997).
19. Ironically, men's employment opportunities in the criminal justice system are premised on the framing of their respective communities as potential sources of criminals. See chapter 2.
20. Waldinger (1996), Stanton-Salazar (1997).
21. Waldinger (1996).
22. Kasinitz and Rosenberg (1996), Kirchenman and Neckerman (1993), Kirchenman (1997).
23. Kirchenman (1997:218).
24. Kasinitz and Rosenberg (1996), Kirchenman and Neckerman (1993).
25. Even Black employers' hiring queues appear to disadvantage men. See Kirchenman (1997).
26. See National Center for Education Statistics (1995:4).
27. First-generation Latina women have better job networks than their male counterparts (Hagan, 1998).
28. See Wrigley (1992:19), Bound and Dresser (1999).

29. Fine and Weis (1998).
30. Cho (1997:204).
31. See Weis (1990).
32. See Waldinger (1996:6).
33. Fuchs et al. (1991).
34. Fuchs et al. (1991).
35. Fine and Weis (1998).

Chapter 8

1. Sierra (1986), Hurtado (1996), Baca-Zinn and Thorton-Dill (1994), Hill-Collins (1990, 1996).
2. Fine (1991), Washington and Newman (1991), Kleinfeld (1998, 1999).
3. Omi and Winant (1994:20).
4. Fine and Weis (1998), Pastor et al. (1996).
5. Portes (1999).
6. Omi and Winant (1994), Sanjek and Gregory (1994), Steinberg (1995).
7. Wacquant (1997).
8. Lubiano (1992), Mullings (1997), Roberts (1997), Espiritu (1997), Davis (1983), Hill-Collins (1990).
9. Leadbeater and Way (1996).
10. Haney-Lopez (1996), Omi and Winant (1994), Wacquant (1997).
11. Meier and Stewart (1991), Kleinfeld (1998).
12. Fine (1991).
13. Meier and Stewart (1991).
14. Meier and Stewart (1991), Kleinfeld (1998).
15. Bowles and Gintis (1976), Oakes (1985), Ogbu (1978).
16. Fine (1991), Oakes (1985), Oakes and Guiton (1995).
17. Hartocollis (1999a, b).
18. Freire (1985).
19. Freire (1985).
20. Fine (1991), Weis (1990a).
21. Freire (1993:66), Delgado (1992), Cummins (1993), Aronowitz and Giroux (1993), hooks (1981, 1994).
22. Freire (1985, 1993).
23. Lopez-Springfield (1997), Paravisini-Gerbert (1997).
24. Lorde (1996), Hurtado (1996), Fine and Weis (1998), Anzaldua (1990), Fine and Zane (1989), Fine (1991), Alvarez (1996), Weis (1990a, b).
25. Hurtado (1996).
26. Anzaldua (1987:84).
27. Fordham (1996), Bourgois (1995).
28. Hondagneu-Sotelo, 1994:193.
29. Hurtado (1996).

30. Kasinitz and Rosenberg (1996), Anderson (1990), Fine and Weis (1998); Kirchenman (1997), Kirchenman and Neckerman (1993).
31. Kirchenman and Neckerman (1993), Kirchenman (1997), Kasinitz and Rosenberg (1996), Kim (1999).
32. Waters (1996), Ogbu and Simons (1998).
33. Stanton-Salazar (1997).
34. Rosenbaum and Binder (1997).
35. Kirchenman and Neckerman (1993), Ogbu (1978).
36. Kirchenman (1997), Kasinitz and Rosenberg (1996), Hurtado (1996), Mullings (1997).
37. Hurtado (1996).
38. Cho (1999:204).
39. Hurtado (1996).
40. Fine et al. (1997:vii).
41. Fine et al. (1997), Frankenberg (1993), McIntosch (1989).
42. Sierra (1986), Hurtado (1996), Washington and Newman (1991).
43. Hurtado (1996:160).

Bibliography

Agger, Ben. 1998. *Critical Social Theories: An Introduction*. Oxford: Westview Press.

Alvarez, Celia. 1996. "The Multiple and Transformatory Identities of Puerto Rican Women in the United States: Reconstructing Discourse on National Identity." In *Unrelated Kin: Race and Gender in Women's Personal Narratives*, edited by Gwendolyn Etter-Lewis and Michelle Foster. London: Routledge.

Alvarez, Julia. 1997. *Yo!* Chapel Hill, NC: Algonquin Books.

———. 1994. *In the Time of Butterflies*. Chapel Hill, NC: Algonquin Books.

———. 1991. *How the Garcia Girls Lost Their Accents*. Chapel Hill, NC: Algonquin Books.

Ammot, Teresa, and Julie Matthaei. 1991. *Race, Gender and Work: A Multicultural Economic History of Women in the United States*. Boston: South End Press.

Anderson, Elijah. 1990. *Streetwise: Race, Class and Change in an Urban Community*. Chicago. University of Chicago Press.

Anyon, Jean. 1997. *Ghetto Schooling: A Political Economy of Urban Educational Reform*. New York: Teachers College Press.

———. 1980. "Social Class and the Hidden Curriculum of Work." *Journal of Education* 162(1):67–92.

Anzaldua, Gloria, editor. 1990. *Making Face, Making Soul, Haciendo Caras: Creative and Critical Perspectives by Women of Color*. San Francisco: Aunt Lute.

———. 1987. *Borderlands: La Frontera, The New Mestiza*. San Francisco: Aunt Lute.

Arnot, Madeleine, Gaby Weiner, Miriam E. David. 1999. *Closing the Gender Gap: Postwar Education and Social Change*. Malden,MA: Blackwell Publishers.

Aroch, Guy; Eve Fowler; Laren Greenfield; Alexei Hay; Jeff Jacobson; Edward Keating; Catherine Opie; Mark Peterson; Joseph Pluchino; Larry Towell; Robert Yager al. 1998. "Being 13: A Photo album of America's Influential, Impressionable, Streetwise, Sentimental and very Young Adults." Cover story. *New York Times Magazine*, Section 6, May 17th.

Aroch, Guy, et al. 1998. "Being 13: A Photo Album of America's Influential, Impressionable, Streetwise, Sentimental and Very Young Adults." *New York Times Magazine*, May 17, Section 6.

Aronowitz, Stanley, and Henry Giroux. 1993. *Education Still Under Siege*. Westport, CT: Bergin and Garvey.

Attanasi, John. 1994. "Racism, Language Variety and Urban United States Minorities: Issues in Bilingualism and Bidialectalism." In *Race*, edited by Roger Sanjek and Steven Gregory. New Brunswick, NJ: Rutgers University.

Baca-Zinn, Maxine, and Bonnie Thorton-Dill. 1994. "Difference and Domination." In *Women of Color in United States Society*, edited by Maxine Baca-Zinn and Bonnie Thorton-Dill. Philadelphia: Temple University Press.

Benmayor, Rina. 1992. *Responses to Poverty among Puerto Rican Women: Identity, Community and Cultural Citizenship*. New York: Centro de Estudios Puertorriquenos, Hunter College, City University of New York.

Best, Amy. 2000. *Prom Night*. New York: Routledge.

Black, Jan Knippers. 1986. *The Dominican Republic: Politics and Development in an Unsovereign State*. Boston: Allen and Unwin.

Blauner, Robert. 1972. *Racial Oppression in America*. New York: Harper and Row.

Bluestone, Barry, and Bennet Harrison. 1982. *The Deindustrialization of America: Plant Closings, Community Abandonment, and the Dismantling of Basic Industry*. New York: Basic Books.

Board of Education. 1995. "The Class of 1995 Four Year Longitudinal Report." New York City: Office of Educational Research.

Bound, John, and Laura Dresser. 1999. "Losing Ground: The Erosion of the Relative Earnings of African American Women During the 1980s." In *Latinas and African American Women at Work: Race, Gender, and Economic Inequality*, edited by Irene Browne. New York: Russell Sage Foundation.

Bourgois, Philippe. 1995. *In Search of Respect: Selling Crack in El Barrio*. Cambridge, UK: University of Cambridge Press.

Bowles, Samuel, and Herbert Gintis. 1976. *Schooling in Capitalist America: Educational Reform and the Contradictions of Economic Life*. New York: Basic Books.

Browne, Irene, editor. 1999. *Latinas and African American Women at Work: Race, Gender, and Economic Inequality*. New York: Russell Sage Foundation.

Candelario, Ginetta, 2000. "Situating Ambiguity: Dominican Identity Formations." Doctoral dissertation. Graduate School and University Center, City University of New York.

Candelario, Ginetta, and Nancy López. 1995. "The Latest Edition of the Welfare Queen Story: Dominicans in New York City." *Phoebe: Journal of Feminist Scholarship Theory and Aesthetics* 7(1/2):7–22.

Cho, Sumi. 1997. "Converging Stereotypes in Racialized Sexual Harassment: Where the Model Minority Meets Suzie Wong." In *Critical Race Feminism: A Reader*, edited by Adrien Katherine Wing. New York: New York University Press, 204.

City University of New York. 1996. "CUNY Student Data Book: Fall 1996." Vol. 1. New York: CUNY.

———. 1995. "Immigration and the CUNY Student of the Year 2000." New York: CUNY.

Crenshaw, Kimberle, editor. 1996. *Critical Race Theory: The Key Writings that Formed the Movement.* New York: New Press.

Cummins, Jim. 1993. "Empowering Minority Students: A Framework for Intervention." In *Silenced Voices: Class, Race and Gender in United States Schools,* edited by Lois Weis and Michelle Fine. Albany, NY: State University of New York Press.

Danticat, Edwidge. 1994. *Breath, Eyes, Memories.* New York: Vintage Books.

Davis, Angela. 1997. "Race and Criminalization: Black Americans and the Punishment Industry." In *The House that Race Built,* edited by Wahneema Lubiano. New York: Vintage Books, 264–279.

———. 1983. *Women, Race, and Class.* New York: Vintage.

Davis, James. 1996. "Who Is Black? One Nation's Definition." In *The Meaning of Difference: American Constructions of Race, Sex and Gender, Social Class, and Sexual Orientation,* edited by Karen Rosenblum and Toni-Michelle Travis. New York: McGraw-Hill.

De Leon, Brunilda. 1996. "Career Development of Hispanic Adolescent Girls." In *Urban Girls: Resisting Stereotypes, Creating Identities,* edited by Bonnie Leadbeater and Niobe Way. New York: New York University Press.

Delgado, Concha. 1992. "School Matters in Mexican-American Home: Socializing to Education." *American Educational Research Journal* (29)3:495–513.

Dovidio, John and Samuel Gaertner, editors. 1986. *Prejudice, Discrimination and Racism.* Orlando, FL: Academic Press.

Driver, Geoffrey. 1980. "How West Indians Do Better at School (Especially the Girls)." *New Society* 17:111–114.

Dunn, James. 1988. "The Shortage of Black Male Students in the College Classroom: Consequences and Causes." *Western Journal of Black Studies* 12(2):73–76.

Eschbach, Karl, and Christina Gomez. 1996. "Choosing Hispanic Identity: Ethnic Identity Switching Among Respondents to High School and Beyond." *Social Science Quarterly* 79(1):73–90.

Espiritu, Yen Le. 1997. *Asian American Men and Women: Labor, Law and Love.* Thousand Oaks, CA: Sage Publications.

Fanon, Franz. 1982. *Black Skin, White Mask,* translated by Charles Lam Markmann. New York: Grove Press.

Farley, Reynolds and W. Allen. 1987. *The Color Line and the Quality of Life in America.* New York: Russell Sage Foundation.

Feagin, Joe and Melvin Sikes. 1994. *Living with Racism: The Black Middle Class Experience.* New York: Routledge.

Fernández-Kelly, M. Patricia, and Richard Schauffler. 1994. "Divided Fates: Immigrant Children In a Restructured U.S. Economy." *International Migration Review* 284(108):662–689.

Fine, Michelle, editor. 1994. *Chartering Urban School Reform: Reflections on Public High Schools in the Midst of Change.* New York: Teachers College Press.

————. 1991. *Framing Dropouts: Notes on the Politics of an Urban Public High School.* Albany, NY: State University of New York Press.

Fine, Michelle, and Janis Sommerville. 1998. *Small Schools, Big Imagination: A Creative Look at Urban Public Schools.* Chicago: Cross City Campaign for Urban School Reform.

Fine, Michelle, and Lois Weis. 1998. *The Unknown City: Lives of Poor and Working-Class Young Adults.* Boston: Beacon Press.

Fine, Michelle, Lois Weis, Linda Powell, and Mun Wong, editors. 1997. *Off White: Readings on Race, Power, and Society.* New York: Routledge.

Fine, Michelle, and Nancie Zane. 1989. "Bein' Wrapped Too Tight: When Low-Income Women Drop Out of High School." In *Dropouts from School: Issues, Dilemmas, and Solutions,* edited by Lois Weis, Eleanor Farrar, and Hugh Petrie. Albany, NY: State University of New York Press.

Flores, Juan. 1997. "The Latino Imaginary: Dimensions of Community and Identity." In *Tropicalizations: Transcultural Representations of Latinidad,* edited by Frances Aparicio and Susana Chavez-Silverman. London: University Press of New England.

Foner, Nancy, editor. 1987. "The Jamaicans: Race and Ethnicity among Migrants in New York City." In *New Immigrants in New York.* New York: Columbia University Press.

Fordham, Signithia. 1996. *Blacked Out: Dilemmas of Race, Identity, and Success at Capital High.* Chicago: University of Chicago Press.

Fordham, Signithia, and John Ogbu. 1986. "Black Students' School Success: Coping with the Burden of Acting White." *Urban Review* 18(3):176–206.

Frankenberg, Ruth. 1993. *White Women, Race Matters: The Social Construction of Whiteness.* Minneapolis: University of Minnesota.

Freire, Paolo. 1993. *Pedagogy of the Oppressed.* New York: Continuum.

————. 1985. *The Politics of Education: Culture and Power and Liberation.* New York: Bergin and Garvin.

Fuchs Epstein, Cynthia, and Stephen Duncombe. 1991. "Women Clerical Workers." In *Dual City: Restructuring New York,* edited by Jose Mollenkopf and Manuel Castells. New York: Russell Sage Foundation.

Gans, Herbert. 1992. "Second Generation Decline: Scenarios for the Economic and Ethnic Futures of the post-1965 American Immigrants." *Ethnic and Racial Studies* 15(2):173–193.

————. 1962. *The Urban Villagers.* Glencoe, IL: Free Press.

Georges, Eugenia. 1990. *The Making of a Transnational Community: Migration, Development and Cultural Change in the Dominican Republic.* New York: Columbia University Press.

Gibson, Margaret. 1988. *Accommodation Without Assimilation: Sikh Immigrant in an American High School.* Ithaca, NY: Cornell University Press.

Gil, Rosa Maria, and Carmen Inoa Vazquez. 1996. *La Paradoja de Maria.* New York: Putnam.

Gilbert, R., and P. Gilbert. 1998. *Masculinity Goes to School.* New York: Routledge.

Gilkes, Cheryl. 1996. "The Margin as the Center of Theory of History: African-American Women, Social Change, and the Sociology of *W.E.B. Du Bois.*" In *W. E. B. Du Bois on Race and Culture: Philosophy, Politics, and Poetics,* Bernard Bell, Emily Grosholz, and James Stewart, editors. New York: Routledge.

Gilroy, Paul. 1993. *The Black Atlantic: Modernity and Double Consciousness.* Cambridge, MA: Harvard University Press.

Ginorio, A., and M. Huston. 2001. *Si Se Puede! Yes We Can! Latinas in School* Washington, DC: American Association of University Women.

Glick-Schiller, Nina, Linda Basch, and Christina Blanc-Szanton. 1992. "Transnationalism: A New Framework for Understanding Migration." *Annals of the New York Academy of Sciences* 645:1–24.

Goffman, Erving. 1964. *Stigma, Notes on the Management of Identity.* Harmondsworth, England: Penguin.

Gordon, Milton. 1964. *Assimilation in American Life: The Role of Race, Religion, and National Origins.* New York: Oxford University Press.

Gramsci, Antonio. 1971. *Selections from the Prison Notebooks,* edited by Quentin Hore and Geoffrey Nowel Smith. New York: International.

Grant, Linda. 1994. "Helpers, Enforcers and Go-betweens: Black Females in Elementary School Classrooms." In *Women of Color in United States Society,* edited by Maxine Baca-Zinn and Bonnie Thorton Dill. Philadelphia: Temple University Press.

———. 1992. "Race and the Schooling of Young Girls." *Education and Gender Equality,* edited by Julia Wrigley. London: Falmer.

Grasmuck, Sherri, and Ramon Grosfuguel. 1997. "Geopolitics, Economic Niches, and Social Capital Among Recent Caribbean Immigrants in New York City: Neglected Dimensions of Assimilation Theory." Transnational Communities and the Political Economy of New York City in the 1990s, Conference, February 21–22, Robert J. Milano Graduate School of Management and Urban Policy, New School for Social Research.

Grasmuck, Sherri, and Patricia Pessar. 1996. "Dominicans in the United States: First and Second Generation Settlement, 1960–1990." In *Origins and Destinies: Immigration, Race and Ethnicity in America,* edited by Silvia Pedraza and Ruben Rumbaut. Belmont, CA: Wadsworth Publishing Company.

Grosfuguel, Ramon, and Chloe Georas. 1996. "The Racialization of Latino Caribbean Migrants in the New York Metropolitan Area." *Centro: Journal of the Center for Puerto Rican Studies* 8(1–2):191–201.

Griffins, M. L. 1994. *Critical Choices: Education and Employment among New York City Youth.* New York: Community Services Society.

Hacker, Andrew. 1992. *Two Nations: Black and White, Separate, Hostile, Unequal.* New York: Random House.

Hagan, Jacqueline. 1998. "Social Networks, Gender, and Immigrant Incorporation." *American Sociological Review* 63(1):55–67.

Halbfinger, David. 1999. "Where Fear Lingers: A Neighborhood Gives Peace a Wary Look, A Special Report." *New York Times*, May 18, A1.

Haney-Lopez, Ian. 1996. *White by Law: The Legal Construction of Race.* New York: New York University Press.

Hartocollis, Anamora. 1999a. "Crew Plans Charter Schools, His Way." *New York Times*, January 29, B8.

———. 1999b. "Private School Choice Plan Draws a Million Aid Seekers." *New York Times*, April 21, A1.

Hawkins, Denise. 1996. "Gender Gap: Black Females Outpace Male Counterparts at Three Degree Levels." *Black Issues in Higher Education* 20–22.

Herman, E., and F. Broadhead. 1984. *Demonstration Elections: U.S.-Staged Elections in the Dominican Republic, Vietnam and El Salvador.* Boston: South End Press.

Hernandez, Ramona. 2002. *The Mobility of Labor Under Advanced Capitalism: Dominican Migration to the United States.* New York: Columbia University Press.

Hernandez, Ramona, and Nancy López. 1997. "Yola and Gender: Dominican Women's Unregulated Migration." In *Dominican Studies: Resources and Research Questions.* Dominican Research Monographs. New York: Dominican Studies Institute at City University of New York (reprinted in *Documents of Dissidence: Selected Writings by Dominican Women*, edited by Daisy Cocco De Filippis. New York: Dominican Studies Institute at City University of New York).

Hernandez, Ramona, and Francisco Rivera-Batiz. 1997. *Dominican New Yorkers: A Socioeconomic Profile, 1997.* Dominican Research Monographs. New York: Dominican Studies Institute at City University of New York.

Hernandez, Ramona, Francisco Rivera-Batiz, and Roberto Agodini. 1995. *Dominican New Yorkers: A Socioeconomic Profile, 1990.* New York: Dominican Studies Institute at City University of New York.

Higginbotham, Elizabeth. 1994. "Black Professional Women: Job Ceilings and Employment Sectors." In *Women of Color in United States Society*, edited by Maxine Baca-Zinn and Bonnie Thorton-Dill. Philadelphia: Temple University Press.

Higginbotham, Elizabeth, and Lynn Weber. 1999. "Perceptions of Workplace Discrimination among Black and White Professional-Managerial Women." In *Latinas and African American Women at Work: Race, Gender, and Economic Inequality*, edited by Irene Browne. New York: Russell Sage Foundation.

Hildalgo, Nitza. 2000. "Puerto Rican Mothering Strategies: The Role of Mothers and Grandmothers in Promoting School Success." In *Puerto Rican Students in U.S. Schools*, edited by Sonia Nieto. Mahwah, NJ: Lawrence Erlbaum Associates.

Hill-Collins, Patricia. 1996. "Toward a New Vision: Race, Class, and Gender as Categories of Analysis and Connection." In *The Meaning of Difference: American Constructions of Race, Sex and Gender, Social Class and Sexual Orientation.* New York: McGraw-Hill.

————. 1990. *Black Feminist Thought: Knowledge, Consciousness, and the Politics of Empowerment*. Boston: Unwin Hyman.

Hondagneu-Sotelo, Pierrette. 1999. "Gender and Contemporary U.S. Immigration." *American Behavioral Scientist* 42(4):565–576.

————. 1994. *Gendered Transitions: Mexican Experiences of Migration*. Berkeley: University of California.

————. Forthcoming. *Gender and U.S. Immigration: Contemporary Trends*, edited by Pierrette Hondaganeu-Sotelo. University of California Press.

hooks, bell. 1994. *Teaching to Transgress: Education as the Practice of Freedom*. New York: Routledge.

————. 1981. *Ain't I a Woman? Black Women and Feminism*. Boston: South End Press.

Hurtado, Aida. 1996. *The Color of Privilege: Three Blasphemies on Race and Feminism*. Ann Arbor, MI: University of Michigan.

Hurtado, Aida et al. 1992. *Redefining California: Latino Social Engagement in a Multicultural Society*. Los Angeles: Chicano Studies Research Center at University of California.

Kao, Grace, and Marta Tienda. 1995. "Optimism and Achievement: The Educational Performance of Immigrant Youth." *Social Sciences Quarterly* 76(1):1–19.

Kasinitz, Philip. 1992. *Caribbean New York: Black Immigrants and the Politics of Race*. Ithaca, NY: Cornell University Press.

Kasinitz, Philip, and Jan Rosenberg. 1996. "Missing the Connection: Social Isolation and Empowerment on the Brooklyn Waterfront." *Social Problems* 43(2):180–196.

Katz, Michael, editor. 1993. *The "Underclass Debate": Views from History*. Princeton, NJ: Princeton University Press.

————. 1989. *The Undeserving Poor: From the War on Poverty to the War on Welfare*. New York: Pantheon.

Kim, Dae Young. 1999. "Beyond Co-ethnic Solidarity: Mexican and Ecuadorean Employment in Korean-Owned Businesses in New York City." *Ethnic and Racial Studies* 22(3):581–605.

Kirchenman, Joleen. 1997. "African American Employers' Attitudes toward African American Workers." In *Racial Attitudes in the 1990s: Continuity and Change*, edited by Steven Tuch and Jack Martin. Westport, CT: Praeger Publishers.

Kirchenman, Joleen, and Kathryn Neckerman. 1993. "We'd Love to Hire Them, But . . . : The Meaning of Race for Employers." In *The "Underclass" Debate: Views from History*, edited by Michael Katz. Princeton, NJ: Princeton University Press.

Kleinfeld, Judith. 1999. "Student Performance: Males versus Females." *Public Interest* 134(Winter):3–20.

————. 1998. *The Myth That Schools Shortchange Girls*. Washington, DC: Women's Freedom Network.

Klor de Alva, J. Jorge. 1997. "The Invention of Ethnic Origins and the Negotiation of Latino Identity." In *Challenging Fronteras: Structuring Latina and Latino Lives in the United States, An Anthology of Readings,* edited by Mary Romero, Pierrette Hondagneu-Sotelo, and Vilma Ortiz. New York: Routledge.

Kowal, Jessica. 2001. "Landmark Win for City Students; Judge: School Funding Has Failed, and Formula Must Change." *New York Newsday,* January 11, A05.

Kozol, Jonathan. 1996. *Amazing Grace: The Lives of Children and the Conscience of a Nation.* New York: Crown.

———. 1991. *Savage Inequalities: Children in American Schools.* New York: Crown.

Kwong, Peter. 1998. *Forbidden Workers: Illegal Chinese Immigrants and American Labor in New York.* New York: New Press.

Ladson-Billings, Gloria, and William Tate. 1995. "Toward a Critical Theory of Education." *Teachers College Record* (97)1:46–68.

Laguerre, Michael. 1984. *American Odyssey: Haitians in New York City.* Ithaca, NY: Cornell University Press.

Landrine, Hope, editor. 1996. *Bringing Cultural Diversity to Feminist Psychology: Theory Research and Practice.* Washington, DC: American Psychological Association.

Leadbeater, Bonnie, and Niobe Way, editors. 1996. *Urban Girls: Resisting Stereotypes, Creating Identities.* New York: New York University.

Lee, Stacey. 1997. *Unraveling the "Model Minority" Stereotype: Listening to Asian American Youth.* New York: Teachers College Press.

Leguizamo, John. 1997. *Freak.* Directed by David Bar Katz, Arielle Tepper, and Bill Harber. February 10. (Demi, semi, quasi, pseudo-autobiographical one-man comedy at the Cort Theater.)

Lewin, Tamar. 1998a. "American Colleges Begin to Ask, Where have all the Men Gone?" *New York Times,* December 6, A1.

———. 1998b. "Public Schools Confronting Issue of Racial Preferences: Growing Number of Parents, Mostly White, Challenge Policies They Deem Unfair." *New York Times,* November 29, A1.

Lieberson, Stanley. 1980. *A Piece of the Pie: Black and White Immigration Since 1880.* Berkeley: University of California.

López, Nancy. 2002. "Race-Gender Experiences and Schooling: Second-Generation Dominican, West Indian, and Haitian Youth in New York City." *Race, Ethnicity and Education* 5(1)(March):67–89.

———. 1998. "The Structural Origins of Dominican High School Dropout." *Latino Studies Journal* 9(3):85–105.

Lopez-Springfield, Consuelo, editor. 1997. *Daughters of the Caliban: Caribbean Women in the Twentieth Century.* Indianapolis: Indiana University Press.

Lorde, Audrey. 1996. "The Uses of Anger: Women Responding to Racism." In *Multicultural Experiences, Multicultural Theories,* edited by Mary Rogers. New York: McGraw-Hill.

Lubiano, Wahneema. 1992. "Black Ladies, Welfare Queens, and State Minstrels: Ideological War by Narrative Means." In *Race-ing Justice, Engendering Power: Essays on Anita Hill, Clarence Thomas, and the Construction of Social Reality*, edited by Toni Morrison. New York: Pantheon Books.

MacLeod, Jay. 1995. *Ain't No Makin' It: Aspirations and Attainment in a Low-Income Neighborhood*. San Francisco: Westview Press.

Mahler, Sarah. 1997. "Bringing Gender to a Transnational Focus: Theoretical and Empirical Ideas." Presentation at the Latin American Studies Association Annual Meeting.

Massey, Douglas, and Nancy Denton. 1994. *American Apartheid: Segregation and the Making of the American Underclass*. Cambridge, MA: Harvard University Press.

Matute-Bianchi, Maria Eugenia. 1991. "Situational Identity and Patterns of School Performance among Immigrant and Non-Immigrant Mexican Descent Students." In *Minority Status and Schooling: A Comparative Study of Immigrant and Involuntary Minorities*, edited by John Ogbu and Margaret Gibson. New York: Garland Publishers.

McIntosh, Peggy. 1989. "White Privilege: Unpacking the Invisible Knapsack." *Peace and Freedom* (July/August) 61 (1–2). New York: Fellowship of Reconciliation Place.

Mead, Lawrence. 1986. *Beyond Entitlement: The Social Obligations of Citizenship*. Glencoe, IL: Free Press.

Meier, Kenneth, and Joseph Stewart. 1991. *The Politics of Hispanic Education: Un paso pa'lante y dos pa'tras*. Albany, NY: State University of New York Press.

Milkman, Ruth. 1987. *Gender at Work*. Chicago: University of Illinois Press.

Model, Suzanne. 1997. "An Occupational Tale of Two Cities: Minorities in London and New York." *Demography* 34(4):539–550.

Mollenkopf, John, and Manuel Castells, editors. 1991. *Dual City: Restructuring New York*. New York: Russell Sage Foundation.

Mollenkopf, John, Philip Kasinitz, Mary Waters, Nancy López, and Dae Young Kim. 1998. "The School to Work Transition of Second Generation Immigrants in Metropolitan New York: Some Preliminary Findings." Working Paper 214. Annandale-on-Hudson, NY: Jerome Levy Economics Institute of Bard College.

Momsen, Janet. 1993. *Women and Change in the Caribbean: A Pan-Caribbean Perspective*. Bloomington, IN: Indiana University Press.

Moraga, Cherrie, and Gloria Anzaldua, editors. 1983. *This Bridge Called My Back: Writings by Radical Women of Color*. New York: Kitchen Table Press.

Mullings, Leith. 1997. *On Our Own Terms: Race, Class, and Gender in the Lives of African American Women*. New York: Routledge.

Murguia, Edward, and Edward Telles. 1996. "Phenotype and Schooling Among Mexican Americans." *Sociology of Education* 69(4):276–289.

Murray, Charles. 1984. *Losing Ground: American Social Policy, 1950–1980.* New York: Basic Books.

Murray, Charles, and Richard Hernstein. 1994. *The Bell Curve: Intelligence and Class Structure in American Life.* Glencoe, IL: Free Press.

Myrdal, Gunnar. 1944. *An American Dilemma*, Vol. 1. New York: Harper and Brothers.

National Center for Education Statistics. 2001–2002. *Dropout Rates in the United States: 1999.* Washington, DC: U.S. Department of Education, Office of Educational Research and Improvement.

———. *The Educational Progress of Immigrant Students: Findings from the Conditions of Education*, 95–767. Washington, DC: National Center for Education Statistics, 4.

Nelson, Candace, and Marta Tienda. 1997. "The Structuring of Hispanic Ethnicity: Historical and Contemporary Perspectives." In *Challenging Fronteras: Structuring Latina and Latino Lives in the United States, An Anthology of Readings*, edited by Mary Romero, Pierrette Hondagneu-Sotelo, and Vilma Ortiz. New York: Routledge.

———. 1985. "The Structuring of Hispanic Ethnicity: Historical and Contemporary Perspectives." In *Ethnicity and Race in the USA*, edited by Richard Ala. Boston: Routledge and Kegan Paul.

Newman, Katherine, and Catherine Ellis. 1999. " 'There's No Shame in My Game': Status and Stigma among Harlem's Working Poor." In *The Cultural Territories of Race: Black and White Boundaries*, edited by Michele Lament. Chicago: University of Chicago Press.

New York City Department of Planning. 1999. *The Newest New Yorkers, 1995–1996: An Update of Immigration to New York City in the Mid-1990s.* New York.

New York Times. 1999. "Police Training Manual Is Criticized," March 17, B5.

———.1998. March 28, B1.

Oakes, Jeannie. 1985. *Keeping Track: How Schools Structure Inequality.* New Haven, CT: Yale University Press.

Oakes, Jeannie, and Gretchen Guiton. 1995. "Matchmaking: The Dynamics of High School Tracking Decisions." *American Education Research Journal* 32(1):3–33.

Obler, Suzanne. 1997. "So Far From God, So Close to the United States: The Roots of Hispanic Homogenization." In *Challenging Fronteras: Structuring Latina and Latino Lives in the United States, An Anthology of Readings*, edited by Mary Romero, Pierrette Hondagneu-Sotelo, and Vilma Ortiz. New York: Routledge.

Ogbu, John. 1995a. "Cultural Problems in Minority Education: Their Interpretation and Consequences—Part One: Case Studies." *Urban Review* 27(3): 189–205.

———. 1995b. "Cultural Problems in Minority Education: Their Interpretations and Consequences—Part Two: Case Studies." *Urban Review* 27(4):271–297.

————. 1978. *Minority Education and Caste: The American System in Cross-Cultural Perspective.* New York: Academic Press.

————. 1974. *The Next Generation: An Ethnography of Education in an Urban Neighborhood.* New York: Academic Press.

Ogbu, John, and Herbert Simons. 1998. "Voluntary and Involuntary Minorities: A Cultural-Ecological Theory of School Performance with Some Implications for Education." *Anthropology and Education Quarterly* 29(2): 155–188.

Oliver, Melvin, and Thomas Shapiro. 1995. *Black Wealth/White Wealth: A New Perspective on Racial Inequality.* New York: Routledge.

Omi, Michael, and Howard Winant. 1994. *Racial Formation in the United States: From 1960s to 1990s.* New York: Routledge.

Orfield, Gary. 1994. "Asking the Right Question." *Educational Policy* 8(4):404–418.

Paravisini-Gebert, Lizabeth. 1997. "Decolonizing Feminism: The Home-Grown Roots of Caribbean Women's Movement." In *Daughters of the Caliban: Caribbean Women in the Twentieth Century,* edited by Consuelo Lopez-Springfield. Indianapolis: Indiana University Press.

Parillo, Vincent. 1999. *Strangers to These Shores: Race and Ethnic Relations in the United States.* Boston: Allyn and Bacon, 426.

————. 1997. *Strangers to these Shores: Race and Ethnic Relations in the United States,* 5th ed. Boston: Allyn and Bacon.

Park, Robert. 1950. "The Collected Papers of Robert E. Park." In *Race and Culture,* Vol. 1, edited by Evert Hugs et al. Glencoe, IL: Free Press.

Pastor, Jennifer, Jennifer McCormick, and Michelle Fine. 1996. "Makin Homes: An Urban Girl Thing." In *Urban Girls: Resisting Stereotypes, Creating Identities,* edited by Bonnie Leadbeater and Niobe Way. New York: New York University Press.

Perez, Lizandro. 1996. "The Households of Children of Immigrants in South Florida: An Exploratory Study of Extended Family Arrangements." In *The New Second Generation,* edited by Alejandro Portes. New York: Russell Sage Foundation.

Perlmann, Joel. 1988. *Ethnic Differences in Schooling and Social Stratification Among Irish, Italian, Jews, Blacks in an American City, 1880–1935.* Cambridge, UK: Cambridge University Press.

Perlmann, Joel, and Roger Waldinger. 1997. "Second Generation Decline? Immigrant Children Past and Present—A Reconsideration." *International Migration Review* 31(4):893–922.

Pessar, Patricia. 1987. "The Linkage Between the Household and Workplace of Dominican Women in the U.S." In *Caribbean Life in New York City: Sociocultural Dimensions,* edited by Constance R. Sutton and Elsa M. Chancy. New York: Center for Migration Studies.

Pessar, Patricia, and Sherri Grasmuck. 1991. *Between Two Islands: Dominican International Migration.* Berkeley: University of California Press.

Piven, Frances Fox, and Richard Cloward. 1993. *Regulating the Poor: The Functions of Public Welfare*, updated ed. New York: Vintage Books.

Portes, Alejandro. 1999. "Immigration Theory for a New Century: Some Problems and Opportunities," In *The Handbook of International Migration: The American Experience*, edited by C. Hirshman, J. Dewind, and J. Kasinitz. New York: Russell Sage Foundation, 21–33.

———. 1996. "Introduction: Immigration and Its Aftermath." In *The New Second Generation*, edited by Alejandro Portes. New York: Russell Sage Foundation.

Portes, Alejandro, and D. MacLeod. 1996. "Educational Progress of Children of Immigrants: The Roles of Class, Ethnicity, and School Context." *Sociology of Education* 69:255–275.

Portes, Alejandro, and Ruben Rumbaut. 1990. *Immigrant America: A Portrait*. Berkeley: University of California Press.

Portes, Alejandro, and Richard Schauffler. 1996. "Language and the Second Generation: Bilingualism Today and Yesterday." In *The New Second Generation*, edited by Alejandro Portes. New York: Russell Sage Foundation.

Portes, Alejandro, and Min Zhou. 1993. "The New Generation: Segmented Assimilation and Its Variants." *Annals of the American Academy of Political and Social Science* 530:74–96.

Reeves, LaVona L. 2002. "Mina Shaughnessy and Open Admissions at New York's City College." *Thought and Action: The National Education Association Higher Education Journal* 17(2):117–128.

Ringer, Benjamin, and E.R. Lawless. 1989. *Race, Ethnicity and Society*. New York: Routledge.

Roane, Kit. 1999. "Minority Private-School Students Claim Police Harassment." *New York Times*, March 26, B5.

Roberts, Dorothy. 1997. *Killing the Black Body: Race, Reproduction, and the Meaning of Liberty*. New York: Pantheon.

Robinson, William. 1993. "The Global Economy and the Latino Populations in the United States: A World Systems Approach." *Critical Sociology* (19)2: 29–59.

Rodriguez, Clara. 1994. "Challenging Racial Hegemony: Puerto Ricans in the United States." In *Race*, edited by Roger Sanjek and Steven Gregory. New Brunswick, NJ: Rutgers University Press.

Rohter, Larry, and Clifford Krauss. 1998. "Dominicans Allow Drugs Easy Sailing." *New York Times*, May 10, A1.

Rolón, Carmen. 2000. "Puerto Rican Female Narratives About Self, School and Success." In *Puerto Rican Students in U.S. Schools*, edited by Sonia Nieto. Mahwah, NJ: Lawrence Erlbaum Associates.

Romero, Mary, Pierrette Hondagneu-Sotelo, and Vilma Ortiz, editors. 1997. *Challenging Fronteras: Structuring Latina and Latino Lives in the United States, An Anthology of Readings*. New York: Routledge.

Rosenbaum, James, and Amy Binder. 1997. "Do Employers Really Need More Educated Youth?" *Sociology of Education* 70:68–85.

Rosenbaum, James, Kevin Roy, and Takehico Kariya. 1995. "Do High School Students Help Some Students Enter the Labor Market?" Paper presented at the Annual Meeting of the American Sociological Association, Washington, DC.

Rosenblum, Karen, and Toni-Michelle Travis. 1996. *The Meaning of Difference: American Constructions of Race, Sex and Gender, Social Class and Sexual Orientation.* New York: McGraw-Hill.

Royster, Dierdre. 1996. "Featured Essay: Ain't No Makin' It: Aspirations and Attainment in a Low-Income Neighborhood." *Contemporary Sociology* 25(2):151–153.

Rumbaut, Ruben. 1998. "Transformations: The Post-Immigrant Generation in an Age of Diversity." Paper presented at the Annual Meeting of the Eastern Sociological Society.

———. 1995. "The New Californians: Comparative Research Findings on the Educational Progress of Immigrant Children." In *California's Immigrant Children: Theory, Research, and Implications for Educational Policy,* edited by Ruben Rumbaut and Wayne Cornelius. San Diego: Center for U.S.-Mexican Studies, University of California.

———. 1994. "Origins and Destinies: Immigration to the United States Since World War I." *Sociological Forum* 9(4):583–621.

Safa, Helen. 1995. *The Myth of the Male Breadwinner: Women and Industrialization in the Caribbean.* New York: Westview.

Sanjek, Roger, and Steven Gregory, editors. 1994. *Race.* New Brunswick, NJ: Rutgers University Press.

Schill, Michael, Samantha Friedman, and Emily Rosenbaum. 1998. "The Housing of Immigrants in New York City." Working Paper 98(2). New York: Center for Real Estate and Urban Policy and New York University School of Law.

Schultz, Katherine. 1996. "Between School and Work: The Literacies of Urban Adolescent Females." *Anthropology and Education Quarterly* 27(4):517–544.

Sedlak, Michael, Christopher Wheeler, Diana Pullin, and Philip Cusick. 1986. *Selling Students Short: Classroom Bargains and Academic Reform in the American High School.* New York: Teachers College Press.

Senior, Olive. 1991. *Working Miracles: Women's Lives in the English-Speaking Caribbean.* Bloomington, IN: Indiana University Press.

Sexton, Joe. 1997. "In Brooklyn Neighborhood, Welfare Fraud Is Nothing New." *New York Times,* March 19, B1.

Sierra, Christine Marie. 1986. "The University Setting Reinforces Inequality." In *Chicana Voices: Intersections of Class, Race and Gender. National Association for Chicano Studies,* edited by Center for Mexican Studies. Austin, TX: University of Texas Press.

Solomon, R. Patrick. 1990. "Black Cultural Forms in Schools: A Cross National Comparison." In *Class, Race, and Gender in American Education*, edited by Lois Weis. Albany, NY: State University of New York Press.

Stanton-Salazar, Ricardo. 1997. "A Social Capital Framework for Understanding the Socialization of Racial Minority Children and Youths." *Harvard Educational Review* 67(1):1–40.

Steele, Claude. 1992. "Race and the Schooling of Black Americans." *Atlantic Monthly* 269(4):68–77.

Steele, Claude, and Joshua Aronson. 1995. "Stereotype Threat and the Intellectual Test Performance of African Americans." *Journal of Personality and Social Psychology* 69(5):797–811.

Steinberg, Stephen. 1995. *Turning Back: The Retreat from Racial Justice in American Thought and Policy*. Boston: Beacon.

———. 1981. *The Ethnic Myth: Race, Ethnicity, and Class in America*. Boston: Beacon.

Stepick, A. 1992. "The Refugees Nobody Wants: Haitians in Miami." In *Miami Now! Immigration, Ethnicity, and Social Change*, edited by A. Stepick and G. J. Grenier. Gainesville, FL: University Press of Florida.

Suarez-Orozco, Marcelo. 1987. " 'Becoming Somebody' Central American Immigrants in U.S. Inner-City Schools." *Anthropology and Education Quarterly* 18(4):287–299.

Suarez-Orozco, Marcelo, and Carola Suarez-Orozco. 1995. *Transformations: Immigration, Family Life, and Achievement Motivation Among Latino Adolescents*. Stanford, CA: Stanford University Press.

Sullivan, Mercer. 1989. *Getting Paid: Youth Crime*. Ithaca, NY: Cornell University Press.

Sum, Andrew, Julia Kroshko, Neeta Fogg, and Sheila Palma. 1999. *The College Enrollment and Employment Outcomes for the Class of 1998 Boston Public High School Graduates: Key Findings of the 1999 Follow-up Surveys*. Boston: Center for Labor Market Studies, Northeastern University.

Takaki, Ronald. 1994. "Reflections on Racial Patterns in America." In *From Different Shores: Perspectives on Race and Ethnicity in America*, edited by Ronald Takaki. New York: Oxford University Press.

Thorne, Barrie. 1993. *Gender Play: Girls and Boys in School*. New Brunswick, NJ: Rutgers University Press.

Tiano, Susan. 2001. "From Victims to Agents: A New Generation of Literature on Women in Latin America." *Latin American Research Review* 36(3):183–203.

Tolman, Deborah. 1996. "Adolescent Girls' Sexuality: Debunking the Myth of the Urban Girl." In *Urban Girls: Resisting Stereotypes, Creating Identities*, edited by Bonnie Leadbeater and Niobe Way. New York: New York University Press.

Torres, Andres, and Frank Bonilla. 1995. "Decline within Decline." In *Latinos in a Changing United States Economy: Comparative Perspectives on Growing Inequality*, edited by Rebecca Morales and Frank Bonilla. London: Sage Publications.

Torres-Saillant, Silvio. 1995. "The Dominican Republic." In *No Longer Invisible: Afro-Latin Americans Today,* edited by the Minority Rights Group. London: Minority Rights Group.

Torres-Saillant, Silvio, and Ramona Hernandez. 1998. *The Dominican Americans.* Westport, CT: Greenwood Publishing Group.

Tyson, Karolyn. 1998. "Debunking a Persistent Myth: Academic Achievement and the Burden of 'Acting White' among Black Students." Paper presented at the American Sociological Association Annual Meeting.

United Negro College Fund. 1997. *The African-American Education Data Book,* Vol. 1. Fairfax, VA: United Negro College Fund.

U.S. Census Bureau. 1998. "Educational Attainment in the United States: March 1998 (Update)," Table 2. *The Official Statistics.*

Valenzuela, Abel. 1999. "Gender Roles and Settlement Activities among Children and Their Immigrant Families." *American Behavioral Scientist* 42(4):720–742.

Valenzuela, Angela. 1999. *Subtractive Schooling: The Politics of Schooling in a U.S. Mexican High School.* Albany, NY: State University of New York Press.

Vera, Elizabeth, Le'Roy Reese, Roberta Paikoff, and Robin Jarrett. 1996. "Contextual Factor of Sexual Risk-Taking in Urban African American Preadolescent Children." In *Urban Girls: Resisting Stereotypes, Creating Identities,* edited by Bonnie Leadbeater and Niobe Way. New York: New York University Press.

Verene-Shepherd, Bridget, et al. 1995. *Engendering History: Caribbean Women in Historical Perspective.* New York: St. Martin's Press.

Vickerman, Milton. 1999. *Crosscurrents: West Indian Immigrants and Race.* New York: Oxford University Press.

Wacquant, Loic. 1997. "Three Pernicious Premises in the Study of the American Ghetto." *International Journal of Urban and Regional Research* 20:341–353.

Waldinger, Roger. 1996. *Still the Promised Cities: African-American and New Immigrants in a Postindustrial New York.* Cambridge, MA: Harvard University Press.

Washington, Valora, and Joanna Newman. 1991. "Setting Our Own Agenda: Exploring the Meaning of Gender Disparities among Blacks in Higher Education." *Journal of Negro Education* 60(1):19–35.

Waters, Mary. 2000. *Black Identities: West Indian Dreams and American Realities.* Cambridge, MA: Harvard University Press.

———. 1999. "Explaining the Comfort Factor: West Indian Immigrants Confront American Race Relations." In *The Cultural Territories of Race: Black and White Boundaries,* edited by Michele Lamont. Chicago: University of Chicago Press.

———. 1997. "The Impact of Racial Segregation on the Education and Work Outcomes of Second Generation West Indians in New York City." Paper presented to the Levy Institute Conference on Second Generation Youth, Bard College.

———. 1996. "The Intersections of Gender, Race and Ethnicity in Identity Development of Caribbean American Teens." In Urban Girls: Resisting Stereotypes, Creating Identities, edited by Bonnie Leadbeater and Niobe Way. New York: New York University Press.

———. 1994. "Ethnic and Racial Identities of Second Generation Black Immigrants in New York City." International Migration Review 8(4):795–820.

———. 1990. Ethnic Options: Choosing Identities in America. Berkeley: University of California Press.

Weis, Lois. 1990a. Working Class Without Work: High School Students in a Deindustrialized Economy. New York: Routledge.

———. 1990b. "High School Girls in a De-Industrializing Economy." In Class, Race, and Gender in American Education, edited by Lois Weis. Albany, NY: State University of New York Press.

West, Cornel. 1990. Race Matters. New York: Vintage Books.

Wilgoren, Jodi. 1999. "Police Profiling Debate Hinges on Issue of Experience vs. Bias." New York Times, April 9, B1.

Williams, Terry, and William Kornblum. 1994. The Uptown Kids: Struggle and Hope in the Projects. New York: Putnam.

Willis, Paul. 1981. Learning to Labor: How Working Class Kids Get Working Class Jobs. New York: Columbia University Press.

Wilson, William. 1996. When Work Disappears: The World of the New Urban Poor. New York: Knopf.

———. 1987. The Truly Disadvantaged: The Inner City, the Underclass and Public Policy. Chicago: University of Chicago Press.

Woodson, Carter. 1972. The Mis-Education of the Negro. New York: AMS Press.

Woody, Thomas. 1966. A History of Women's Education in the United States, Vol. I. New York: Octagon Books.

Wrigley, Julia. 1999. "Is Racial Oppression Intrinsic to Domestic Work? The Experiences of Children's Caregivers in Contemporary American." In The Cultural Territories of Race: Black and White Boundaries, edited by Michele Lamont. Chicago: University of Chicago Press.

———. 1995. Other People's Children. New York: Basic Books.

———. 1992. "Gender, Education and the Welfare State." In Education and Gender Inequality, edited by Julia Wrigley. New York: Falmer Press.

Ybarra, Raul. 2000. "Latino Students and Anglo-Mainstream Instructors: A Study of Classroom Communities." Journal of College Student Retention Research, Theory and Practice 2(2):161–171.

Zavella, Patricia. 1987. Women's Work and Chicano Families: Cannery Workers of Santa Clara Valley. Ithaca, NY: Cornell University Press.

Zephir, Flore. 1996. Haitian Immigrants in Black America: A Sociological Portrait. Westport, CT: Bergin and Garvey.

Zhou, Min, and Carl Bankston. 1998. Growing Up American: How Vietnamese Children Adapt to Life in the United States. New York: Russell Sage Foundation.

Index